Customized
Schooling

Customized Schooling

Beyond Whole-School Reform

Frederick M. Hess and Bruno V. Manno
Editors

HARVARD EDUCATION PRESS
CAMBRIDGE, MASSACHUSETTS

Library of Congress Control Number 2010942133

Paperback ISBN 978-1-934742-07-5
Library Edition ISBN 978-1-934742-51-8

Published by Harvard Education Press,
an imprint of the Harvard Education Publishing Group

Harvard Education Press
8 Story Street
Cambridge, MA 02138

Cover Design: Sarah Henderson
The typefaces used in this book are Minion and Helvetica Neue.

The Educational Innovations Series

The *Educational Innovations* series explores a wide range of current school reform efforts. Individual volumes examine entrepreneurial efforts and unorthodox approaches, highlighting reforms that have met with success and strategies that have attracted widespread attention. The series aims to disrupt the status quo and inject new ideas into contemporary education debates.

Series edited by Frederick M. Hess

Other books in this series:
Bringing School Reform to Scale
by Heather Zavadsky

What Next?
Edited by Mary Cullinane and Frederick M. Hess

Between Public and Private
Edited by Katrina E. Bulkley, Jeffrey R. Henig, and Henry M. Levin

Stretching the School Dollar
Edited by Frederick M. Hess and Eric Osberg

Contents

Acknowledgments

IMAGINE AN ENTITY THAT provides a critical service to the public and spends half a trillion dollars each year but rarely asks or examines what consumers want. Rather, it relies on what analysts and experts think the public should want. It would seem impossible for such an enterprise to exist and remain solvent, right? Unfortunately, this is the case of K–12 education today, where little or no thought is given to the study and understanding of the services that parents and educators want and need for children.

For far too long we have turned a deaf ear to these needs, tacitly accepting the one-size-fits-all school system that has hindered the ability of entrepreneurs to emerge and better target particular populations and needs. As we have seen, cases of entrepreneurship in K–12 schooling have generally focused on efforts to boost the supply of familiar things: more good schools, more talented teachers, and more effective school leaders. Consequently, the best known and most celebrated endeavors have tended to be whole school solutions like charter operations KIPP, Green Dot, and Achievement First or efforts like Teach for America and New Leaders for New Schools, which are focused on recruiting better teachers and leaders into the same aged job descriptions. Too often absent has been careful analysis of how differentiated solutions, innovative tools, and outside providers may supplement and support efforts to meet the demands for schooling in smarter ways.

This volume follows two earlier Harvard Education Press volumes that have sought to understand how new, more agile, and specialized providers can help spur breakthrough improvements in twenty-first-century schooling. Those earlier volumes, *Educational Entrepreneurship* (2006) and *The Future of Educational Entrepreneurship* (2008), emphasized the value of new providers and suggested what it will take for them to succeed. In this volume, we turn our angle of vision to the beneficiaries of these efforts—students, families, teachers, and schools—to ask what it will take for new and traditional providers to serve more effectively their diverse and often-overlooked needs.

To explore how those various needs might be better met in a more customized world of schooling, we recruited a select group of preeminent researchers, entrepreneurs, and policy analysts to help navigate the challenges and opportunities ahead. The collected analyses were first presented at a December 2009 conference at the American Enterprise Institute. After extensive discussion and revision, you hold here the final iterations of those same efforts.

We want to thank the discussants who contributed such valuable guidance and feedback at that initial conference: Gina Burkhardt, CEO of Learning Point Associates; George Cigale, founder and CEO of Tutor.com; Jeff Cohen, president and CEO of Educate, Inc.; Josh Edelman, deputy chief at the District of Columbia Public Schools Office of School Innovation; Deborah McGriff, partner at NewSchools Venture Fund; Cathy Mincberg, vice president and chief academic officer at KC Distance Learning; Eva Moskowitz, founder and CEO of Harlem's Success Charter Network; Tom Vander Ark, partner in Revolution Learning and former director of education for the Bill and Melinda Gates Foundation; Robert Waldron, president and COO of Curriculum Associates; and Charles Zogby, senior vice president of education and policy for K12 Inc.

We are, of course, indebted to the unwavering support provided by both the American Enterprise Institute (AEI) and the Annie E. Casey Foundation, especially that of their respective presidents, Arthur Brooks and Douglas Nelson. Financial support for this project was generously provided by the Annie E. Casey Foundation and the Bill and Melinda Gates Foundation, and we express our deepest gratitude for it. We also thank the terrific staff at AEI, whose hard work coordinating the December 2009 conference as well as compiling and editing the contributions herein made this volume possible. In particular, we thank Juliet Squire and Olivia Meeks for their diligent efforts, as well as Whitney Downs, Raphael Gang, Daniel Lautzenheiser, Claire Moore, and Jenna Schuette for their vital assistance. Finally, we would like to express our gratitude to the Harvard Education Press team, in particular our publisher Doug Clayton and production manager Marcy Barnes, who once again proved to be remarkably skilled and thoughtful collaborators in crafting this volume.

Introduction

Bruno V. Manno and Frederick M. Hess

TWENTY-FIRST-CENTURY SCHOOL reformers have inherited a model of K–12 public education that dates from the early-twentieth-century Progressive movement and was borne of an era marked by one-stop shopping and bureaucratic provision. This creaking model is antithetical to specialization and is an awkward fit for a world in which technology and tools have made it possible for new providers to deliver high-quality, customized services to targeted children or educators. The challenge of using new tools to rethink schooling in the information age is not unique to the United States but is one that policy makers are wrestling with around the globe.

Geographically defined systems governed by a central bureaucracy and charged with serving the varied needs of all children in a community were perfectly sensible responses to the educational challenges of a century ago. Given the limited tools for delivering instruction over distances, collecting and managing data, identifying particular student needs, or assessing performance, the effort to improve schooling via large, routinized "one best system" bureaucracies made sense in the decades from 1900 until World War II. In the period from World War II until the 1980s, efforts to desegregate schools, adequately serve children with special needs, and expand and extend the availability of traditional schooling to underserved populations were jobs that still seemed a good fit for the bureaucratic systems that the Progressives had built. By 1983, however, when *A Nation at Risk* mounted its fierce critique of America's K–12 system, the limitations of the one-size-fits-all machinery for a diversifying nation were becoming increasingly apparent.[1]

The then-century-old, centrally managed model was held responsible for providing all operational and instructional services to every school in a given geography, and, unsurprisingly, its operators were finding it difficult—if not impossible—to do everything well. The nation's successful school districts were increasingly those that possessed massive natural advantages: educated families, involved parents, a rich supply of talented teachers, and supportive communities.

For many reform advocates, this state of affairs prompted a deliberate effort to help students escape the unjust confines of geographically dictated education by allowing for greater movement between schools. However one feels about *school choice*—including various forms like charter schooling, school vouchers, and tuition tax credits—debates over school choice routinely assume schools to be the basic unit of educational delivery and then approach demand as the simple question of enabling families to choose among schools. The contributors here seek to push past this constricted view of choice and talk not only about selecting a better school but about creating an environment that welcomes increasingly customized and student-centered schooling. This entails a right to make a formal choice among providers but also a responsibility to attend to the kinds of information, outreach, flexibility in spending, and policy design required for such efforts to work as intended.

At the school level, the familiar building block has been based on the *whole-school model,* which served to bring together teachers and students in a single building at a time when there was no other practical way to connect students with instructors, tutoring, or educated adults. Today, of course, the proliferation of online instruction, multimedia instructional programs, tutoring providers, mentoring programs, and so forth means that those old ties no longer bind in the same way. Yet, this framework continues to presume that a school will be able to provide an array of services that will meet the range of needs of every child, ensuring that these schools will be overburdened and have a difficult time doing everything—or, in some cases, anything—especially well. The whole-school mind-set impedes opportunities for specialty education providers and leaves educators hard-pressed to meet the needs of unprecedented numbers of students or to customize instruction and supports to meet those needs.

While few batted an eye at the centralized school system in an earlier era, when bureaucratic, industrial giants were the norm, educators and analysts of all stripes are increasingly convinced that the old model is an anachronism in today's world of specialized services. In an era where providers routinely segment services in accord with a variety of consumer wants and needs, it seems ludicrous to take something as ultimately personal as learning and then force educators to provide it through systems designed on the presumptions that teachers are interchangeable, that students (other than those with special needs) are indistinguishable, and that instruction should be provided in predetermined, time-bounded blocks limited to twenty-four students at a time.

In a world where such trivial services as cell phone plans and television sports packages are routinely customized to meet individual needs, it is bizarre that school districts are so often tripped up when identifying the concerns of different families, seeking ways to provide extra tutoring to particular students, or finding means to satisfy demands for particular advanced or elective instruction. Old policies, practices, and habits of mind mean there is often far too little opportunity in today's education space for entrepreneurs to enter the business of training providers and delivering services outside preexisting district arrangements or institutions.

Recent efforts to reform K–12 schooling through both district-based and new sector solutions have generally focused on efforts to boost the *supply* of familiar products and services—for example, more good schools, more talented teachers, more effective school leaders, or high standards with linked assessments. One consequence is that even today's best known and most celebrated entrepreneurial endeavors in K–12 education reform, like KIPP, Achievement First, YES, Green Dot Public Schools, Teach for America, The New Teacher Project, and Uncommon Schools, have stayed within the general boundaries of existing policies and structures to try and fix education problems at the whole-school level. Terrific charter schools like these are deserving of admiration, but they also look very similar to any other familiar school—with the same array of services and approaches to staffing. While many of these less traditional endeavors are justifiably praiseworthy and do foster significant improvements in student achievement, we believe that their focus on building better whole schools is ultimately constrained. Given the finite amount of time and energy that can be devoted to creating and managing schools and the surplus of providers itching to serve students in some smaller way, it is surprising how limited the attention is for how providers might use new tools to deliver or customize services that do not conform to conventional policies or structures.

When we survey contemporary efforts by practitioners, policy makers, philanthropists, and would-be reformers, we see decided inclinations to focus on improving aged machinery and replicating familiar whole-school models and to rely on assumptions embedded in the one best system. Based on years of intimate involvement in K–12 policy and practice, we believe this emphasis is not the considered product of careful reflection but a default response to the world as it exists. The result is insufficient attention in the education community to the diverse needs of consumers—to the *demand* side of K–12 education. This dynamic is self-fulfilling, since a failure to think rigorously about diverse needs, opportunities for customization, or the needs and demands of various parties will continue to leave these needs unarticulated.

The reliance on the traditional whole-school approach impedes opportunities for decentralized specialty education providers to satisfy the wants of their consumers—including parents, students, teachers, and communities. No one suggested that Amazon creator Jeff Bezos should travel around the country shilling his new plan to sell books and music online to established stores until he found a taker. Nor was he told that the only way for his plan to be taken seriously was if he opened a chain of brick-and-mortar stores and sought to do everything Barnes & Noble already did, but better. Yet, in schooling that is very much the norm. It is our hope that this volume contributes to a shift in focus toward delivering the instruction and services that our children need rather than those that fit into the conventional school structure.

The key insight that contributors leverage in the chapters that follow is that, precisely because it is hard to do everything well, breakthroughs in efficiency and productivity are frequently the result of specialization. That requires finding ways to let providers figure out what students, families, and educators need; answer those needs in increasingly useful and powerful ways; and then provide their services to large number of students and educators across classrooms and schools.

EXTENDING INSIGHTS ABOUT ENTREPRENEURSHIP AND TECHNOLOGY

This volume builds on two distinct bodies of work that have gained momentum in recent years: one, efforts to understand the role and preconditions for educational entrepreneurship; and two, examinations of the transformative potential of educational technology. Frederick Hess has been an early leader at this nexus of research, editing volumes such as *Educational Entrepreneurship* and the follow-up *The Future of Educational Entrepreneurship* and *Education Unbound*.[2]

At the same time, advances in technology have often been championed for their potential to foster virtual school models and distance learning. Books chronicling this trend include John Chubb and Terry Moe's *Liberating Learning: Technology, Politics, and the Future of American Education* and Clayton Christensen, Michael Horn, and Curtis Johnson's influential *Disrupting Class: How Disruptive Innovation Will Change the Way the World Learns*.[3] These two books highlight the opportunities for new tools and technologies to transform the face of American education. However, as Chubb and Moe note, technology's impact is strongly dependent on the rules and policies that govern school practice.

In the era of No Child Left Behind, concerns about accountability are omnipresent, and the vast majority of attention on that front has emphasized whole-school assumptions, focusing on schoolwide achievement measures or treating traditional classrooms as the unit of analysis. In an effort to identify and analyze such countervailing trends, we sought out and assembled an esteemed roster of leading education researchers, practitioners, and policy makers to delve deeper into the obstacles to customization and a new class of more specialized education problem solvers. After surveying these difficulties, the contributors point out some key approaches to how we might start to extend and complement those efforts, suggesting smart ways to develop data and accountability measures, ensure availability of innovative tools, and better understand the consumer base for customized providers operating outside the boundaries of traditional classrooms, schools, or districts.

THE NEED TO UNBUNDLE

Today, practitioners and education school experts speak frequently of the need to differentiate instruction for a variety of needs, like those of children with disabilities, gifted students, and English language learners. Meanwhile, those in the world of education technology wax grand about new possibilities for streaming individualized instruction, devising personalized tutorials, and allowing experts to conduct face-to-face sessions with students halfway around the world. These aspirations, however, are routinely frustrated by policies, data systems, routines, and habits of mind that are geared toward the bureaucratic machinery of school systems. Financing systems, district analyses of familial needs, and resources for parents are not geared to facilitate the kind of high-powered customization that practitioners and technologists envision. Creating the room and resources for these efforts to unfold requires altering policy and familiar practice, and our hope is that the contributions in the pages that follow can help serve as a bridge between entrepreneurs and practitioners focused on meeting the wide range of student needs.

Becoming comfortable with customized schooling options requires first unbundling familiar notions of what is meant by education, shifting the conversation from school to schooling, from teacher to teaching. If we reimagine schools as mechanisms providing students with an assortment of services instead of delivering an indivisible package of "education," we can start to disentangle the components of that package and customize them to fit specific student needs and abilities. Harnessing new technologies and crafting policies that support such customization are vital steps to successfully upending our familiar approaches to delivering education, all for the benefit of students' families or for the educators, schools, and systems of schools that serve them.

Promoting customization through policy and investing in new providers and technology holds out a possible path to transformative improvement. The potential of this path is reflected by new providers tackling these challenges, such as Wireless Generation's mobile assessment software, the national network of afterschool mentors at Citizen Schools, or the online tutoring services available to students through SMARTHINKING. However, these organizations and others like them often encounter three chokepoints in their development and expansion: customized providers have to market to districts who cannot gauge or do not value productivity gains; foundations tend to fund whole-school approaches that have more easily discernible and localized impacts; and existing data systems often lack good ways to judge the quality or success of new education products.

The contributions that follow explore the questions of unbundling and customization and provide examples of how customization plays out in practice and the possibilities that loom in pursuing this course. The first section sketches the landscape for customized education provision. These chapters review the current providers, services, and global trends in the industry and use a thought experiment to challenge readers to think outside the box on how the public selects and consumes educational services. The second section provides concrete snapshots from on-the-ground efforts by schools and education entrepreneurs who are exploring the challenges and opportunities of customized education. These chapters report findings from an analysis of what customers (school leaders, teachers, parents, and students) want in educational services; whether and how schools can be designed to deliver these customized services to diverse students; the extent to which new technology and tools can be leveraged to meet differentiated needs; and a profile of participating entrepreneurs and how they understand and adapt to changing needs. Despite the potential of increasing customization, crucial challenges remain when it comes to service coordination, quality control, and policy implications. The final section seeks to address the practical concerns about policy and implementation by using the higher education example to address questions of coordination and related concerns; looking at the metrics and data needed for accountability in a more customized system; and, finally, exploring the implications of customization for policy making. As the final section of the volume alludes, the editors do not presume to have settled these issues. However, the absence of prepackaged solutions should not hinder the discussion of how to address differentiated student needs with new tools and new providers.

We hope that this book can help policy makers and practitioners think through the challenges of shifting our system of schooling to one focused on customizing instruction and services to serve students with diverse needs. Absent such attention, well-meaning reformers will continue to design policies and practices that stifle the emergence of more promising problem solvers.

THE BOOK AHEAD

Here we take just a moment to sketch the chapters that lie ahead. In chapter 1, Kim Smith and Julie Peterson launch the discussion of customization by trying to better understand the various consumers involved—including students, families, educators, and administrators. They explore how to identify the types of schools and services that different students and parents want and the kinds of instructional environments that teachers, principals, and students seek. The process and purpose of understanding key market segments is valued highly in most sectors but is little more than an afterthought in education. Smith and Peterson explain the notion of market segmentation, apply it to public education, and explain how it can create opportunities for new kinds of problem solvers to tailor customized services.

In chapter 2, Chester E. Finn Jr. and Eric Osberg undertake a thought experiment. If parents and students are the customers driving educational decisions, how might they be empowered to ensure that student needs are being more effectively served? Currently, parents and students exert influence on schools in a variety of ways, including through their choice of school, residence, teacher, and school boards and by paying directly for schooling. While such options afford parents some limited and relatively crude opportunities to customize schooling, Finn and Osberg explore how intraschool choice among classroom materials, teachers, and extracurricular activities can be expanded and bolstered through such mechanisms as weighted school funding, virtual schooling, and individualized education spending accounts. Pushing past conventional notions of school choice, they sketch a concrete vision of how financing and school organization need to be reorganized to facilitate a greater array of choices for parents and students.

In chapter 3, Chris Whittle demonstrates that trends in the macro economy are giving rise to private educational institutions that upend familiar geographic boundaries and provide services on a global basis. In the new international marketplace of schooling, Whittle notes, the emerging student populations in China, Korea, India, and elsewhere are becoming hungrier for Western higher education, while American parents increasingly look to broaden their children's exposure to the economic superpowers of the near future. Meeting the growing demand for the worldview only a globalized education can offer presents a new challenge for providers here and abroad. In this chapter, Whittle pinpoints the difficulties in identifying international customer preferences for educational services while also offering insights into rethinking how new institutions can resegment the marketplace, harness the potential of private providers, and leverage new advances in virtual learning to best serve particular student needs across geographic boundaries.

In chapter 4, Tamara Battaglino and JoEllen Lynch examine how districts can better serve a range of student needs by operating a portfolio of distinctive schools. New York City's "multiple pathways" approach to helping support and graduate special-needs students, Battaglino and Lynch note, offers a nearly comprehensive range of school options, paying particular attention to the highly heterogeneous needs and abilities that are largely neglected by today's one-size-fits-all schools. Drawing from experience with districts and school networks across the country, the authors identify core strategies for fostering differentiated schooling models, tracking resource requirements, and measuring the relative return on investment based on how well individualized programs are able to improve student outcomes.

Chapter 5, by Thomas Stewart and Patrick Wolf, presents cutting-edge research from their evaluation of the District of Columbia's Opportunity Scholarship Program. Stewart and Wolf provide a new level of insight into how parents negotiate a choice-based environment and identify their child's needs. The shift from the tradition of residential school assignment to a model of parental school choice, the authors argue, is equivalent to the change from shopping at the corner store to shopping at a sprawling shopping mall: consumers have significantly more options but are also faced with increased search costs and quality-control concerns. This study of low-income family participants indicates that some are not currently prepared for the shopping mall experience. Access to accurate comparative school information from a reliable and independent source—essentially a site map for the mall, or consumer reports about the different options—appears to be a key resource for urban school choosers, as is an extended network of concerned adults to help them navigate the marketplace. As Stewart and Wolf explain, participating families' engagement in the program evolves from client recipient of services, to educated consumers, and finally to citizen participants, providing us with a constructive way of viewing the effects of school choice and the implications for greater customization for families.

Much has been made about the potential of technology in education, but how can these new tools be leveraged to provide education customers with better-suited schooling options? In chapter 6, Douglas Lynch and Michael Gottfried tackle this challenge by first describing what these tools look like and then considering targeted ways in which they can be leveraged to increase customization. Anything that helps in the production of a good, Lynch and Gottfried explain, can be considered a tool, and using these tools to measure and promote quality in a more individualized, consumer-focused model can better serve student and school needs. Like computer shoppers looking to buy only those products with the Intel Pentium processor inside, education consumers (once they've been given information on the tools their districts use) can better assert their demand for high-quality school partners and thus choose only the best-fitting schools. The chapter also explores how new tools can help distribute better information, breaking the monopsonistic hold of traditional public education that currently dominates the education market and hinders incentives for innovation. Lynch and Gottfried then close with some thoughts on how to restructure the market conditions so that entrepreneurs such as Wireless Generation and SchoolNet can assess and meet demand.

In chapter 7, Joe Williams profiles how an emerging class of education reform organizations—a charter school management organization, a human resources-focused nonprofit that works with public school systems, and a nonprofit that trains teachers in reading comprehension strategies—responds to the diverse needs of their targeted customers. Williams also offers a taxonomy of players in education who respond to the latent demands of consumers in a number of ways, such as directly corresponding to needs, enabling needs to be better articulated, and nurturing a sense of demand among parents and schools. The journey of these players as exemplified in Williams's on-the-ground profiles showcases the promising opportunities and serious cautions raised as new providers attempt to identify the needs of clients and to question the extent to which they must adapt their products to fit those needs.

In chapter 8, Burck Smith discusses lessons learned from his pioneering work in customized higher education and applies them to course-level choice in K–12 education. New technological tools, Smith explains, allow for students from separate schools to be rearranged into specialized teaching cohorts, for differentiated content to be systematically coordinated and delivered, and for new online learning options to be integrated into face-to-face environments. However, because the mechanisms for intraschool choice in K–12 are limited by the inflexible regulations of compulsory public providers and by a host of coordination challenges, few have been created or explored. Postsecondary education, by comparison, is *not* compulsory, and colleges must compete for students who are more mobile and self-directed, who have many more educational models from which to choose, and who have greater options within those models. With years spent navigating the business of course provision, Smith identifies these structural barriers and echoes other chapters with his call for increased awareness of cost-effectiveness, a critical component to pushing schools to be more efficient while allowing families to spend education resources strategically. K–12 entrepreneurs are also provided with several seasoned insights into how to coordinate the raft of services between public and private education providers in order to satisfy a set of heterogeneous needs, as well as being given a glimpse into what greater schooling customization will look like on a systemic level.

Chapter 9, by Jon Fullerton, zeroes in on the significant data challenges facing customization efforts. Getting past one-size-fits-all schooling requires getting past one-size-fits-all metrics and accountability. Potential providers must understand the needs of parents, teachers, and administrators in order to tailor education options to them, and parents, teachers, and administrators need to understand what they are choosing among. However, Fullerton explains, today's monolithic data collection system often ties the hands of would-be customizers because it cannot capture the array of diverse needs of customers, nor can it be used to hold decentralized providers accountable. It is still not feasible to get information on how effective a provider is compared to their competitors, how effectiveness has changed over time, or how past customers rate providers on the issues that matter most. Given these challenges, Fullerton focuses on potential solutions to the challenge of data-based accountability for customized schooling, including a more robust and standardized assessment system, a transformation of state roles to give them more responsibility for warehousing data, and the potential rise of third-party market researchers and more advanced IT systems to capture and share critical information.

In chapter 10, Cutis Johnson and Ted Kolderie ask what it will take for policy at the school, district, and state levels to allow demand for customization to flourish. Drawing from their decades of experience in attempting to stimulate innovation in schools and schooling, Johnson and Kolderie assess the current governance and regulatory structures that block efforts to reform the creaky, centuries-old machinery that we still rely on today. The authors suggest we consider the case of school districts: these building blocks of American education are scaled-up arrangements from a time when standardization and geographic constraints ruled decision making. However, given the new opportunities created by technological advances, such systems have in some ways outlived their usefulness, blocking efforts to allow for alternate methods that deliver customized learning choices to districts. The new policies needed to bring schooling into the twenty-first century will require substantial rethinking of the way we approach K–12 schools, such as freeing funding flows, engaging in aggressive market research of consumer demand, rethinking the parameters of the classroom, and removing barriers to entry. By enabling change both inside and outside districts, policy makers can move beyond the roadblocks erected by the narrow consequentialism of the whole school choice debate and instead begin to craft policies that encourage and support providers of tailored schooling.

Finally, in the closing chapter Frederick Hess and Olivia Meeks try to draw through some of the common threads of the volume and discuss a few takeaways for policy and practice.

In this twenty-first-century world, individuals take for granted the ability to cheaply and easily talk face to face with family around the globe, to casually and instantaneously message dozens of friends around the nation, to carry on virtual debates with many far-flung experts, to search encyclopedias on a cell phone, and to access libraries of data and knowledge from a desktop. In this world, the routines of the nineteenth-century schoolhouse and the twentieth-century school district are an increasingly clumsy fit. Efforts to bend new tools, technologies, and practices to fit these old boxes have proven frustrating. Needed are new arrangements and ways of thinking that can allow educators, families, and communities to better seize on new tools and to individualize teaching and learning in a manner suited to an evolving world.

1

Creating Responsive Supply in Public Education

Kim Smith and Julie Petersen

THE FIRST STEP TOWARD improving public education is to strengthen and deepen our understanding of the diverse needs and preferences of its most important stakeholders: the parents and students it is intended to serve as well as the educators at the heart of the institution. Despite the very real differences between individuals in these groups, public education institutions have too often aimed straight down the middle, developing monolithic approaches that push aside these differences in the name of equity and fairness. But setting out to treat everyone the same has not led to equitable outcomes for students or to fair treatment of educators. We believe that a more attentive understanding of these characteristics, beliefs, and behaviors would lead to a supply of schools, tools, and services that is more tightly linked with student success.

In this chapter, we call for a new mind-set, *responsive supply*, that not only acknowledges the diversity of needs and preferences among education's central stakeholders but also seeks to better understand it and harness that knowledge to develop a variety of educational options anchored in these differences. This approach has the potential to dramatically improve public education by enhancing satisfaction, increasing student achievement levels, and improving the productivity of educators, programs, schools, and school systems. Not only could existing providers of education use this approach to adjust the way they do their work, but this information would also encourage a new crop of education entrepreneurs to address more richly defined market niches.

The road toward such responsive supply in public education begins with a serious commitment to placing students, parents, and educators at the center of our efforts and making a significant investment in what the business community calls *market segmentation.* This technique consists of education providers—including school systems but also teacher training and certification bodies, large curriculum and assessment publishers, and a range of entrepreneurial organizations—gathering detailed data and information about the characteristics, needs, and preferences of those on the receiving end of schooling. This information is then used to inform decisions about whether to address the resulting groups in a homogenous way, to differentiate approaches according to the needs of different groups, or even to tailor methods for reaching individuals. Without detailed information, though, we tend to make sweeping assumptions about what people want or need, defer to ideology or intuition, and end up with suppliers who unknowingly waste valuable time, money, and energy—not to mention frustrated consumers who do not get the products, services, or outcomes they are hoping for.

Although such segmentation has been more limited in public education than in other sectors, our recognition of diverse demand—and the resulting differentiation in supply—has increased bit by bit with every passing era. Gone are the days of the one-room schoolhouse, in which children of all ages were educated as one large group; we now have districts divided up into attendance zones that were initially intended to match students with schools based on their neighborhood's needs and schools that further segment students by grade and increasingly by developmental level. Still, most public education institutions—including the vast majority of districts, nearly all educator preparation programs, and even many entrepreneurial organizations—adhere to a one-size-fits-all mentality, with little responsiveness to the underlying diversity of demand. There has been an increasing amount of what we will call *diverse supply*. This is most familiar at the classroom level with the rise of differentiated instruction but can also be seen at the school level in portfolio districts that seek to treat different groups of students and families in unique ways by providing them with a variety of school options. There are also experiments under way to take this increasing differentiation to its logical endpoint by matching diverse individual needs with an equally diverse array of modular products and services that can be combined in exceedingly tailored ways. We call this approach *specialization* and believe that it holds important potential but at the same time presents some challenges that are of special concern to those seeking to improve outcomes for the students in low-income communities whom public education has often failed.

This chapter explains the concept of market segmentation as a foundation for understanding the demand side of education and explores how these principles could advance responsive supply in three areas: in breaking up the current one-size-fits-all mentality that pervades the human capital market, in furthering the diversity of public school options, and in pioneering ways to deconstruct and recombine the various elements of schooling in ways that are tailored to individual students. Ultimately, we make the case for a more open acceptance of the differences among students, parents and educators—and for redesigning our systems to explicitly account for and address those differences.

MARKET SEGMENTATION 101

In order to lay the groundwork for an understanding of what market segmentation is and how its principles could inform a more responsive approach to supply in public education, it is important to turn all the way back to the concept at the heart of it: a market. Simply put, a market is an economic system in which demand and supply—usually buyers and sellers—meet and exchange something of value. Suppliers provide goods or services that can be acquired, and demand is generated by the buyers or recipients of these products or services. The boundaries of markets can be formed in a variety of ways, including by geography—for example, the North American market, the urban market—or by product or industry, such as the market for coal or for cell phones. However, advances in technology are accelerating two divergent trends: markets are becoming simultaneously more global and more specialized, or niche. The former trend has been famously explained in books like Thomas Friedman's *The World Is Flat*, which points out the way technology is leveling the playing field so that even people in far-flung corners of the globe can transact with one another.[1] At the same time, explains *Wired* magazine editor Chris Anderson in his book *The Long Tail*, our culture and economy are shifting away from a focus on a relatively small number of products that reach a broad market and toward a very large number of small niche players who serve smaller and more precise markets.[2]

Within any market, suppliers and consumers attempt to maximize their own gain for the lowest cost. There is an implicit assumption that buyers and sellers are able to make choices—suppliers can choose who to focus their supply on, and buyers can choose freely from among a range of suppliers (or choose to exit the market). We believe such choice is important not only because it introduces accountability among suppliers but also because it increases the engagement of the stakeholders who make these choices. Together, these dynamics put pressure on suppliers to understand the demand side's needs and preferences so they can compete effectively with other suppliers. Of course, buyers and sellers are human beings, and therefore not always entirely rational, and they rarely operate with perfect information. The recent emergence of behavioral economics has illuminated the way people bring personal values and emotions to bear on their buying and selling decisions, which complicates these market dynamics.

When a customer identifies a need, she gathers some information and considers the available products and services, often grouping the potential options or vendors in order to make the decision easier. Should I shop at a single-category store like a specialty bakery or are my needs today better met at a superstore like Wal-Mart?

Do I need a regular cell phone or a tricked-out camera-and-Internet-enabled gadget that also makes calls? Often consumers will ask for advice from friends or family with whom they have something in common, and some will even consult with expert sources like *Consumer Reports*. But suppliers use an even more sophisticated range of information to understand their potential customer base. One important part of the analysis they do is market segmentation, in which the demand side is broken down into different distinct parts, or segments. This analysis is used to inform decisions within individual organizations about what kind(s) of supply they will provide. When paired with good information about supply that is made available to the buyer or consumer, such segmentation can help optimize the match between supply and demand in a given market over time.

What this optimization looks like can vary widely. In the business sector, where this approach is most widely and typically used and where moneymaking is the name of the game, the goal of segmentation is to increase profit by focusing the company's resources on products that are most likely to be purchased by consumers, resulting in maximized revenue for minimized cost. For example, many companies have seized on the baby boomer demographic segment as an attractive target for everything from health and wellness services to genealogy Web sites that capitalize on the aging group's concerns and have chosen to plow their resources into products for this market because of its sheer size and perceived spending power. However, maximizing supplier profit is not the only potential goal: increasingly, public agencies and nonprofit organizations are using this approach to target resources accordingly. For example, the consulting firm Bridgespan Group created a model for San Francisco's Communities of Opportunity initiative that categorized families in the city's isolated southeastern neighborhoods into three segments—"families in chronic crisis, families in a fragile state, and families that are self-sufficient—which allowed the city to direct support toward those families in different ways based on their needs.[3]

The nonprofit organization Social Compact has developed the detailed "Neighborhood Market Drill Down" analysis that has been used in places such as Washington, DC, to entice vendors like organic grocery stores to locate in inner-city neighborhoods by painting a detailed picture of the unmet needs and spending potential of residents.[4] This can surely be a win for the new vendors, but it also benefits residents by increasing their satisfaction with the retail options in their neighborhood and potentially their health and well-being by offering healthier food options. As such, segmentation is not just a cold approach to improving a market's efficiency and profits; it is also an empathetic way of figuring out how to improve outcomes for everyone by aligning the needs, preferences, and priorities of customers with thoughtful supply that is responsive to their needs.

Market segmentation seeks to group people according to some common characteristic or set of characteristics. The most familiar of these dimensions are *geographic* (urban or rural, specific ZIP code) or *demographic* (age, gender, race, ethnicity, socio-economic status), both of which are relatively simple to gather, thanks to the accessible tools like the U.S. Census and the objective nature of the data, and are generally used to classify broad segments. However, demographic and geographic attributes are no longer enough for most suppliers, who have found that far more useful results come from understanding *psychographic* attributes like values, attitudes, opinions, aspirations, and interests and *behavioral* attributes like what products people actually buy and how they are used. For example, Porsche sells its cars primarily to a demographic segment—male college graduates over age forty who earn more than $200,000 a year—but in order to boost sagging sales in the 1990s, they identified five psychographic segments, including Top Guns, who are driven by power and ambition who want to be noticed, and Fantasists, for whom a luxury car is an escape and a bit of a guilty pleasure. Porsche tailored its marketing and advertising according to these different segments, and sales skyrocketed.[5] On the behavioral front, online retailers like Amazon.com use recommendation engine software to monitor and analyze users' behaviors—including what they search for and what they end up choosing—as a way of predicting future purchasing decisions and making recommendations accordingly. The promise that such software holds for increasing sales is so high that Netflix just awarded a $1 million prize to a group of developers who came up with a more successful algorithm for such recommendations.

These examples show how segmentation analysis can lead to a tighter fit between what suppliers offer and what consumers want, particularly when it goes beyond basic geographic and demographic data to get at the heart of people's motivations. But because psychographic and behavioral data are more subjective and nuanced, they are harder to gather and interpret and require the use of sophisticated tools like surveys, focus groups, product demonstrations, and interviews. Moreover, it takes a big dose of judgment and a lot of energy to capture and interpret this kind of complicated data. As such, most industries have a bevy of market research and analysis firms that focus on gathering and analyzing information about demand, and businesses stand ready to pay them top dollar for this customer intelligence. For example, in the technology sector, Yankee Group focuses on demand for telecommunications products and services, while other firms like Forrester Research and Gartner gather information about a wide array of technology markets.

At its best, market segmentation is part of an ongoing, data-driven cycle of learning and adaptation. New companies often emerge to fill the gaps that such analysis identifies, while existing companies use the results to determine how they might tweak existing products (or just market them, as Porsche did) or whether to introduce new ones. In either case, suppliers may choose to use the results of segmentation analysis to serve one or multiple segments in a one-size-fits-all way (by offering a single product with no tailoring beyond it) or to serve different segments with different products or brands. For example, while a local bed-and-breakfast offers the same experience to all its guests, Hilton Hotels has a wide portfolio of hotels that range from Hampton Inns for "value conscious and quality-minded travelers" to Doubletrees for business travelers to the high-end Waldorf Astoria brand. In either case, businesses have found that it behooves them to be clear about what segment they are serving, to understand thoroughly the needs and preferences of that segment or segments, and to tailor their marketing information accordingly. It is the rare business that aims its product or service blindly at whoever might stumble on it.

Moreover, it is becoming increasingly possible for suppliers to serve individuals in a tailored way, with examples ranging from news Web sites that allow users to choose the topics their page will display to Converse shoes allowing customers to design their own athletic shoes online. The economy as a whole—fueled in part by technology advances—is moving simultaneously toward a more global, far-reaching playing field and to more personalized or niche treatment of individual groups and customers on that field. As such, market segmentation no longer requires companies or other organizations to default to targeting customers who are geographically close, nor does it mean that they need to go only so far as to differentiate between large groups. It is now possible to serve the diverse needs of many customers in many places and in very individualized ways.

These dynamics are playing out in public education as well, albeit much more slowly and too rarely informed by segmentation data about the differences in needs and preferences among students, parents, and teachers. Although the one-size-fits-all mentality is eroding, with more support than ever for increased differentiation and even specialization, the shift has been fraught with resistance to the idea of intentionally treating people differently.

SEGMENTING DEMAND IN PUBLIC EDUCATION

To apply this segmentation framework to education, it is important first to acknowledge some of the ways public education is, and is not, like a classic market. Public education is both a public and a private good, which introduces a legitimate tension about the extent to which it should prioritize the needs of society and communities as a whole versus the needs of individual students. Mark Schneider and Paul Teske have pointed out that "schooling is characterized by only an indirect link between the payment for and the receipt of the service, which blunts some of the power consumers have over private goods, such as the ability to withhold payment."[6]

Another dynamic that distorts the system is the lack of a user- or learner-centric approach in policies and buying decisions. For example, state textbook adoption processes and purchasing cycles often adhere to timelines and criteria that reflect the state's ability to consider or purchase materials rather than the pace of change in the content or the needs of teachers, let alone student utility. Despite these complicating factors, analyzing supply and demand in education is still a useful way to increase the diversity and responsiveness of our approaches.

The education market looks something like this. States are divided up into districts, which then operate some number of public schools. By default, students generally attend the public school in their neighborhood, so that the buying decision is based on where their parents have decided to live. However, parents and students are not the only consumers, nor are schools the only suppliers. Districts and schools buy products and services from outside providers, so in that equation they become the demand, with vendors of things like transportation services, student meals, and classroom computers as the supply. Yet another conception of supply and demand in education has to do with educators themselves. Although few currently think of them this way, current and prospective teachers and leaders are the customers of preparation and certification programs and also choose what school they want to work in. Across this landscape, notions of supply and demand are complicated, and who is playing which part depends very much on which part of the market dynamic is under consideration. For the most part, education policy is arranged to support the conventional view of the education market, with federal, state, and local dollars flowing to local education agencies and then to physical schools, with districts and schools spending the vast majority of their funds on staff, and with other monies used to procure products and services from outside providers for things like materials, transportation, food services, and so forth.

The growing number of entrepreneurial education organizations has begun to unsettle this familiar marketplace. In earlier work, we defined education entrepreneurs as innovators who have a vision for a better way of doing things despite the constraints of existing rules and resources. These visionaries create new nonprofit or for-profit organizations to realize this vision and, through their success, redefine our sense of what is possible, inspire others to follow, and inform changes to policies.[7] Across the public education landscape, entrepreneurs are challenging familiar roles and expectations for what students can achieve, what teachers can accomplish, what role schools and systems should play in supporting student success, and what other tools are necessary. In some cases, these organizations are doing things differently in relatively familiar roles, such as operating public charter schools in place of district-operated schools, preparing teachers and leaders for roles in such schools, and creating smart student assessment and analysis tools that address needs left unaddressed by large education publishers. Often, these organizations disrupt the old dysfunctions in the education market by taking a more user-centric approach, such as the way charter schools must market themselves to parents in order to secure student applications. This trend is on the rise as an increasing number of families choose to supplement their student's education at home with additional content or even attend entirely online or virtual schools.

When it comes to entrepreneurial supply, therefore, the question of what the relevant demand is and how it might be segmented comes down, in part, to the kind of approach the organization is taking. What most of today's most promising entrepreneurial education organizations have in common is their shift toward a more user-centric approach, often one anchored in the use of data, as a way of improving student outcomes. However, they differ in whether they are appealing to parents (to choose their charter school over district offerings, say, or to choose their tutoring service), teachers (to choose their preparation program), school systems (to choose their content, product, or service), or some other consumer.

Before turning to the ways in which market segmentation can inform smarter supply in public education, it is important to consider one final dynamic that makes education such a complicated market: the role of choice. As noted earlier, markets work best when buyers have the option to make other choices; otherwise, while there will still be suppliers and users, there will be little dynamic or responsive interaction. Economist Albert Hirschman has explained how an organization's ability to improve hinges on the interrelated ability of members, citizens, consumers, or employees to exercise voice in attempt to effect change or to exit.[8] This holds true in education and has been a subject of heated debate. Many have resisted allowing parents to more actively choose a school for their child, and public policies like certification regulations and collective bargaining agreements make it difficult for administrators to choose the staff that best fits their needs. School choice supporters tend to trust that competition will motivate improved behavior by suppliers, while opponents often distrust markets as harmful, impersonal forces that benefit only the wealthy. Both of these conceptions miss the point. As inconvenient as it is for pure free market supporters, markets actually require quite complex and thoughtful regulation—witness the recent developments in the financial industry.[9] Meanwhile, those who fear market forces fail to consider the potential for choice to have a broad positive impact on a system that can be made more dynamic and responsive through the existence of competition.

It is not just the abstract system that benefits, though; individual participants reap the rewards. Organizations simply work better when the people who gather within them agree on a common purpose and approach, and they ignore this reality at their peril. When people gather in an environment to work together (as teachers do) or learn together (as students do) and they have divergent ideas of what they should be accomplishing or how they should be operating, leaders and managers must spend a lot of time and energy trying to resolve these issues. Such misalignment often masquerades as disgruntled employees or customers; but because the problem runs deeper than that, it often detracts from the work at hand and makes it that much more difficult to achieve positive outcomes. Choice, together with clear information about what is involved in making that choice, is a proactive way to channel energy away from attending to the squeaky wheels and toward actual learning.

Choice is also critical for a third important reason: it increases the agency of the stakeholders who make these choices. The ability to make choices is crucial to our sense of well-being and our motivation, which, in turn, leads to increased engagement—exactly the sort of behaviors educators hope to foster among teachers, parents, and students. "Choice has a clear and powerful instrumental value: it enables people to get what they need and want in life," notes author Barry Schwartz in his book *The Paradox of Choice*. "Freedom to choose [also] has what might be called expressive value. Choice is what enables us to tell the world who we are and what we care about." Research has shown that the very act of choosing leads people to demonstrate an "escalation of commitment" to what they have chosen. Moreover, the lack of choice can lead to what psychologist Martin Seligman has called "learned helplessness," a belief that one has no power to influence an outcome, which leads to an inability to take action *even when* circumstances are changed and the opportunity to choose is offered and has been linked to everything from poor health to low academic outcomes.[10] As such, inherent in our analysis of how market segmentation can inform smarter supply in education is the implicit assumption that doing so will yield the most benefit if users—whether students or educators—have a choice in the matter.

Perhaps due to the legacy of tracking and other systems that were misused as tools of bias and exclusion, we have been reluctant as a field to explore beyond the surface similarities within our public school communities and really understand the differing needs and priorities that might benefit from being tackled in different ways. Likewise, we have ignored the different skills and strengths among teachers and school leaders and have shied away from creating diverse approaches to preparing and supporting them. However, we are at a unique moment in education in which a better understanding of the characteristics, needs, and values of students, parents, and educators can have a significant impact. Policies like No Child Left Behind have pushed us toward disaggregated student data and have put a spotlight on the unaddressed needs of entire groups of students. The current administration is building on that by pushing for fewer, clearer, and higher common standards; more sophisticated assessments; and a stronger data infrastructure that will support measuring student need. At the same time, frustration with the pace of improvement in traditional schools has made low-income communities more receptive than ever to innovative approaches to learning, and technology has likewise made it possible for entrepreneurs to experiment with such approaches in affordable ways.

Indeed, it seems that we as a nation are finally moving away from an almost universal acceptance of one-size-fits-all schooling toward increasing differentiation and even specialization of the means we use to achieve our educational goals. In order to better understand how improved market segmentation can help us move forward, we consider three different areas of the education market. First, the labor market for teachers and leaders is largely undifferentiated and so will serve here as a case study for an area where little segmentation and responsive supply has happened and where there is a great deal of work ahead. Second, some differentiation has begun to occur in the realm of school options for parents and students, but such differentiation in supply has not generally been mapped to actual demand among parents and students. Finally, we consider the trend toward more personalized learning that is targeted directly at the needs of individual students, which implies both a detailed understanding of preferences, motivations, and needs and a similarly granular approach to how other resources would need to be reconceived in order to support those needs.

ONE SIZE FITS ALL: EDUCATORS AS WIDGETS

It is somewhat shocking that the segment of the education market that still clings the most to the one-size-fits-all mentality is the market for teachers and leaders. Despite the fact that we are dealing with professional adults who are mature enough to choose a profession, select a course of training, and find a place of employment, we constrain these choices at every turn. Moreover, as The New Teacher Project showed in its recent report *The Widget Effect: Our National Failure to Acknowledge and Act on Differences in Teacher Effectiveness*, even once teachers have found their way into a classroom, we persist in treating them as interchangeable in the way we evaluate them, with less than 1 percent of teachers receiving unsatisfactory ratings and half of districts studied not dismissing a single teacher for poor performance in the past five years. It is absurd to pretend that teachers are interchangeable widgets that can be prepared in the same way or moved seamlessly from one environment to another, yet that is just what we do today across teacher preparation programs and most districts. Given that education is a service business where the vast majority of operating budgets are allocated toward salaries, it seems ludicrous that we do not yet organize this market in a way that would enhance preparation and licensure and engender more productive working environments that correspond with the diverse needs, preferences, and skills of educators.

The failure to recognize this begins with preparation. The vast majority of traditional teacher education programs treat teachers in a one-size-fits-all way, beyond the generic variables of what grade level they want to teach and what subject matter they might specialize in. Regulation distorts market forces here, causing these institutions to behave as though their customer is neither their students (or, for that matter, the students those teachers go on to instruct) nor the schools who hire their graduates but, rather, state certification and accreditation regulators. With a few notable exceptions, like the Stanford Teacher Education Program (STEP), which is focused on teachers who want to serve diverse populations, and Columbia University's Klingenstein Center, for teachers who want to work in independent schools, few higher education institutions proactively identify a specific market segment or niche to serve. Fewer still gauge the demand among prospective teachers for instruction in particular pedagogical approaches, nor do they consider the demand among placement schools for different types of teachers or skills. Perhaps even more troubling is that few preparation programs bother to track and assess their own effectiveness over time, as measured by their graduates' ability to bring about successful student outcomes.

Entrepreneurial providers have made some progress in this market. On one end of the spectrum, new online providers of teacher education like Capella, Western Governors University, and 2Tor consider their primary customer to be the aspiring teacher and thus emphasize priorities like convenience. Some observers fear this comes at the expense of quality and call for these providers to consider school placement sites as customers whose satisfaction and outcomes should also be tracked. On the other end of the spectrum, new preparation programs anchored in specific charter school models like Teacher U (born out of the needs of Achievement First, Uncommon Schools, and KIPP) and High Tech High Graduate School of Education (housed at San Diego's High Tech High, the first charter school authorized by the state of California to fully credential teachers) consider placement schools as their primary customer and thus take a highly specialized approach to selecting and preparing teachers for success in a specific kind of work environment.

We do not yet know if this placement-based approach is more effective, but many of these entrepreneurial providers are tracking their graduates to measure whether such alignment and customization leads to better teacher performance and better student outcomes. Some segment their customers according to the specific types of educators they believe will be successful in their program and beyond. For example, from the moment she started Teach for America (TFA) in 1989, Wendy Kopp was clear about the segment she sought to recruit into education: young leaders who were community minded and who would help reform education over their lifetimes, from whatever careers they ended up in, and who would begin by committing to teaching at least two years in an underresourced classroom. As such, TFA focuses on the demographic of recent college graduates that bring psychographic traits like an internal locus of control, a passion for community service, and a high degree of grit or tenacity. Over the last twenty years, TFA has found that these characteristics correlate with effectiveness in the underresourced classrooms and makes them more likely to carry out the program's longer-term mission of public service.

Once educators have been certified or credentialed, there is equally little differentiation applied to the various types of work environments in which they can choose to work. Currently, educators are divided primarily by grade level (elementary versus secondary), subject, and students taught (comprehensive, Advanced Placement, special education) and, beyond that, by compliance-oriented mechanisms like certification, years served, and tenure. School systems generally resist further segmentation of educators based on management style (their own and the type of structure they work well within), preferred pedagogy, and desired school culture. However, as former Gates Foundation official and teacher David Ferraro has described, allowing educators to make active choices among schools can help create much more effective and productive work environments by aligning them with colleagues and organizations that match their deeply held values and beliefs—and that is before we have even tried to match them with roles that take advantage of their actual skills.[11] Certainly, some teachers are more motivated and successful in a highly constructivist environment, while others might prefer a more structured one; still others prefer to design much of their own curriculum, as compared to those who would rather follow an established set of lessons and assessments. And these preferences may very well change over time as an educator becomes more comfortable with the craft of teaching or as their lifestyle changes.

Although school systems and training programs have begun to invest energy and resources in measuring teacher and leader effectiveness, most of that work mistakenly assumes that "effective" is more or less the same in all environments. Pragmatically, good educators understand that these differences exist, and good principals seek to hire teachers who are a good fit with their school model, culture, management style, and values, just as good teachers seek to find schools and leaders aligned with their own preferences and talents and values. Charter school management organizations (CMOs), have embraced this mind-set, understanding that the clearer they are about what their school stands for and how it will operate, the more likely they are to attract and retain professionals who want to be in that environment and can be successful there.

Based in large part on our work with entrepreneurial organizations developing new approaches to preparing educators, as well as with nearly two dozen different charter management organizations, we believe that a better understanding of the underlying preferences of the labor market for different work environments—preferred pedagogy, culture, team values, operating principles, work schedules, structure of the day and year, leadership styles of principal, and compensation approach—would dramatically improve productivity and satisfaction on both sides of the equation. "If we knew [what their preferences and skills were], we could create schools and work environments to maximize productive and happy teachers, which we know equals great gains for students," agrees Kaya Henderson, deputy chancellor of District of Columbia Public Schools, who oversees the district's human resources work. "This would also force us to make sure we have a portfolio of options for teachers the way we are working to have a portfolio of diverse options for students."[12]

Such analysis should be conducted and tracked over time in order to figure out if there are some stable segments of the market we should be treating differently in order to improve effective instruction and strengthen student outcomes. Are there relatively stable groups of educators who want different environments, or do their preferences adjust in tandem with changes in their skill level or lifestyle outside of work?

Some research does segment teachers into newer or younger teachers and older, more experienced teachers and examines differences in opinions and attitudes. But as long-time market researcher Steve Farkas said, "One of the things we most need to know is: what are the characteristics of the segment that stays motivated and continues learning and pushing their practice over long periods of time?"[13] This is the kind of information that could help us understand what types of environments would draw educators in and keep them engaged. A recent study from Public Agenda and Learning Point Associates entitled "Teaching for a Living: How Teachers See the Profession Today," took a step in the right direction by dividing current teachers into three psychographic clusters: the Disheartened, who tend to feel unsupported by their school's administration; the Contented, who see teaching as a lifelong career; and the Idealists, who see teaching as a way to help underserved students get ahead but are likely to move on to other careers. The report encourages school systems to consider how to address these groups in different ways, determining how best to support the Idealist's passion with skills and resources while at the same time determining whether the Disheartened is in the wrong career or just the wrong school.[14] Clearly, more and deeper research such as this must be done to probe into the behaviors teachers exhibit through the choices they make, the results of the instruction they provide, and what that implies about how we might structure different kinds of teacher preparation programs that respond to those needs as well as a range of working environments for educators that take advantage of those differences.

A few organizations are coming up with ways to identify good matches between teachers and leaders and the schools they choose. For example, the Haberman Foundation provides online surveys and interview tools that are intended to help school systems hire educators who will be more effective in serving low-income and at-risk students in urban environments. They do this by tracking behavioral and outcomes data across a large group of educators in order to identify attributes that correlate with high success rates. Their Star-Teacher Pre-Screener can be combined with an interview protocol that they claim leads to a "95 percent accuracy rate in predicting which teachers will stay and succeed and which ones will fail or quit."[15] Still a relatively blunt instrument, in the sense that it considers all at-risk and urban environments as essentially the same, it nonetheless provides a greater degree of market segmentation analysis of the potential teacher and leader labor pool than these environments often have. Similarly, the Knowledge Is Power Program (KIPP) has designed a leadership selection rubric to help identify prospective leaders most likely to succeed in operating schools that follow the KIPP model and serve low-income students, and it has refined this rubric over time based on linking these attributes with successful school outcomes. The rubric has eleven major characteristics, some of which are rooted in skills like communication but many of which are psychographic attributes like adaptability, relentless achiever, self-awareness, and student-focused.

Better segmentation analysis of the education labor market might also allow school managers to do a thoughtful redesign of staffing models, including differentiating among the kinds of roles teachers and leaders can play based on their skills and preferences. More in-depth understanding of how different kinds of teachers excel in different ways—this one on instructing large groups, that one on coaching struggling learners, another on leading teams of teachers, still another masterminding curricula or assessments behind the scenes—could lead to new ways of addressing instructional needs and to innovative ways of mapping the diverse labor pool against those needs. Indeed, this differentiated approach to career progression is taking hold in the corporate sector, where "career lattices" that allow for employees to chart their own progress in a variety of ways are beginning to replace the antiquated notion of the corporate ladder, with its rigid, linear path from one role to the next.[16] This could even allow schools to offer more flexible and part-time positions that could either draw certified teachers back in new roles or allow other talented people to contribute to schooling.

A recent Education Sector report on school designs aimed at maximizing teacher effectiveness cited a number of promising new approaches, including the variety of community partnerships that the Brooklyn high school Generation Schools has established, such as with the nonprofit organization ReServe, which places retired professionals in schools and other organizations. In a low-income Latino community near Boston, public elementary school Gardner Pilot Academy even has an extended services director on staff to coordinate the contributions of fifteen community partners. "This kind of support, where aides and interns are assigned to oversee recess, lunch, and before- and after-school programs, means that teachers' work at Gardner can be designed almost entirely around improving instruction," notes report author Elena Silva.[17]

DIFFERENTIATION: DIVERSIFYING THE SUPPLY OF SCHOOLS

In contrast to the lack of differentiation we apply to educators, we have slowly been increasing our recognition that students are different at the classroom and school levels, and there are even some limited experiments to create differentiated options. In spite of this progress, there are too few examples of school providers who are segmenting the demands of students and parents (or educators) as a way to inform the development of more effective and more diverse supply that is responsive to those demands. As enrollment swells or shrinks in a district, the response is usually to find ways to accommodate additional students in existing schools or to close entire schools, rather than using this as an impetus to get underneath the reasons for the enrollment change and to determine how the system might adapt accordingly.

Moreover, although entrepreneurial providers of schools like CMOs are often more customer oriented—creating a coherent and consistent brand to appeal to parents and educators and gathering frequent data about student progress and parent satisfaction—their models tend to correspond with founder ideology or experience rather than with specific knowledge about student and parent demand. So, ironically, although in aggregate they provide diverse supply to the market, individual entrepreneurial leaders often demonstrate the same kind of one-size-fits-all mentality that plagues district leaders, believing that their own model is the only size that will fit right.

In cases where schools have wait lists—a sure sign of demand outstripping supply—it is rare for anyone to mine the information on those lists, whether it be a district considering how demand for specialized magnet schools might inform its own programs or a charter school operator determining what kinds of unmet needs exist in a community. One researcher told us that he works with a district where roughly 75 percent of parents report considering a school other than their default. But when he asked for data on historical wait lists to analyze the specifics of unfulfilled demand, he learned that wait lists were managed at the school site and often discarded once empty seats had been filled, with no attention paid to what this latent demand could tell them about how to adjust supply.

Some districts and entrepreneurial school operators perform limited marketed segmentation using the relatively blunt instrument of demographics. For example, CMOs assess prospective neighborhoods and communities for their next school site based in part on an analysis of areas of high poverty and the often corresponding low school performance. In Montgomery County, Maryland, Superintendent Jerry Weast segmented his community into Red and Green zones in an effort to differentiate between the needs of different parts of the community. Based largely on demographic information (which correlated to large and persistent achievement gaps), Weast used this simple segmentation to allocate resources differently across the zones in an effort to increase equity of academic opportunities.[18] The complex work of leading this community through this change was anything but simple, but the segmentation analysis itself and the overarching supply response rationale were relatively straightforward: using demographic analysis, apply more funds to the schools where chronic failure correlates with poverty and minority student concentration.

A more sophisticated approach can be seen in *mandatory choice* districts where all eighth graders must actively choose a high school, as Boston and New York have done, and in *portfolio districts,* where leaders seek to manage portfolios of schools rather than directly operating all of them, as cities like New Orleans and New York have done across the board and Chicago has done in a more limited way with its Renaissance 2010 initiative. Even in mandatory choice and portfolio districts, leaders have not yet segmented their market in a way that would inform a differentiated supply of schools for students, parents, and educators to choose from. More often, leaders will create or seek out school models that are perhaps tailored to broad demand in a geographic neighborhood (such as around a failing school) or to a specific grade level and then survey parents once a year to assess satisfaction. In districts that have instituted mandatory choice, the policy has created more awareness of what supply is most popular among parents and in some instances has begun to create a responsive adaptation by districts (with replication of a few popular college-prep high schools and the increase of programs like art or band), but neither has taken a systematic or proactive approach to optimizing the match between what it offers and what communities seem to want.[19]

Meanwhile, Paul Hill, at the Center on Reinventing Public Education, is working with a network of portfolio management districts and indicates that they are most often responding to the school providers that approach them, not investing in market research to proactively consider how to meet parent and student demand with optimal supply. And no district we found was putting all of these parts together by applying this logic to better understand how their labor pool of teachers and leaders mapped to parent and student demand.

The responsive supply mind-set is taking hold first in areas where the traditional model has been most inadequate. For example, in New York City's District 79, created to serve a demographic and behavioral segment of over-age, under-credited students, entrepreneur-turned-superintendent Cami Anderson and her team realized that "in spite of the fact that failing kids are often seen as a monolithic group, they are actually a quite diverse group." They set out to segment the 150,000 students in their district in an effort to dramatically improve outcomes by providing much more responsive supply. Their work built on earlier efforts under the leadership of Michele Cahill, which began with an in-depth analysis of demographic and behavioral data that identified some predictive triggers for students who ended up in this situation and then led to the closing of some large comprehensive high schools that were responsible for more than two-thirds of this pool of students. At the same time, they identified that a set of transfer schools and other recuperative programs were having much greater success and so almost doubled the supply of these kinds of seats, including programs like the South Brooklyn Community High School and Young Adult Borough Centers and revamped GED programs such as GED Plus and Access GED.[20]

Moreover, when Anderson's team analyzed the transfer schools that were achieving the best results, it found that one key factor was the way the schools combined academic rigor with a case management approach to the social and emotional challenges of the students. It also found that that there were different psychographic and behavioral attributes that led students to fall behind in credits, which in turn affected which kinds of interventions were most likely to be effective. So the district pursued a more advanced market analysis to better understand these diverse segments of students. With the help of the consulting firm Parthenon Group, the district administered a student survey with more than four thousand respondents that uncovered three primary segments of students: those who had real and significant learning challenges, those who were reading and thinking at high levels but were behind in credits for some reason (ranging from too little time in class to low test scores to significant social or emotional issues), and those whose challenges stemmed from some major life event, like the death of a parent, a pregnancy, or being a victim of violence. Following up on this general segmentation, District 79 formed in-depth focus groups on more detailed subsegments, such as girls who had dropped out to have babies and then returned to school, in order to better understand what kind of responsive supply might have kept them in school all along. The district leaders learned that guidance counselors had advised these girls to drop out once they became pregnant; however, these girls shared that after becoming pregnant, they felt an even greater appreciation for the importance of succeeding in school, and what they needed was someone to push them *not* to give up as well as some adaptive services like study groups and mentoring by other girls who had succeeded despite pregnancy. As Anderson describes:

> We decided to close the schools that offered segregated programming with really poor outcomes and to invest the money in the Living for the Young Family through Education (LYFE) program—school-based childcare centers with a dual mission of providing access to excellent early childhood experiences so parents can stay in school while helping them transition successfully to parenthood and a toolkit of resources for principals to help student parents stay on track toward graduation in their schools. The focus groups helped to sharpen the action plans for both—still very much works in progress. For example, many of the students' quotes and suggestions will appear in the tools for principals. As another example, many of the LYFE centers are piloting parenting groups and curricula in response to the expressed needs of the students.

Although efforts to create more diverse school environments have been helpful in better meeting the varying needs of students, parents, and educators, too often this differentiation has been based not on data-driven analysis, as in the District 79 example, but on the intuition and ideologies of those making supply-side decisions—including district and charter school system leaders, school leaders, and philanthropic funders who choose which school models and networks to support. Billions of dollars have been invested based largely on hunches about what teachers and parents want and what students need. This has led to a school supply market that combines various mixtures of pedagogy, school culture, content emphasis, and activities into loosely differentiated models. There is a spectrum based on pedagogy and culture that ranges from, on the one end, experiential learning (such as Outward Bound) and constructivist project-based learning (High Tech High, Big Picture Company, Envision Schools) to, at the other end, more structured programs like Achievement First and KIPP, with those school models that offer features from both approaches, like Aspire Public Schools, in the middle of the spectrum. Other kinds of differentiated supply include specialized approaches such as single-sex schools (e.g., Excellence Academy in Brooklyn, Young Women's Leadership School of East Harlem) and content-specific schools (e.g., Denver School of Science and Technology).

Despite the number of parents on wait lists and teachers who have been attracted to these new public charter schools and others, those that have developed and funded these charter schools do not really know whether they collectively provide the right mix and proportion of models to reflect the priorities and desires of parents, the learning needs of students, or the working styles of educators. When we created NewSchools in 1998, we hypothesized that there was a very diverse underlying demand among parents, students, and educators and have since invested a great deal of time, energy, and money in supporting a variety of CMOs in low-income communities. However, we have not been able to raise philanthropic funds for corresponding market research that would explain the demand-side perspective so that we could map supply accordingly; nor have we seen anyone else take on this work, outside of rare exemplar districts like Edmonton, Canada. As a result, we simply do not know what portion of urban parents want a constructivist school environment over a more traditional one or how many would prefer single-sex schools or subject-specific schools, let alone what proportion of students are positioned to best succeed in these and other models. Is the popularity of traditional school environments—as measured by high numbers of applications for any new school opened by KIPP, Uncommon Schools, and Achievement First—a reflection of true parent demand or of a limited supply of quality options? We simply do not know.

In this section, we focused largely on *parents as demand* for whole schools because they act as proxies for student need and it is their actions that often dictate what school students end up in—whether by residential choice or specific school choice. The little research that has been done in this area has indicated that for parents, the act of choosing a school for their child is quite complicated and involves many values-laden considerations as well as personal judgment about what environment might best serve their child's needs. Some have hypothesized that there may be a hierarchy of needs akin to the one psychologist Abraham Maslow developed for basic human needs, where survival and safety must be attended to first, followed by social interaction and then individual accomplishment: parents attend first to the immediate safety of their children and beyond that begin to differentiate along values-based lines.

There is little research to determine what needs—academic quality, convenience, school culture, extracurricular options, diversity or homogeneity of the school's population— are next in line and why. All of these qualities probably matter, but in differing order for each customer. To inform smart supply among those who make decisions about providing schools to students, parents, and communities—including districts but also entrepreneurs and their funders and policy makers, like charter school authorizers—we need market research that is sophisticated enough to combine both empirical, evidence-based preferences and more subtle values- and personality-based preferences. At that point, there may well be a public policy debate about whether to meet that demand head-on or take a page from behavioral economists like Cass Sunstein who might encourage us to "nudge" parents toward the most effective environment for their students.[21] However, we cannot even engage in a productive debate until we understand where parents, students, and educators are actually coming from.

SPECIALIZATION: PERSONALIZING LEARNING FOR STUDENTS

At the opposite end of the spectrum from a one-size-fits-all mind-set is personalized learning, which harnesses technology advances to deliver educational products and services directly to students and teachers and either meets a specific need by design or can be customized to do so. This vision was perhaps best laid out by author Clay Christensen in his book *Disrupting Class: How Disruptive Innovation Will Change the Way the World Learns*: "The proper use of technology as a platform for learning offers a chance to modularize the system and therefore customize learning. Student-centric learning opens the door for students to learn in ways that match their intelligence types in the places and at the paces they prefer by combining content in customized sequences."[22]

While technology has facilitated this movement toward specialized or personalized learning, it is also motivated by the recognition that despite the progress that public schools have made over the last several decades, there are still too many students whose needs are not being met, particularly in low-income communities where few read and do math on grade level and even fewer graduate and go on to receive the college education they will need to succeed in the knowledge age of the twenty-first century. This dynamic has also had an impact on the most advanced K–12 students, as the intense focus on improved equity has in some cases meant less attention and fewer resources directed toward gifted students. The pace of this change is being accelerated by a policy environment supportive of common standards and assessments as well as by technology that makes it far cheaper and easier to build, maintain, and distribute sophisticated software. Together, these advances make it more possible for entrepreneurs and other innovators to devise creative ways of addressing very diverse student and educator needs through content, tools, assessments, support services, virtual schools, hybrid schools (which combine offline and online elements), and other approaches we have not yet dreamed of. Done right, these shifts could also generate more data about the needs and preferences of parents and students and, therefore, help us better understand the different segments of demand, which could in turn lead to dramatic improvements in productivity and academic success.

In some ways, this trend is a natural progression from the increasing differentiation of instruction at the classroom level, in which a teacher groups the many students in their class as a way to acknowledge the different pace at which they may master content or the response they may have to different instructional strategies. This development has been increasingly coupled with adaptive software tools that allow the pace of instruction and assessment to be hastened or slowed based on student progress and for teaching modalities to shift based on student responsiveness. For example, Carnegie Learning created a cognitive tutor for algebra that recognizes the different kinds of mistakes students make along the way and adjusts instruction accordingly. A more recent example is Apangea Learning, which uses a huge database of historical student performance data to track individual behavioral patterns and provides real-time human tutoring online once a student has maxed out his potential for self-directed computer-generated tutoring. Generally, these approaches allow educators to treat individual students in a more personalized way but still within the traditional staffing, management, and policy environment.

Meanwhile, an increasing number of parents have expressed their dissatisfaction with the public school structure itself by either choosing to homeschool their children, enroll them in virtual schools or online programs, or supplement their school experiences with some sort of out-of-school instruction. Homeschooling and virtual schooling account for more than 2.5 million students—compare that with just 1.5 million students enrolled in charter schools.[23] This trend speaks to an increasing sense that students should be treated as individuals and that traditional brick-and-mortar schools are not necessarily the best way to meet their needs. Historically, schooling has meant that resources and personnel have been concentrated in the same geographic place as the students and where they do all of their learning. The increasing openness of parents and students, combined with the rising sophistication and affordability of technology, is enabling these elements to be unbundled and could make for a much more a la carte approach to public education—and, with it, for new concepts of how to learn, to teach, to supervise, to lead, to allocate resources, to sell products, and to provide services. "When I think about where we are going to be in fifty years, I think we are going to have a marketplace model for education where the student is in control of their education and they determine who is going to educate them, when, where, and how," said venture capitalist Fred Wilson. "I'd like my kids to be able to avail themselves of the quality classes and teachers they have in their physical space but then opt out of those [classes] that aren't good and go get that knowledge somewhere else."[24]

For example, a state might allocate to each child a weighted formula of funds based on their socioeconomic and learning characteristics, and then educators or parents might be able to use these public funds to select a customized combination of educational services rather than have them simply be directed to a single school. The parent or learning advocate might have either a general roadmap of subjects that would need to be covered over the course of time in order to meet state standards or an individual education plan, and then they might choose within that framework a variety of content and services in keeping with their child's needs. For example, they might choose online foreign language instruction from Rosetta Stone, AP math from Apex Learning, college counseling services from College Summit, science lab simulations from Lockheed Martin's Virtual World Labs, courses in accounting at the local community college, and so forth. Furthermore, technology can be harnessed to ensure that content is meeting the needs of individual students: the software platform developed by the start-up Guaranteach allows the user to choose online math instruction videos based on preferences for simpler or more complex concepts, fast-paced or slow-moving tutors, verbal descriptions or pictures. The idea is that the user (the parent, on their child's behalf, and in consultation with their child as appropriate) would become more of an active shopper, piecing together the various parts of an education from different suppliers using public dollars.

This kind of modular system would enable learning to be highly customized in both the individual parts of instruction and how they come together to form a coherent education. Having a parent do the work of assembling the pieces is not the only way to conceive of this, though. A state, district, school, or educational advocate could take a more modular approach to managing providers of instructional services for the students under their supervision (just as they manage providers of services like food and transportation today). For example, at the limited end of the spectrum, the Florida Virtual School is already serving seventy thousand district students in 150,000 classes, initially filling gaps in curriculum options at traditional high schools in the state rather than operating as a degree-granting institution, and more recently has moved into the role of of being a complete virtual school of record. The school receives per-pupil funds for those students who successfully complete and pass their courses, making the school more responsive to student demand and more accountable for results than many traditional schools. Meanwhile, the school district of Alpine, Utah, has created a hybrid approach, establishing an online K–8 school to support its homeschooled students using courses from K12 Inc. and other online school providers rather than developing its own curriculum, thereby allowing them to quickly switch providers for specific subjects when necessary.[25]

As content is delivered from multiple providers in a variety of configurations, we will need dramatically different approaches to assessments and the traditional notions of courses and credits. More than two decades ago, education professor Frank

Smith described a system like this as "like a 'student outcomes ATM-card' for tracking progress and data management. As they demonstrate performance mastery, students could swipe their 'ATM card' at various school and community locations to keep track of their progress."[26] What was a futuristic story two decades ago is now close to what the state of New Hampshire is rolling out as they combine new staffing and assessment approaches to better support Extended Learning Opportunities for high school students. Students can learn from independent study, private instruction, performing groups, internships, community service, and online courses and can participate in new competency-based assessments that determine whether students really are learning in this new context.[27]

Perhaps the most sophisticated and far-reaching version of this customized environment is the School of One in New York City. In the summer of 2010, the district piloted the School of One inside an otherwise ordinary middle school. Parents and students selected the school. Students equipped with laptops worked in different configurations throughout the day—individually and in groups, with a laptop or with a teacher. End-of-day computer-based assessments determined what the next day would bring for each student. The model is still early and so far only covers math, but founder Joel Rose, chief executive of the city's Department of Education's human capital office, envisions that a technology-based learning platform at the heart of the School of One would eventually gather student information (learning styles, preferences, interests, progress), analyze the school's resources and constraints (teachers, content, physical space), and generate a tailored "playlist" of learning activities for each student, with teachers recast as much more specialized instructors. This could be a radically different way to deliver a more personalized learning experience to students based on their unique academic needs, learning styles, and motivations—and a new means of using teachers in a more differentiated and focused way, allowing them to take on more specialized roles based on their own content expertise, instructional style, and skill level. In fact, early indications show that the playlist algorithm ensures that students have already mastered precursor skills and content before each new module. This allows teachers to focus on their current lesson without having to juggle between students who are ready and students who really are not yet ready for the current lesson, which, in turn, has led to increased productivity and satisfaction.

Certainly, staffing arrangements can and should be adjusted to make the most of more personalized learning environments and could allow resources to be allocated in new and creative ways. Supervisors or coaches—competent adults with less instructional expertise than teachers (and likely less expensive as a result)—could oversee the progress of a group of students learning online; certified teachers might even be able to supervise slightly larger classes given the personalization of technology-enabled learning. California charter school management organization Rocketship Education is experimenting with this kind of creative staffing approach by using technology to reallocate resources away from teacher salaries and toward other school needs. It may even be feasible for some students to be paired with a rigorous technology-based instructional program and a case worker or other adult whose skills more closely match the needs of disconnected youth with significant emotional needs. Historically, our system tries to split these students in two, asking certified teachers to teach them in one setting while a case worker or coach helps them address their emotional needs in another setting. Integrating these services might better meet the needs of these students.

Unbundling educational supply—entirely or partially—creates the opportunity for a diversity of supply to meet very specialized segments of student need. This is happening throughout the economy in a phenomenon described as the "long tail," in which a large number of sales of niche products, when taken together, earn more revenue than those of a smaller number of so-called "hit" products.

"In an era without the constraints of physical shelf space and other bottlenecks of distribution, narrowly-targeted goods and services can be as economically attractive as mainstream fare," writes author Chris Anderson, who popularized the concept in his book *The Long Tail*. "People gravitate towards niches because they satisfy narrow interests better, and in one aspect of our life or another we all have some narrow interest (whether we think of it that way or not)."[28] It is likely that this personalization will lead to much greater effectiveness for public education, particularly for students with special needs that are difficult to meet in a bundled school environment that often needs to aim its resources at larger groups of students in order to be cost-effective.

CONCLUSION

No one in education really argues that one size fits all. However, there has been too little acknowledgment of diversity among and across stakeholders in public education; too much reluctance to address that diversity by investigating characteristics, needs, and preferences; and not enough of the cultural shift we need to adjust the way we deliver education to more dynamically optimize productivity, effectiveness, and satisfaction for both educators and students. Too often we create policies that place the onus for personalizing education on educators and parents but don't give them the context, the resources, or the support they need to do this well. Educators do a heroic job of trying to navigate the different skill levels and learning styles of their students, often in a school structure that runs counter to the way they prefer to work and alongside colleagues whose philosophies and approaches to education may be different. Meanwhile, we give most parents just one high-stakes moment to choose the public education environment that will serve their student best—when they choose a home—even though we know that choice is bound up in other requirements ranging from the job market to where their extended family is located. After that moment, they must be vigilant to ensure their child's needs are being met, and only in rare circumstances will they choose to go through the laborious process of finding supplemental services, let alone switching to a different school.

It is incumbent on those who provide public education and create new supply—whether that is the public policy makers who establish the rules and regulate funding streams, the foundations that support new supply, or the entrepreneurs who are busy devising innovative new approaches—to figure out how to account for and address the diverse needs and preferences of educators and students. This requires the development of public policies that support a more comprehensive approach to data, invite both parents and educators to make more choices, conceive of content as more than textbooks and learning as delivered by organizations other than local education agencies and schools, and allow funding to flow in more user-centric ways, such as weighted student formulas.

Furthermore, we will also need to invest in the systems and infrastructure needed to make this shift. For example, current assessment models, which are largely annual summative tests that rely on one delivery methodology (pencil and paper bubble scans), will become less relevant as education shifts to become more tightly attuned to interim and formative assessments and more responsive to specific needs and modalities (including things like computer-delivered simulations). We will need new approaches to assessment that allow students to demonstrate mastery of individual learning modules at their own pace as well as systems that can track this progress in a nonlinear way and across a variety of potential learning environments—in school, at home online, in a workplace, and in the community. In addition, we will need robust technology infrastructure on the supply side to help deliver content, organize resource allocations, allocate instruction and supervision in new ways, and ensure quality oversight of an increasing number of education providers.

Indeed, this shift toward increased differentiation and personalization thrusts education's myriad stakeholders into new roles. School systems and schools will need to focus more on developing strong academic standards and acting as arbiters of educational quality and less on being the sole providers of instruction. Teachers and principals would no longer be cogs in a standardized system but true professionals who are able to act on their preferences and maximize their contributions in a variety of ways. Parents would exercise not just residential choice, and then agitate for the best opportunities within a monopolistic framework, but would wield greater degrees of freedom—and responsibility—to choose between whole schools and tailored programs for their students. Even students themselves would become more engaged participants in designing their own educational opportunities from a raft of possibilities.

However, these new roles could quickly spiral into an unmanageable set of choices if we are not careful about how we aggregate and present information. Scholars of choice have found that people can be easily overwhelmed not just by the sheer number of options but also by difficult or complex choices that have weighty consequences. For instance, one study showed that while most people say they would want control of the very personal issue of cancer treatment, after diagnosis almost everyone actually prefers an expert to tell them what to do.[29] Similarly in education, we will need to strike a delicate balance between an increased number of options and the complexity of those decisions and come up with ways to present information in much more transparent and user-friendly ways.

Rather than guessing about how this might work, we should begin immediately by identifying what parents, students, and educators want by not only asking them but by offering pilot experiments that show them how such options would actually work and then track how they actually behave and what it tells us about the kinds and degrees of choice they actually want to exercise and what the benefits and trade-offs are. This implies near-term investment by the public, philanthropic, and even for-profit sectors in market research studies and firms and in starting and growing expert information sources patterned after organizations like Consumers Union and JD Power & Associates that provide unbiased and detailed recommendation information to consumers of retail products like cars and electronics. These efforts must be supplemented by investment in the kinds of robust data systems needed to manage this information, and in a wide variety of small providers that can test out new niche approaches to instructing students and preparing educators. Ideally, this would all lead funders to invest in a greater diversity of school providers and more diversified supply of adaptive and modular learning tools that address demonstrated needs and stated preferences, especially if there is data to show that such responsive supply leads to smarter use of philanthropic and investment resources and greater outcomes for students. However, in the short term this may require for-profit capital providers to make a greater number of smaller investments—which is at odds with how venture capitalists prefer to work—and philanthropic funders to support riskier experiments than foundations generally prefer to support.

Once we have better data about what such differentiated efforts look like and lead to, we can then engage in broader discussions about the modularization and personalization of the public good called *education*. Would it be the most underserved who would thrive from customizing their education, which could be a major improvement for productivity overall, or would it be only the most technologically savvy and empowered learners and their parents who simply want to advance their own progress? Is the promise more about increasing equity by meeting the needs of those who the current system is failing, or is it about increasing the adaptability of the system so that it accelerates the pace of learning for all students, including those who are advanced and those who are struggling? Certainly, since personalized education generally involves more independent work and individualized choices, many will be concerned about the weakening of public schools' role in creating a coherent society out of many diverse communities. There will also be some who believe that having students attend neighborhood schools and having teachers instruct groups of students face to face is necessary for social and emotional development. These are legitimate concerns, but the reality is that today's students are comfortable with technology and using it and other means to meet their individual needs, and the society we are preparing them for is moving increasingly toward differentiation and personalization. So now is the time to engage directly in these debates and redesign public education policy so that we are no longer constrained by rules that were created during the agricultural and industrial eras but instead can create a system that optimizes the mix between public and personal good in the twenty-first century.

Kayakers have an adage: in order to steer, you must paddle faster than the water you are in. Similiarly, for those of us in education, not embracing the future doesn't mean it will not happen; it simply means we will not be prepared to to take advantage of it for the most productive benefit of educators and the students and communities they serve.

2

Reframing the Choice Agenda for Education Reform

Chester E. Finn Jr. and Eric Osberg

AN EDUCATION SYSTEM RESPONSIVE TO—and guided by—the priorities of parents and children would have many merits. The top-down nature of public schooling would change as *consumers* acquire at least as much leverage in this marketplace as the *producers*. No longer would a child's school experience be dictated primarily in distant board rooms, legislative chambers, government agencies, and faculty lounges. As is already the case in preschool, in higher education, and in most other spheres of American life, the customer would have plentiful choices and numerous opportunities not only to select among them but also to shape the options themselves. A culture of innovation and customization would emerge as educators and school systems continuously adapt to the preferences and requirements of their diverse clients—and as they find themselves obliged to compete for those clients and their patronage. Schools would focus more directly on what matters to children and parents rather than on bureaucratic compliance, job protection, and the other familiar habits of organizations that lack outside pressure to perform. Taken together, these changes would produce a dramatically altered education system, significantly different classrooms, and a more contented, more empowered, and better educated citizenry.

We see two overlapping and complementary rationales for giving consumers greater say in education, twin arguments that derive from basic economics. First, better-functioning education markets will more fully satisfy the consumers. Their needs and preferences will be met more precisely, affordably, and flexibly than is possible in a top-down system. Second, the competition fostered by such markets will lead to a more ample supply of diverse, high-quality, and cost-effective schools and other education providers by rewarding those that succeed and marginalizing or eliminating those that are undesirable or unable to keep pace with the competition.

Buyer-responsive markets can easily be imagined at the school level, not least because a fair amount of it already exists. But it can also be visualized *within* schools—among courses, teachers, even instructional materials. Here we describe what such a dynamic could entail and how it might change education, customizing the work of schools in accord with the needs of students and parents while also improving school quality, productivity, and effectiveness.

It is true that if such changes were as easy—and incontrovertibly desirable—to accomplish as to imagine, they would be upon us today. So we will also note some barriers and trade-offs inherent in such a demand-driven education system, beginning with the fundamental truth that education is both a public and a private good. It must address larger societal needs even as it provides for individuals and families. On the public side, we expect our schools to lay the groundwork for civic participation, higher education, a competitive workforce, a robust economy, and a sturdy culture. Education is not ice cream or skateboarding; it is an essential good, and it performs a vital public function. Moreover, we expect it to serve all pupils fairly and competently, regardless of race, income, physical condition, mental prowess, or prior education. We also impose on our schools public burdens that are not strictly academic, such as tending to the health of children and imparting basic values and work habits. Alongside such contributions to the commonweal, we ask our schools also to meet the diverse needs of millions of young people, providing them the education that they and their families crave, maximizing their potential, readying them to support themselves, and accommodating their myriad idiosyncrasies, dreams, and circumstances. Quite a balancing act. Quite a challenge.

HOW PARENTS AND STUDENTS ALREADY
INFLUENCE SCHOOLS

Consumers have long possessed many mechanisms by which to signal and sometimes act on their schooling preferences. Families with the financial means can move to neighborhoods with superior public schools or enroll their children in private schools. For some, teaching their kids at home is an avenue for avoiding schools altogether. In recent years, magnet, charter, and virtual schools have provided additional options. Some districts operate selective schools for high achievers, such as New York's Stuyvesant and Bronx Science. Some states allow children to attend schools in adjoining districts or (as in Minnesota) anywhere in the state. Adding it up, one can reasonably estimate that at least half of American students—most from the upper half of the income distribution—are enrolled in schools that entailed some form of choice on the part of their families. And those families have greater access than ever before to information that can facilitate their school selections—not just school-level report cards posted on state Web sites but also private information providers and interpreters such as GreatSchools.org and SchoolMatters.com.

But selecting among schools is not the whole story. Particularly at the secondary level, students and parents have long enjoyed options: among vocational, academic, and honors tracks; between French and Mandarin; between physical education classes or the track team. Gifted and talented programs, Advanced Placement, and International Baccalaureate courses create additional within-school opportunities, as do arrangements that allow students to take courses at the community college- or university-level while still in high school. And then, of course, there are the innumerable extracurricular options (school newspaper, drama club, ROTC, Future Farmers), as well as supplemental offerings outside the school altogether, like ballet lessons, internships, and summer science camps. Such opportunities have burgeoned in recent years as America has become more diverse, as political pressure for choice and equal opportunity has intensified, and as technology and prosperity have facilitated access to such options. The advent of online or virtual courses, for example, has enhanced our capacity to elect courses, modes of study, daily schedules, and even some choice among teachers, as well as our ability to supplement regular schooling with outside offerings.

At the same time, there has been pressure in the opposite direction—from uniform academic standards and testing, for example, and certainly from resistance by teachers unions and other influential elements of the public school establishment. In some ways, then, public education has become *less* responsive to parents as districts have focused on state and federal accountability requirements and found themselves bound more tightly by regulations, collective bargaining contracts, and court precedents. Still, the dominant trend has been toward amplification of consumer-driven education options among, within, and outside schools.

Parents also exert indirect influence over their children's schooling by voting in school board (and other) elections; by participating in school affairs via PTAs and PTOs, classroom volunteering, or field trip chaperoning; by testifying at school board meetings; and by using their influence with board members, principals, teachers, and others to get their daughters and sons into certain classes, clubs, and programs. With the help of special education and civil rights statutes and (sometimes) litigation, the parents of disabled children in particular wield substantial control over their student's educational experience (though here, as elsewhere, the well-connected and well-to-do generally exert greater clout than the poor and powerless).

Students, too, exert influence over their own schooling, increasingly so as they progress to high school, where they face a plethora of choices among electives, clubs, sports, and more. Education visionary Ted Kolderie notes that "Minnesota now has schools in which young people make more decisions, individually about the pace and nature of their learning and collectively about the rules by which their school runs."[1]

Yet, today's education market displays multiple gaps, dead ends, and shortcomings. Good information remains limited. Though private data providers augment objective statistics like test scores, student demographics, and course offerings with subjective parent reviews and comments, such information is often sketchy. For example, the profiles of Maryland's Montgomery Blair High School, a school of nearly three thousand students in a middle-class suburb, contain not a single parent review on School-Matters.com and just eleven on GreatSchools.org (three of which are more than five years old).[2]

Even if parents had better information, many families would still find too few viable options. The public school establishment's pushback against most forms of choice is well documented.[3] The political battles over charters in many states—whether to allow them at all, what constraints to place on their growth and funding—have been intense, so that today, nearly two decades after the first such school opened in Minnesota, less than 3 percent of all public school students study in charters. Eleven states still have no charters at all.[4]

Choices among districts are also constrained. Only eighteen states insist that students be allowed to cross district lines to find other public school options, and many of those policies incorporate severe limitations. In Arkansas, for instance, the transfer is conditional on its desegregation impact; Missouri's program is limited to those who live unreasonably far from their assigned school or whose district has no accredited school; and several states restrict their required transfer programs to only students in low-performing schools.[5]

Within individual districts, too, many parents enjoy few choices. Only half the states require local school systems to offer choices, and many such offerings are skimpy. In Massachusetts, for example, they are restricted to students assigned to racially imbalanced schools. Thirteen jurisdictions limit their required alternatives to students attending low-performing schools.[6] And while the federal No Child Left Behind Act (NCLB) of 2002 sought to expand public school choice, at least for students in faltering schools, just 1 percent of the 6.9 million eligible students participated in that option in 2006–2007, and "a majority of parents . . . say they were not notified of those options, even though the districts documented that they had sent out written notifications."[7]

While plenty of large high schools offer ample menus of classes and programs, many students attend small, rural, or poor schools where they find far less variety—scanty Advanced Placement (AP) offerings, few foreign language choices, little choice among small seminars or lab-style classes, and no say over whether they are placed in front of a didactic or student-centered teacher.

In short, despite the proliferation of education options in recent years, many families enjoy far too few choices among and within schools.

WHAT COULD BE DIFFERENT TOMORROW

The present situation need not describe the future. One can picture many paths by which students and parents could gain greater power over their own education and over the offerings and practices of schools and districts. Although consumer supremacy in public education may seem like a pipedream in 2010—and would surely come with trade-offs and drawbacks—in a host of ways, schools *could* adapt and customize their offerings to satisfy their consumers more fully than they do today. In the process, the education delivery system would become more open to the benefits of innovation and efficiency rather than remain focused mostly on costs, as it does today. If we can muster the political will, technological capacity, and vision to see past the status quo, parents and students could wind up with many more choices among schools, courses, teachers, and instructional materials.

More School Choices

To align public education more precisely with the preferences of families, we can continue to create more new schools, more choices among existing schools, and more of the financial and political mechanisms whereby such choices can be exercised by a widening sector of the population. Programs allowing parents to choose among public schools, both within their district and across district borders, should certainly be expanded. And voucher and charter programs should be allowed to flourish and grow. But such changes, though desirable and probably inevitable, are apt to continue to be gradual—and too slow for the millions of students now relegated to inadequate schools.

A faster form of change—one far harder to block through traditional politics—is heralded by virtual schooling. Technology holds great promise for conferring education options on families. It helps remove the physical, logistical, and geographic constraints created by school locations, classroom capacity, teacher availability, calendars, and more. As Terry M. Moe and John E. Chubb write in *Liberating Learning*, technology points to a future in which "schools will do a better job serving needy constituencies."

Cyberschools provide a vehicle for incorporating the nation's million-plus homeschoolers into the education system, providing them with high-quality curricula and an organized schooling experience. Dropouts can readily take the classes they need for graduation, aided by the choice and flexibility that cybers provide them—and the graduation rate should climb. Rural kids can escape the limitations (usually due to small size and budget) of their local districts, use cybers to enroll in a full range of specialized and advanced courses, and take advantage of what the larger education system has to offer. Gifted kids, so often held back by the "least common denominator" norm in regular schools, can zoom ahead at their own speed."[8]

Technology creates opportunities both to grow choices *among* schools and to create more options *within* schools. Consider the Florida Virtual School, now with 84,000 students.[9] Other states have similar statewide offerings, and an additional 100,000 students attend virtual *charter* schools in twenty-two states.[10] Virtual courses have been growing for years, creating options within and alongside schools. Starting with Utah's Electronic High School in 1994, 1.03 million students participating in virtual classes of one form or another in 2007–2008, and forty-four states now "offer significant full-time or supplemental online learning options for students."[11] All of these give students and parents the flexibility to customize their educational experiences. When changing schools can be accomplished by altering the Web address on one's computer rather than moving homes or busing across town, parents gain abundant market power, as do students—particularly at the secondary level—with interests and passions of their own.

How might such options be further expanded? Certainly the six states without significant online course offerings (Oklahoma, Maine, New Jersey, New York, Rhode Island, and Vermont) and the twenty-eight states with no virtual charter schools represent wide-open opportunities for growth.[12] Virtual coursework is also destined to accelerate, as has happened in other industries in the wake of new technologies. In *Disrupting Class: How Disruptive Innovation Will Change the Way the World Learns*, Clayton Christensen, Michael Horn, and Curtis Johnson predict that within a decade half of all high school courses will be online, driven there by a superior cost structure, ever-better technology, and looming teacher shortages in brick-and-mortar schools.[13] The growth of online learning will occur both within traditional schools and in the less corporeal environments of charter and virtual schools, where the swiftest diversification is likely. As Moe and Chubb explain, "The proliferation of autonomous schools, combined with their differentiation as they seek out niches and constituencies to attract enrollment, will give students and parents a much broader array of alternatives to choose from: some cyber, some hybrid, some neither, with many variations on each theme."[14]

There are, to be sure, many relentless foes of choice and plenty of good and bad arguments against it. The most squalid arise out of self-interest—that of school systems which stand to lose funding, unions that fear shrinking power and membership, or bureaucracies bent on maintaining control. Nearly as bad are arguments that stem from ideology or misinformation, such as the fear of letting private ventures gain a larger foothold in public education, the concern that competition will harm rather than strengthen public schools, and the belief that choice will inevitably siphon the best students from traditional public schools. These concerns have been debated for years and refuted with skill, so we will not rehash them here. Nor will we linger over the opposition to cybereducation in particular, which is no less intense and self-interested. Unions, for example, understand that virtual education may portend fewer conventional teachers. But there are also legitimate concerns about educational efficacy: Will children learn as well from a computer? For what ages and subjects is virtual learning really suitable? Is it practical for lower-income students? Does it diminish pupil interactions with other children? As such options expand, the opportunities for analysts—and parents—to evaluate them will increase and clearer answers will emerge.

In the meantime, however, we must acknowledge several important barriers to a high-performing, parent-driven marketplace of schools. One important concern is the paucity of good consumer information. Another is the risk that giving schools the incentive to appeal to parents' demands could yield perverse outcomes, since we know that academic success is only one among families' priorities. Parents may, for example, prize safety, convenience, or sports above academic performance. Others may judge schools by their appearance and facilities. Will schools respond by devoting excessive time to cosmetic matters? Will they fret too much about keeping parents happy and hesitate to send stern messages to those who need them? Do such concerns undermine the potential for parental choice to force schools to compete on grounds of academic quality?

Plainly, this market needs a safety net. The default school option must be adequate. When it comes to restaurants, we assume that the health inspector and the FDA ensure that what we eat is safe, even if not necessarily tasty. But safety is not enough in schools, which are more like medical devices (at least in the United States) that are obliged to demonstrate both their safety *and* their efficacy. Society's interest in education demands that all schools not only meet minimum legal standards but also produce acceptable academic results.

A set of strong academic standards, suitable assessments, promotional gates, and graduation requirements can provide a reasonable academic safety net. Combined with an effective blend of sanctions, interventions, and help for schools that fall short, both parents and society can be reasonably confident that the choice among schools is not fraught with educational peril.

Another objection to school choice is that it will foster a fragmented society in which people sort themselves into likeminded clusters, becoming isolated in communities with people who look like themselves and share their values.[15] Will such sorting weaken the shared public nature of schooling and undercut the common experiences we hope all students receive at school? It is possible that some of this will occur, and, within limits, it is not all bad. For example, enrolling students whose families share similar educational priorities or who themselves have similar needs helps a principal who seeks to focus his school's mission, strengthen its culture, and customize its programs.

The negative effects of such sorting could also be mitigated by a strong common core of academic standards and course requirements ensuring that all schools cover the essentials of history, science, and other topics. Curriculum expert E. D. Hirsch is perhaps the foremost proponent of such an approach, which he deems especially important in the primary and middle grades when students must acquire essential knowledge in core subjects.[16] With this safeguard, we need not unnecessarily restrict parents' freedom to select among schools for fear that pursuit of their own preferences would undercut the public good in public education. Hirsch suggests that the common core might comprise half of the curriculum in grades K–8 and that schools would be free—and perhaps encouraged—to differentiate themselves in the other half. (He also expects high schools to differ considerably from one to the next.)

A final, important concern about school choice is that too many parents will turn out to be passive consumers, accepting the school they are assigned—or the one closest to home—rather than seeking out better alternatives. For example, under NCLB's choice provision, "parents have shown a low propensity [t]o avail themselves of the options offered to their children."[17] That further argues for a robust system of standards and accountability to ensure that the default choices are sound for families that do not make the most of the education marketplace.

Evidence from other sectors is instructive, too. Economists have found that markets can function well so long as a reasonable fraction of consumers is truly active. Economists have estimated that perhaps 15 percent of customers in the United States are information seekers who make product comparisons and strive to make an informed decision—for example, which brand of soap or toothpaste is most effective and most economical—while the rest of us simply grab what is on sale that week or has the snazziest label.[18] Economists have argued that these active consumers help make the market more efficient for all buyers, since manufacturers and sellers strive to satisfy that small minority. As a result, the other 85 percent of shoppers, though more passive about their selections, are reasonably assured of quality products.

Schools, to be sure, work differently than supermarkets and soap companies, and the number of active, fussy consumers may need to be higher for those who run schools or districts to respond to pressure to improve and compete. But with a sufficiently free market, a growing number of better-informed consumers, and enough choices, all parents can benefit, even if some are better than others at navigating the complicated process of selecting a superior school.[19] Furthermore, because research suggests that parents can be induced to become more active by giving them choices, some of the challenges we perceive in getting parents more involved in their children's education may simply be an artifact of the weak control they have today.[20]

Regardless of whether all parents ever become fully engaged in choosing schools, the fact that some ride on the coattails of others is not an obstacle in creating a better market for schools, nor should it deter our quest to widen options for students and families.

Choice Among Courses

Not only do parents need more choices *among* schools, they would also benefit from more having choices *within* their children's schools. The most straightforward approach is to increase the variety of courses and programs available to students. Certainly, many schools do supply a considerable variety of individual courses as well as curricular pathways. *The Washington Post* reported that "Virginia offers a growing menu," including an "advanced diploma" that "requires more math, science, social studies and foreign language credits." "About half the Virginia students who completed high school last spring [2008] earned one," and in 2010 "students who prefer to learn by doing will be able to earn one of two technical education diplomas."[21] Many other high schools course choices across many subjects. Even in a field like art, a large high school—Maryland's upscale Walt Whitman, for example—may furnish a plethora of art choices, from the basic to advanced levels and covering specific genres like drawing, photography, digital art, and more.[22]

A school must ordinarily be large enough and wealthy enough to offer much variety beyond the traditional elective choices of French versus Spanish, AP Biology versus basic life sciences. But classes could be differentiated in other ways, even in smaller, poorer settings. For example, tenth-grade English could offer a choice between a thirty-five-student lecture and a nine-student seminar. Likewise, physics could be either primarily lab based or textbook based, depending on the teacher's experiences and preferences and on market demand. If teachers were judged on their results, they could be freer to deviate from their colleagues in instructional styles while still assuring parents that education quality will not suffer. Indeed, such pedagogical freedom might lead to its improvement.

Students would also benefit from continued expansion of within-school options. Consider, for example, multigrade classes, team-taught classrooms, homogeneous versus heterogeneous grouping of students on the basis of prior achievement, as well as more all-embracing programmatic options (such as International Baccalaureate [IB], art-centric, or language immersion programs). Although we tend to suppose that high schools provide course options while elementary schools do not, this need not be so. Even if all schools were to adopt a Core Knowledge–style curriculum for a sizable chunk of the school day, there is still room in elementary and middle schools for pre-IB programs, gifted and talented programs, accelerated math, and other choices. And while schools charged with imparting basic skills and knowledge to younger pupils may never become curricular multiplexes, they need not be art houses either, serving up only a single take-it-or-leave-it offering. Parents and students need at least a few key choices that are not unduly costly or disruptive for schools.

Once again, technology makes much of this easier, more economical, and more accessible for small schools. Offering classes online is a relatively direct way to provide students with more curricular choices and sidestep some of the constraints imposed by school buildings, faculties, and budgets. Such courses can span an impressive array of subjects, as entrepreneurs and innovators push the virtual boundaries. For example, the online Virtual ChemLab "serves some 150,000 students seated at computer terminals across the country."[23] Even gym and music classes can deploy imaginative technologies. Consider Nintendo's Wii, which allows users to participate physically in any number of games and sports in their living rooms. Some teachers are already incorporating Wii Music into their classrooms. Given the high cost of supplying real instruments to students, it creates learning opportunities that are otherwise out of reach for some schools. As an MSNBC broadcast recounted, "Using the Wii Remote and Nunchuk controller, players can experiment with more than 60 different virtual instruments ranging from bagpipes to ukulele. They can play mini-games such as 'Handbell Harmony' and 'Pitch Perfect.' And they can jam or improvise as part of an ensemble."[24]

Some people fear that providing more curricular choices—actual or virtual—within a school will undermine the institution's culture or distinctive educational mission. Successful schools often feature a coherence that may be threatened if they turn into a smorgasbord of individual preferences. This is, of course, one argument for choice *among* schools: when options are limited within a given school, students can find alternatives in other schools. Thus, school choice and within-school choices are complementary: a rich diversity of schools means that none of them must cater to all preferences and needs.

Yet, a modicum of variety *within* schools is important, too, if education is to be more responsive to students and parents. A 2007 survey by Civic Enterprises found that only 30 percent of parents in low-performing schools reported that their schools "do a good job . . . giving parents an opportunity to be involved in selecting the courses their children take," compared to 68 percent of parents in high-performing schools.[25]

To foster more options within schools, a creative mechanism is needed to balance parent and student preferences with resource and logistical constraints. Most parents might prefer their children to be in small classes all the time, but that is not budgetarily realistic for all students. Today, such rationing is typically managed by the school or district, which determines that physics classes will take a certain form, that a preset selection of English classes will be offered, and that students will be allotted to courses in prescribed ways. But like any top-down allocation, such a system relies on guesswork, past experience, or merely the preferences of suppliers—the school, principal, and teachers—to determine the mix of offerings that the consumers, in this case parents and students, can choose among.

A more efficient way of allocating such choices is to create a market by attaching a price to each and giving every student a budget with which to construct a semester's or year's worth of courses. This could grow overly complex, but we can readily imagine moving in that direction. Whereas in the past, calculating the cost of a small class versus a large one would have been a challenge, today's amplitude of data simplifies it. The work of analysts like Marguerite Roza enables us to see, for example, that in one district core classes like English and math cost $950 per student, while electives average $1,206.[26] Parents could then decide that Shawanna should get intensive attention in physics rather than in English, because she is a voracious reader on her own time anyway. Or Madeleine could get maximum exposure to track and field, tennis, and music while settling for larger classes in math and history. Even in the lower grades, a small class in reading might be offset by a larger one in science or art, or vice versa. And as the students get older, they could choose inquiry science over the didactic approach, and more.

The prices set by the school could be adjusted annually depending on the popularity of courses and the demand for each offering. This would be novel, even revolutionary, albeit alien to the prevailing culture of public education in which economic considerations seldom sully the romantic ideal of a school that meets all the needs of all its students. But such price-point rationing would acknowledge the reality that parents and students have distinctive preferences and the premise that schools should respond to those needs tomorrow more than they did yesterday. Without the invisible hand of the market, school leaders are likely to guess wrong—or not care much—about what their students and parents value most.

As with choice among schools, a system of uniform academic standards and results-based accountability, plus perhaps a universal core curriculum, would help ensure that students do not neglect the vital ingredients of a sound basic education. Though testing and accountability are more difficult in the outer reaches of the curricular universe, so long as all are becoming proficient in math, reading, history, and science, we may not need as much external accountability in the arts or in the advanced and elective versions of history, science, and so on.

Greater choice among classes will revive some sticky questions around the teaching of controversial topics like abstinence and contraception, evolution and creation or intelligent design, a European or a multicultural focus in literature, and which events to focus on in history and social studies. Here, the role of public policy is to ensure that all students receive a solid core education, leaving to parents the no-consensus decisions about which supplementary courses to add to the menu and leaving to teachers the decisions about how to teach such courses. Choice among courses may provide parents an outlet for avoiding or seeking out some touchy topics, but it would not erase the obligation of schools to determine which topics and courses to *require*. We can only suggest that schools err toward giving parents as much flexibility as feasible, so that more value-laden judgments can be made in homes rather than in district headquarters or principals' offices.

Choice Among Teachers

Few parents now have much say over which teachers instruct their children—or whether those teachers are effective. The fussiest and most persistent (or influential) parents may be able to lobby a principal to get his child into a certain instructor's class (or perhaps to have that teacher praised or reprimanded for something that caught the parent's attention). And parents and students often have only indirect choices among teachers when selecting high school electives or online courses.

Yet none of these versions of teacher choice gives parents a sure way to match instructors' varying pedagogical and personal styles with the needs or learning styles of their children. None ensures that parents' preferences influence teachers. None incorporates market signals from parents and students when teachers are reviewed, promoted, reassigned, or let go. Hence, schools' human resource decisions are made without direct regard to the impact these teachers have on their students.[27]

Can parents exercise more choices among teachers within their schools? Should they? Certainly there are ways to create more options for a school's clients while accommodating the principal's obligation to structure the course offerings and in-structional assignments within the confines of his teaching staff, classroom sizes and numbers, and so on. For example, parents could indicate their first, second, and third teacher choices. Computer software could then assist administrators to mesh those preferences with their resource constraints. As with course selection, basic markets could be created, with prices set for teachers. It is a controversial proposition. But it could be done. Indeed, it would be natural for any market in courses to deal jointly with teachers.

Such prices need not literally reflect the exact cost of any one teacher or class in order to be useful. For example, students needing to select fifteen classes over the span of tenth grade could be given a hundred points with which to assemble their set. Most teachers or courses might be worth five points, but those with the smallest class size or most experienced teacher (and thus the highest cost) or the longest waiting list (greatest demand) might require twenty or thirty points to secure a seat. One could thus imagine a student selecting a dozen basic default courses and thereby husband-ing her points to reserve seats in the costliest or most popular classes or in those that matter most to her.

It needs to be acknowledged that few parents or students are experts in pedagogy. Their opinions about whether Ms. Jones is a good eighth-grade math teacher may focus too heavily on the experience of their child, or a neighbor's child, and miss the mark about whether she is effectively helping her class as a whole. (And nobody benefits if teachers compete to become "most popular" in the eyes of students and parents.) Principals need to keep careful watch on this. One of their core responsibilities is to oversee their teachers and make expert judgments about the optimal matching of instructors with courses and pupils. Small schools pose additional problems.[28] Yet here, once again, technology can assist. If Billy could use the Internet to access the award-winning English teacher across town, this virtual teacher might prove to be better than the uninspiring flesh-and-blood instructor in his own school. Technology will also help teachers sort themselves. In Moe and Chubb's vision, "Teachers will have a great variety of schools to choose from, and a greater variety of roles they might play. The typical teacher will no longer be standing in front of a classroom of twenty-five children. Indeed, there will no longer be a typical teacher: specialization and differentiation will become the norm, and the bland uniformity of the past will die a well-deserved death."[29]

Demand-Driven Instructional Materials

Parents and students have scant influence over the choices their schools and districts make about which textbooks and other instructional materials to use. Much of this is logistical—the combined effects of bulk purchasing, state textbook adoption, textbook series that span multiple classrooms and grades. And the curricular materials that accompany those books—handouts, lesson plans, and the like—are typically selected by teachers, principals, or subject specialists who have greater knowledge about curriculum than most parents. Moreover, a teacher's style and classroom techniques bear on the types of materials that work best for her. It is not out of line to suggest that parents should stick to parenting and let educators worry about curriculum. Yet, if parents could exercise somewhat greater influence over the selection of instructional materials, everyone might benefit. Unlike many other aspects of schooling, this is an area where significant scale exists for reviews, ratings, and other such data to inform parents about what their children are learning and for parents to provide ratings or feedback that in turn inform (if not control) the purchasing decisions of schools and districts. TripAdvisor and Zagat provide reviews and customer feedback about hotels, vacation destinations, and restaurants, empowering consumers to make better-informed decisions while at the same time pressuring inns and eateries to improve. There is no reason why education would not benefit from an equivalent arrangement for textbooks.

When combined with working markets among schools, courses, and teachers, such reviews and ratings would give parents several ways to vote with their feet if their child's teacher or school purchases shoddy or offensive textbooks. Publishers, in turn, would have incentives to improve their reviews and ratings.

Yet again, technology is apt to speed the move toward a better market for instructional materials, one less dominated by a limited number of textbooks and in which the concentration of publishers and the often-political adoption processes in many states thwart real competition. As Christensen, Horn, and Johnson argue in *Disrupting Class*, "When disruptive innovators begin forming user networks through which professionals and amateurs—students, parents, and teachers—circumvent the existing value chain and instead market their products directly to each other . . . the balance of power in education will shift. Administrators, unions, and school boards will capitulate to the *fait accompli* of larger and larger numbers of students acquiring and using superior, customized learning tools of their own."[30]

Technology also curbs the influence of and dependence on textbooks by making it far simpler for schools, teachers, and even individual pupils to assemble their own materials from multiple sources, mixing and matching to serve more individualized needs than mega-textbooks can. In this way, parents and students (and teachers and schools) gain additional control and customization.

THE POLICY AND MARKET ENVIRONMENT

For the types of choices envisioned here to proliferate and thereby help make public education more demand driven and client responsive, changes are needed both in school governance and in the operation of the education marketplace. Most obviously, parents need better information, school funding needs to be reengineered, and the politics of schools need to become more mindful of consumers and less in thrall to producers.

Better Information

Markets with poor consumer information work poorly. Consumers with an approximation of complete information about their choices are empowered. Producers in every sector understand this; that is part of the reason why the public education establishment has made it difficult for parents (and taxpayers) to obtain clear, up-to-date, trustworthy information about school and teacher performance, costs, comparisons, and the like.

Attentive grocery shoppers can access troves of information about the ingredients, nutritional values, and unit costs of bread loaves, cans of peas, or hot dogs. The information available to parents shopping for schools pales in comparison, and the problem worsens in schools delivering weak academic results. Civic Ventures found that "73 percent of parents with a child in a high-performing school say they have good sources of information beyond school-provided materials to help them decide which courses their child should take to prepare for success after high school, compared with only 51 percent of parents with a child in a low-performing school."[31]

We should also acknowledge that gaining deep understanding of what makes a school tick demands a sizable commitment of time and effort. One must wander its corridors; talk with the principal, teachers, other parents and students; and spend time comparing these many factors to all the alternatives. Some parents have the time, wherewithal, and motivation to do all this, but many do not—and, as a result, their decisions are imperfectly informed. They may be passive consumers who find a school or course that satisfies a handful of criteria that matter to them rather than exhaust all their options and learn everything there is to know about other schools or courses.[32]

Is this an indictment of school choice? Not really. In no market is every participant perfectly informed; yet a satisfactorily functioning market can exist even when information about choices is spotty or unevenly available. When shopping for a new pair of jeans, some would-be purchasers may visit dozens of stores to inspect and try on hundreds of varieties and then comb the advertising circulars for coupons to find the perfect combination of price, style, and fit. But most of us do not shop that way. We visit one or two stores, depending on how rushed or desperate we are, and buy the first pair of jeans that meet some basic criteria: the price is reasonable, we like the style, and they fit well enough. Yet there is still robust competition among jeans manufacturers, in part because some active consumers are persnickety shoppers. And, certainly, with more complicated and consequential purchases—like a new car or house—many people do put in more time.

Choosing a school is more like buying a car than buying jeans, so it is important that parents have every opportunity to make the best possible decision. Until very recently, however, one could get far more information about one's choices of cars, movies, and hotels than one's school options. Of late, federal and state report card requirements and private Web sites have improved this situation, although significant challenges still confront parents wishing to determine which school in their community is the best—or, more importantly, which is best for their child. A concerned parent might reasonably want to be able to compare many different school elements, from its teachers and their pedagogical styles to its textbooks and curricula, from its financial health to its demographics, from safety to culture to parental involvement. Some of these are easily quantifiable and thus more available in written form, but others, like a school's culture, must be experienced to be well understood.

Part of the problem in sharing such information about schools is scale. *Consumer Reports* and *Car and Driver* can provide detailed reviews on cars because there are a limited number of new models every year, each with thousands of buyers. The United States has about 100,000 public schools, most of them attended by a few hundred or, at most, a few thousand students.[33] Virtual schools and courses help address this issue. With more students per class, there is greater scale to induce ratings. And when classes (and whole schools) can be more easily viewed by outsiders, reviews become easier to produce, and students and parents find it easier to sample and look in on classes before making a choice.

Technology can also do much to keep parents in touch with their child's school and his or her progress, as end-of-week reports and other feedback loops become simpler for the teacher to produce and easier for parents to access. In that way, parents become better-informed consumers and perhaps also better parents. Some of these interactions between home and classroom occur today, yet parents, teachers, and principals all say that more would be beneficial. This can be done on a one-on-one basis but can also be done on a larger scale. In New York City, for example, 850,000 parents responded to a 2009 survey about the quality of their schools and teachers, the results of which count for 10 percent of each school's progress report grade.[34]

Aggregate achievement data from teachers' classes, past and present, could also be made available to parents, linkage that is somewhat easier today thanks to states wiping out bans on it so as to qualify for Race to the Top funding. Though one must be cautious in interpreting such data, the increasing availability of longitudinal data, particularly the value-added kind, enables parents and others to observe the size of student gains over time and thus to appraise the role of teachers in such gains (or the absence thereof).

Feedback from other parents could also be aggregated and shared, creating multiple impressions of individual teachers and perhaps a group consensus. Student input might also be harnessed. As education analyst Bryan Hassel has noted, "RateMyTeachers.com enables students and their parents to rate K–12 teachers on 'easiness,' 'helpfulness' and 'clarity.' As of June 2008, this site contained 10 million reviews of 1.5 million teachers nationwide."[35]

Finally, in increasing the quality of information that parents use in comparing schools, teachers, courses, and programs, common standards and metrics would be helpful, together with achievement reports (preferably from trusted third parties) keyed to those standards. Such data would equip parents with a sound base on which to rest the choices that they must make, including monitoring the progress of their own children's education.

Fussy comparison shopping is not new to education. Many parents and students are accustomed to time-consuming information gathering, comparison, and selection processes among preschools, private schools, and colleges. So it is easy to imagine many more becoming accustomed to and adept at making such choices within K–12 education.

Educators and schools also benefit in sundry ways from a healthy, two-way flow of information with engaged consumers that is not limited to times of decision making or other major "transactions." In any market, this improves the quality of goods and responsiveness of services. Education could do more to emulate sectors that have such robust feedback loops enabled by, for example, Web or phone surveys, hotel and restaurant complaint cards, and chefs asking their patrons how they have enjoyed the meal. By doing more of this, schools would enhance their capacity to deliver solid academic results while fostering better-informed and more engaged parents.

Weighted Student Funding

No market functions well unless resources flow to and away from providers in synch with the choices that consumers make. This is obvious in the private sector where, for example, only the airline or restaurant or soap manufacturer that John Doe patronizes on a given day receives the money that he spends for the purchase. In portions of the public sector that function like vouchers—food stamps, Pell Grants, Medicare, housing vouchers—similar mechanisms are at work: the consumer makes a decision that causes a certain amount of public funding to flow to a particular vendor. But public education, by and large, causes its monies to flow on a completely different basis according to complex budgets, allocation formulas, staffing ratios, and programmatic rules. Only by happenstance do those monies end up in the particular school that parents may choose for their child, much less in the paycheck of a particular teacher.

Such a system may work satisfactorily if the goal is simply for schools to replicate last year's funding, perhaps with a small boost, or if the objective is to control centrally the distribution of teachers, extracurricular offerings, and special programs. But if the goal is for resources to be allocated where they are most needed and for education services to be attuned to children's needs, then a more dynamic system is needed to signal whether schools are succeeding or failing, whether parents are satisfied or disgruntled, and whether resources are being used smartly or carelessly. For such a funding arrangement to work, it must hinge on the family's decision as to what school(s) its children attend. In other words, the flow of resources must be student based and fully portable rather than tied to teacher salary, staff position, or program. When a dissatisfied family switches schools, one school's budget shrinks and the other grows. In that way, every school's future is tied to its success in attracting, satisfying, and retaining students rather than its success in appealing to the district office for dollars, personnel, or programs. And if the amounts that follow children are adjusted according to their needs—attaching more dollars, for example, to youngsters who cost more to educate for any number of reasons—the system further empowers those parents who today are the least powerful.

Under such a weighted, student-based funding system, principals also gain greater authority to lead their schools, deciding who works there (and how they are deployed and compensated) and how to use their resources and structure their academic programs. Initially some principals will not do this well. But they will learn, and people desirous and capable of wielding such authority will gravitate to the principal's office. Even in the near term, their errors are apt to be fewer and smaller than those regularly made by bureaucracies—especially those burdened by politics, complex rules, and elaborate contractual stipulations—trying to divine the optimal mix of teachers, classes, or programs at dozens or even hundreds of schools.

Under a weighted student funding system, parents sort their children into the schools that fit them best. That sorting in turn reinforces the unique nature of each school, drawing to it more pupils and parents who share the principal's distinctive vision and goals. That principal has the budgetary autonomy and authority to implement the programs that work best for these students, customizing services; responding to individual, family, and neighborhood circumstances; and breaking down central office barriers against innovation and adaptation. Over time, this will foster better, more entrepreneurial principals.

We recognize that a more dynamic funding system is also less predictable. It could become harder for a school to plan ahead when next year's enrollment and funding cannot be known with precision. But organizations of all types deal with such challenges, making projections and contingency plans to account for various futures, then working as hard and intelligently as possible to realize the future they desire. Within the education realm, examples of this sort can be found among preschools, colleges, tutoring programs, summer camps, and more, most of which cannot be sure of their enrollments—or revenues—until the year or session actually commences. Public schools, too, can learn to cope with this kind of uncertainty, and it seems like a fair exchange for a better-functioning market.[36]

Politics and School Governance

Schools will never be terribly responsive to parental preferences and student needs as long as their politics and governance are little influenced by such priorities. That does not mean parents must run school systems, serve on school boards, or dominate the voting for school referenda. Insofar as they seek policy influence, other mechanisms are often available to parents. Schools frequently have parental advisory bodies. For example, Chicago's schools have long had local school councils, which select principals and develop school budgets and improvement plans. And in New York City and Los Angeles, charter school leaders have started parents unions like Harlem Parents United and the Los Angeles Parents Union, in part to create a political counterweight to the teachers unions.[37]

Yet all of these are means and not the desired end of a dynamic school system in which new school options can flourish, in which control of schools rests at the school level rather than in central bureaucracies, and in which technology is welcomed and mobilized toward its full potential to create a high-quality, customized education experience for each student.

While fully describing all the political and governance-related steps toward achieving that goal is beyond our scope here, it seems clear that bureaucratic control must be replaced, at least in substantial part, by market dynamics and that the political sway of provider groups must be diminished. The education establishment must become more comfortable with markets and competition. These are not simple challenges. Yet there is hope, some of which stems from today's fast-moving technologies. As Moe and Chubb explain, technology helps thwart the establishment's "politics of blocking." Indeed, they optimistically assert that it "spells the end of monopoly in American education."[38] Moreover, charter schools and voucher programs have created new constituencies that are now deeply invested in the success of education markets (even if few would use that terminology). As the new parents unions demonstrate, along with grassroots organizations such as the Black Alliance for Education Options, parents and community members can be stirred to fight for their right to a quality school option. In these ways footholds are created from which greater competition, more options, and vigorous customization can spring, eventually accelerating us toward a more parent-centered, consumer-oriented education system.

WHOSE JOB IS THIS?

Moving these ideas and kindred reforms from drawing board to classroom and school system is a heavy lift. Public education remains slow to evolve, even in the face of changed circumstances and altered needs. Witness the immortal summer vacation, the durability of rigid teacher pay scales, and the persistence of classroom-based, grade-by-grade brick-and-mortar schools. Such attributes of America's K–12 enterprise have endured for generations even as everything around them has changed. It is no secret that the public education establishment has powerful incentives to resist disruptive change. The control, compensation, and job security of those who run schools and school systems are threatened by it—and never more so than when the goal of change is to shift power from them to parents and students, from producers to consumers, from suppliers to demanders.

Thus, reformers wishing to customize the experience of public schooling and make it respond more fully and swiftly to the needs of its clients face a major challenge, all the more so because it is not obvious who will lead this campaign. Today's education reformers fall into four rough categories, each with plausible reasons for devoting scant time or energy to the quest for more choices among teachers, classes, or instructional materials.

First, there are general education reform organizations. Many of these are state-based advocacy groups, like ConnCAN in Connecticut and EdVoice in California, and their national counterparts, such as Education Sector or the Education Trust. Each has its own priorities and policy portfolio, such as raising academic standards, strengthening teacher quality, or reforming school funding. While those priorities may coexist comfortably with a more parent-friendly system, and while many of these organizations favor more choice among schools, more innovative schools, and so on, none treats this as its top priority.

Second, we find reform organizations that focus on school choice per se, groups like the Foundation for Educational Choice, the Alliance for School Choice, and the National Alliance for Public Charter Schools. They certainly do their part to increase the supply and diversity of school options for parents; they support reforms like weighted student funding (to varying degrees) and would welcome better consumer information. But it is simply beyond their current mission to argue for more choices within schools, among teachers, or in the realm of instructional materials.

Third, we find well-intended groups that stand for reform but are also customers of or vendors to the school system and therefore predictably wary of unsettling their relationships by pressing for changes not integral to their own interests. Teach for America relies on districts to hire its corps members, and New Leaders for New Schools counts on them to train and hire its would-be principals. Charter management organizations, though competitors to district schools in some respects, often need the cooperation of districts to approve their charters, bus their students, and loan them facilities.

A fourth category of reformers and reform groups may offer a bit more hope and potential leadership on this issue. Plausibly termed *agenda-setters,* these reformers consist of the philanthropists, columnists, thought leaders, prominent academics, and perhaps even secretaries of education who have the independence, gravitas, and outsider standing to agitate, advocate, fund, and guide such deep, systematic reform. These folks tend not to fear establishment retribution, and they need not be distracted by myriad other organizational priorities. To be sure, each has its own agendas and interests; but if each made it a priority to put students and parents first in K–12 education, it would make a difference.

TRADE-OFFS AND CONCLUSIONS

In a hundred ways, K–12 education consumers could be empowered more than they are today, and there are a hundred arguments for why this is a worthy goal, beginning with the near-certainty that parents and students will be better off when their educational needs are met. American education will also be better off—and its pupils better schooled—when it is propelled by competition, innovation, and a focus on results.

Yet making the system more consumer responsive is no simple proposition. Aside from the many logistical and practical challenges entailed in giving parents greater say in their selection of schools, teachers, courses, and more—alongside the challenge of creating markets in education—this discussion raises some important questions for policy makers and reformers.

First is the classic trade-off between the *unum* and the *pluribus*—between what should be uniform in American education and what should be different or varied. While schools should give greater deference to the needs and desires of individual students and parents, we also recognize that schooling serves both private and public ends. That is why many (us included) favor national standards and assessments and a substantial core curriculum. Yet we also remain aware that public education has long been more concerned with the needs of its pupils as a collective than as individuals. It has been too slow to customize its offerings for students. We want to push it further in this direction, even as we want it to fulfill its role on behalf of the commonweal. It is not easy to do either of those things, much less both.

A second, more specific dilemma concerns the tension between promoting choice *among* schools and choice *within* schools. Greater proliferation of school choices would imply smaller schools, which inevitably limits the capacity of a given school to offer multiple courses or teacher choices to its students. Likewise, any school wishing to expand its offerings will find the task easier to accomplish as it grows larger. That portends a reduced supply of schools. This trade-off is not to be avoided.

Third and finally, we offer more of an opportunity than dilemma. Astute observers of education often note how rarely this field learns from and then adopts the best practices of other sectors. There are innumerable reasons for this, but it is undeniable that other segments of our economy and society that also provide essential services, with both public and private components, have done better at addressing the needs of individual users or consumers while also grappling with the public interest. Transportation is an example: its primary purpose is to help individuals get from point A to point B, but public concerns abound and are among the reasons we invest in buses and subway systems, subsidize ridership, and tax cars, gasoline, and drivers licenses. Yet, despite this ample government involvement and oversight, one's transportation options are nearly boundless. A traveler from Washington, DC, to New York, for example, can drive his own car, ride a motorcycle, or hitchhike; he can take a train, bus, plane, taxi, limousine. And once aboard a train, he can choose a quiet car, ordinary car, or cafe car; he can sit by the window or the aisle; he can spend time eating, reading, sleeping, or talking on the phone. And so on. The permutations for such a trip are practically limitless.

What can education learn from transportation? What about scrutinizing health care, communications, energy, and myriad other sectors for sound models? How can policy makers and education reformers distill lessons from those worlds that could be applied constructively in our schools?

Our goal is to devise reforms that enhance the market power of parents and students without fundamentally weakening the public nature or societal contribution of primary-secondary schooling. Yes, trade-offs and compromises will need to be made and lessons drawn from elsewhere. But these ought to be manageable—and are surely worth making. The United States in 2010 needs a system of schooling that places parents and students at the center, where they can exert a strong gravitational pull on the schools, principals, teachers, and others that orbit in this cosmos. Finding that balance is no easy task, but the benefits are great enough to justify the effort.

3

The Rise of
Global Schooling

Chris Whittle

FOR CENTURIES, K–12 EDUCATION around the world has been organized at the municipal, provincial, or national level with educational institutions rarely operating in a meaningful way beyond their country's boundaries. This state of affairs is likely to continue in publicly funded schools, as they are tasked to serve students and families within certain geographies. However, trends in the macro economy are giving rise to private educational institutions that upend these familiar boundaries and provide services on a global basis.

A quick read of any major newspaper or magazine reminds us of the highly connected nature of our world, from *global* climate change to *global* financial crises to *global* media. A perusal of any school's mission statement will show that locally funded public schools and single-city private schools recognize the importance of graduating students with a global view. Few, however, are in a position to rethink the assumptions behind their own geographic limitations. Here I identify global trends in the demand for educational services and show both how new institutions can serve particular needs across geographic boundaries and how the education marketplace can be resegmented by new providers. Some educational snapshots of schools and school systems around the world serve as a backdrop for the themes that I explore later in the chapter.

THE WEST'S GREATEST EXPORT

In Shanghai, the American School has two sprawling campuses covering fifty acres and serving nearly 3,000 students. One campus is in the older part of the city, Puxi, and the other is on the farthest outskirts of Pudong, the sprawling newer section of this 20-million-person megalopolis. The second campus was built to accommodate the huge demand that the initial site, all 600,000 square feet of it, was unable to fill. The desire for these American Schools is so great that some students commute an hour and a quarter each way to the Pudong facility while waiting to get into the more convenient Puxi.

When I visited both campuses in 2007, I expected to find a slice of America imbedded in Shanghai, a school filled with American expatriates living and working in Shanghai. Wrong. I was surprised to discover that Chinese students constituted a significant percentage of the enrollment, a fact made more puzzling since in China only foreign passport holders are allowed to attend international schools. In one classroom I observed, most of the children were locals. I asked one Chinese parent, "Why did you choose the American School?" Her answer was immediate: "I want my child to go to college in the United States and this is the best path." I then inquired how she was able to get her child into the school. "Oh, I have a second passport from Chad. All the Chinese citizens here have dual citizenship and an additional passport from somewhere else," she said in flawless English, without missing a beat.

America may have a problem exporting its manufactured goods, but as this Shanghai mother indicated, American education (actually English-language education, of which America is the leading provider) is in great demand the world over. That demand is driven by multiple factors. At its core is admiration for American and other English-speaking cultures and our way of life. Another factor is that a huge percentage of the world's outstanding universities and colleges are in the United States, England, Canada, and Australia. Look at these facts, all drawn from the October 2009 *Times Higher Education* ranking of the world's universities:[1]

- Of the top 100, 83 percent are in the U.S., U.K., Australia, Canada, and Western Europe
- Of the top 100, only two are in mainland China
- Of the top 100, *none* are in Brazil, India, or Russia, three of the BRIC countries vaunted for their growth
- *None* of the top 100 are in sixteen of the world's largest twenty countries, including those just noted and also Indonesia and Mexico
- Of the top twenty universities in the world, all are in the U.S., U.K., Australia, and Canada

What does this mean? If you are a student in mainland China, you have a miniscule chance of getting into one of the two ranked universities. In India the number of school-age children is greater than the entire population of the United States—and there are no ranked universities. In most countries of the world, the higher education options for children are not very attractive. Many parents who have the necessary resources hope to send their children to the United States for college (as illustrated by my daughter's recent college visit to Brown, where hundreds of South Korean applicants toured the campus along with a handful of Americans).

This demand for Western higher education has a trickle-down effect on K–12 demand in all of these countries. The K–12 needs of parents planning to send their children to the West for college are different from those of parents who expect their children to attend higher education institutions in their home country. Their children *must* achieve English fluency and have an understanding of Western ways. And such results are not likely to be produced by traditional local schools, public or private.

They are looking west.

MEANWHILE, BACK IN NEW YORK, PARENTS LOOK EAST

If the West currently has a lock on the quality higher education market, then the East, particularly China and India, owns a big part of the economic future of the world. Sophisticated Western parents know it—and know that their children must be prepared for a world in which "there are two or three chefs in the kitchen," as one Chinese businessman recently said to me. They understand that a Western-centric education is not a modern one; that, in the century ahead, French, however classy, will not serve someone nearly as well as Mandarin and that a semester abroad in Florence, however beautiful, is no longer sufficient international exposure.

Yet, just as Chinese local K–12 schools are not preparing their children for Western higher education, American local schools, whether public or private, are not graduating students truly ready for a global economy. Even the finest private schools only graduate a tiny percentage of students fluent in a second language; many still start languages in later grades and do not approach it with the seriousness required for mastery. Indeed, a report commissioned by the British Council concludes that "monoglot English graduates face a bleak economic future as qualified multilingual youngsters from other countries are proving to have a competitive advantage."[2] Participation in foreign exchange programs is low, and for the most part these programs are European-oriented. And history and literature courses are mostly domestic or Western.

Also, unlike their Asian counterparts, American parents do not have nearly as rich an offering of international schools that could serve as windows to the East. The result is that in Western societies the demand for a much more globally minded education at the K–12 level is unmet.

ARMANI AND PRADA MEET CORNELL AND HARROW

Walk through any high-end mall in Hong Kong, Dubai, or London and the names are all the same: Hermes, Polo, Calvin Klein, Yves St. Laurent, Armani. These global brands transcend all national boundaries and are in high demand by consumers the world over.

Although many in the educational community view brands as superficial and even meaningless, consumers do not see it that way. *Brand* is just another way of saying *reputation,* and that is something hard-earned. Not only in fashion and cars but increasingly in schools and colleges as well, consumers trust brands, and that trust is a form of demand not to be underestimated. In the world of education, that used to be a local phenomenon. No more.

The Cornell School of Medicine recently graduated the first class at its Qatar campus. Qatar is currently shopping for top K–12 schools from around the world through its Outstanding Schools Initiative, which has as its mission "the recruitment of top private international schools to open branch campuses in Qatar."[3] The Harrow School, founded in 1572 by a charter from Queen Elizabeth I, now has campuses bearing its name in Bangkok and Beijing, with a Hong Kong campus opening in 2012.[4] Similarly, Dulwich, dating to 1616 and King James, has a campus named after it in the Pudong section of Shanghai.[5] And while not using its name, King's Academy, created by King Abdullah of Jordan, virtually imported the concept of Deerfield and is even nicknamed by some "Deerfield in the Desert."[6] College du Leman, a fifty-year-old, two-thousand-student international school in Geneva, just opened a campus in Chengdu, China.[7] These brands represent local institutions morphing into global entities. An equally successful strategy already being worked on by companies around the world is the creation of new educational entities conceived from the beginning as global brands. These may not have the running start of an existing brand, but they have the advantage of being able to seize a more modern innovative positioning not burdened by pesky legacy matters.

Perhaps the earliest K–12 global brand is the United World Colleges, a network of twelve International Baccalaureate (IB) programs around the world (which, in full disclosure, both my wife and one of my daughters attended). The vision of the school, which was founded at the height of the cold war by German educationalist Kurt Hahn, is to bring students from around the world together during their last two years of high school in order to overcome religious, racial, and cultural misunderstandings. Graduates of United World Colleges from locations such as Wales, India, and Singapore (totaling nearly forty thousand since it was founded in 1962) are sought after by universities around the world.[8]

JEJU ISLAND GOES GLOBAL

Jeju Island sits off the coast of Korea and is dubbed "Korea's Hawaii" by some because it is a favorite of Asian tourists. This resort community, however, anticipates offering a different kind of tourism in the near future.

Motivated by (1) the fact that 436,000 Korean students (including tens of thousands of preteens and teenagers accompanied by parents) have already gone abroad to study; (2) the rapid expansion of this trend, up 160 percent from 2001; and (3) Korea's educational trade deficit of nearly $3.4 billion, Jeju's provincial government is taking action to seize an opportunity. It plans to build a $785 million global education city consisting of twelve new international schools serving more than ten thousand K–12 students.[9] It will recruit these schools in a manner similar to the way Qatar approached Cornell. A report in the *Korea Times* said, "The project aims to draw students planning to study abroad to the island, offering cheaper tuition, easy access and better education. The plan will also contribute to fostering the education industry, as well as improving national competitiveness, the Jeju provincial government predicts."[10]

ABU DHABI ONE-UPS PHILADELPHIA

Most of the demand noted above is consumer demand, or *B to C*, the phrase used in business to connote business-to-consumer relationships. But there is another type of demand also growing in the world of international education, *B to B*, or business-to-business or institution-to-institution. In the case of education, this tends to be governments seeking out educational entities—for example, Qatar recruiting Cornell.

The earliest large-scale example of such B to B educational activity in the United States was Philadelphia's recruitment in 2002 of half a dozen private U.S. organizations to manage more than forty public schools. EdisonLearning (formerly Edison Schools), a company I founded, was the largest of those. This was an example of a U.S. school system recruiting U.S. organizations to manage U.S. public schools. Abu Dhabi is taking that to a new level.

Over the past few years, the Abu Dhabi Education Council has recruited educational firms from around the world to manage more than thirty of its public schools. Their objective is to increase academic performance within their schools, and they are turning to organizations such as SABIS (Lebanon), Nord-Anglia (U.K.), Mosaica (U.S.), Center for British Teachers (U.K.), and GEMS Education (UAE). This move represents a breakthrough in the development of global schooling. To put in perspective how advanced the United Arab Emirates' activity is, imagine if Kansas City were to recruit French, Saudi, and Chinese entities to manage a group of its public schools.

THE MOBILE GLOBAL

In the early days of the rise of the American domestically oriented corporation, executives were often assigned to multiple locations over the course of their careers—four years in Cincinnati, five in Los Angeles, and several more in Raleigh. Such career paths were common. Children of those executives typically attended a series of schools, more often than not good suburban public schools in different locations. Though often upsetting for spouses and children, the educational transition was not that difficult. More or less, it was simply a matter of parents advising a public school that they would be enrolling their children there.

Flash to a completely new level of educational trauma. Imagine for a moment that your New York–based company suggests that you should have experience in Europe and Asia in order to move up in the organization. This means relocating your three children from New York to Hong Kong to London and then back to New York, say, over twelve years. As a starter for your new educational adventure—unless your children speak fluent Mandarin—a Hong Kong public school is ruled out, which limits your alternatives to private institutions. You know none of them, but you quickly learn that a key initiative of the American Chamber of Commerce in Hong Kong is the creation of new private schools because it is so difficult to get into the few that do exist. Indeed, a practice of some well-heeled companies is reserving seats in private schools, often at a price of several hundred thousand dollars per seat. Your company is not so well-heeled, however, so you are left on your own to determine whether the Chinese International School, Concordia, or Hong Kong International School is right for your child and then to figure out how to get your child in. If you are lucky enough to solve that problem, you can anticipate doing it again in London in a few years and then once again back in New York, where your old school long ago sold your seat.

Does this picture make sense? To answer that, contrast it to another experience of mobile families. When you travel, more likely than not you have a preferred hotel that you stay in, whether the high-end Four Seasons or more modest Sheraton. When you arrive at a hotel destination around the world, they know your name and your preferences, aid you in booking accommodations in your next city, and provide you with preferred rates and upgrades. Why should the same services and conveniences not exist in something much more important, such as schooling?

ENGLISH—MORE A CURRENCY THAN THE DOLLAR OR THE POUND

There are more than 6,900 languages in the world.[11] Mandarin is spoken by the largest number of people, with roughly one billion speakers worldwide. Hindi, Spanish, and English are more or less tied as the world's second most spoken languages, with each having approximately half a billion speakers.[12] This situation is expected to change radically over the next two decades. Although the teaching of Mandarin and Spanish as second languages is on the rise, a report by the British Council projects that the number of people learning English will reach approximately two billion within the next fifteen years, roughly 30 percent of the Earth's population and more than five times the number of native speakers of English.[13]

Long the language of science, global business, and smaller global matters such as aviation, English will likely continue its emergence as the world's language. The rise of English has already impacted educational institutions worldwide. Philip Altbach, director of the Center for International Higher Education at Boston College, says that "the nations using English, particularly the United States, have become the academic superpowers. Size and wealth matter a great deal in determining the academic pecking order. The United States alone spends almost half the world's R&D funds and is home to a large proportion of the top universities on the world's increasingly influential league tables. The English-speaking academic systems host more than half the world's international students."[14] This hegemony will impact primary and secondary education as well. Schooling entities rooted in countries where English is the native language will have an important competitive advantage—at least for awhile.

PREDICTION

What the above snapshots demonstrate is that consumers and governments worldwide are facing a new kind of educational demand versus that of twenty or thirty years ago, specifically:

- Parents in the East want to prepare their children for Western higher education
- Parents in the West want to expose their children to cultures and economies that will play increasingly important roles in the coming century
- Governments want to bring the educational resources of other cultures to their shores
- Educational consumers desire brands, old and new, that they can trust, and in education those tend to be the Western ones
- Mobile families desire seamless educational transitions

As reliably as water always finding a way to flow downhill, these new educational demands will be met. However, legislatively restrained, cottage industry, domestically oriented schools or school systems are not well-positioned to do so.

Three new types of schooling institutions are likely to emerge, the earliest versions of which we can already see examples:

- Global private school companies, both of the brick-and-mortar and virtual forms
- Global providers of public schools or related public school services
- Organizations that do both

Such schooling entities will provide parents and governments with the types of benefits noted above. Equally important, because of their scale-driven ability to invest in substantial research and development (R&D) and the absence of political constraints, they will play an important role in driving innovation in pedagogy.

MANY GLOBAL NETWORKS

Today's global traveler can choose from a variety of airlines and receive in return various loyalty-driven perks. Over the past fifty years, British Airways, American, Continental, Delta, Emirates, and Singapore Air have aspired to serve the world with a global footprint of routes. Similarly, hotel companies such as America's Hyatt, Canada's Four Seasons, France's Sofitel, China's Mandarin or Peninsula, or Singapore's Raffles have established locations in most of the world's leading ports of call. And, as discussed above, a mall in Beijing or Dubai contains storefronts very similar to those in Berlin and Dallas.

The future world of schooling will have much in common with these players. Thirty years from now, imagine perhaps a dozen global systems of schools giving parents a much wider array of options than those currently available. These new systems will have much in common, and yet they will offer wide variety as well. Parents will be able to choose from different school designs (some schools will offer the IB while others will create designs from scratch); different price points (some will be premium-priced, competing with top-tier schools, while others will provide education for the budget-conscious); different geographic strategies (some will focus on world capitals while others will locate in second- and third-tier cities); different funding sources (some will be private pay and some will be public, often recruited by government school systems to offer different choices to local educational consumers); and some will be for-profit while others will be global nongovernmental organizations (NGOs). Their similarities may include operating under a global brand, having multiple campuses around the world that adhere to a particular school design or pedagogy, and being supported by a central infrastructure (think of them as international school districts).

Fully formed versions of such entities do not exist today, but there are both forerunners and early corporate examples that may well emerge into what is imagined here. Country-related international schools can be found around the world. An example is the American School of London and the American School of Shanghai. Although these schools have common roots, often having grown up in the backyards of American embassies to serve American citizens abroad, they are not part of any real system or organization, and their pedagogy and curriculum vary. There is the International Baccalaureate, which is a common curriculum but not an actual system of schools. Perhaps the closest parallel is the French Lycee. Although each campus operates with great independence, it does so under a common brand, with a common curriculum, and under some supervision from a central office. It differs from the networks of the future in that it gives priority, though not exclusively so, to French citizens.

On the corporate side of the ledger, there are also several examples. Meritas, a U.S. company, is acquiring private schools around the world and now owns campuses from Mexico to Switzerland. Meritas functions as a family of schools, with each school continuing to operate under its original name, although, as noted above, Meritas's College du Leman has expanded from its Geneva campus to Chengdu, China. GEMS, a significant operator of private schools in the UAE, has expanded into India and England. Like Meritas, it functions more as a family of schools than a global brand, as do the schools of Nord Anglia and Cognita, both British concerns that operate locally branded international schools from Bratislava to Beijing.

THE SOCIAL IMPORTANCE OF THESE SYSTEMS

The scale of these systems even twenty years from now will be tiny relative to the number of children in the world. Perhaps the largest systems will by that time have fifty to two hundred campuses and serve from 100,000 to 200,000 students within the four walls of their particular campuses. Although that level of enrollment would be equivalent in size to one of the larger public school systems in the United States, the number is immaterial when you consider that India alone has nearly 400 million children under the age of eighteen.

These new institutions, however, may have an importance that extends far beyond those students they directly serve. When the history of education and education reform in the twenty-first century is examined, these new global systems of schools may well be highlighted as having played meaningful, even seminal roles. They could be forerunners of the largest K–12 schooling companies, important R&D centers for new school designs, bridges of international understanding, and platforms or staging areas for global virtual schools of the future.

HIGHLY POSITIVE R&D ENVIRONMENTS

K–12 schooling companies began to emerge in a significant way in the early 1990s, mostly in the United States and mostly focused on the management of public schools and either as subcontractors to school systems or as managers of public charter schools. Most of these companies invested (some to a very significant degree) in the creation of whole-school designs. The work of such organizations (including KIPP, EdisonLearning, and others) has had an important impact on American public education. It has contributed directly to the education of hundreds of thousands of children within the schools these organizations created and/or managed, and it has indirectly enriched the conversation of school reform both in the United States and in other countries.

However, many who have participated in these efforts over the past two decades would agree that there has not been as much improvement in school design or academic performance as early reformers had anticipated. In no small way, that is a result of the terrain on which these pioneering organizations labored. The public schools they were asked to manage were provided relatively low per-pupil spending, including charter schools that often received per-pupil funding materially lower than peer public schools. Often companies and organizations were assigned management of the most dysfunctional schools in a city. In virtually all cases, there were significant political, legislative, and bargaining agreement constraints. And these reform organizations frequently operated in environments of intense political controversy. That none of these organizations was operating in ideal settings for innovation or in highly controlled test conditions is an understatement. Instead, their efforts to create and implement new designs occurred under harsh, battlefield-like conditions. While this may have some benefits—working in a highly realistic environment being one of them—it stunted the development of innovative designs.

But the new global schooling companies will enjoy multiple benefits that should result in design breakthroughs. First, international private schools typically enjoy a per-pupil tuition level (some over $30,000 per year) that is significantly greater than what early education companies received. These robust economics make allocations for research and development easier and provide a well-funded environment in which to conceive and execute innovative techniques. Once educational effectiveness is demonstrated, the focus can shift to the development of scalable economic models. Second, international schools are typically exempted from local, domestic educational regulations, operating effectively in regulation-free zones, much like duty-free shops at airports. In many respects, they can be thought of as global charters—but even better, since charters are often burdened with local educational regulations. Third, the fact that these new schooling companies will have a direct perspective on schooling in the world's leading cultures will inform and improve their educational designs, making them a synthesis of excellent pedagogy worldwide versus that of a single setting.

These new enterprises will encourage new areas of emphasis in school design. Of paramount importance will be an increasing focus on the acquisition of a second and third language. Given the rise of English mentioned earlier, some may ask, "Why do students need a second language when the entire world is learning English?" Learning a second language is important beyond its utility; it provides a deeper understanding of other cultures. Moreover, exhibiting proficiency in a language is a demonstration of respect and, therefore, a good defense against a certain arrogance that can creep into any highly successful or dominant culture. Measured as a whole, the language programs of even America's finest schools lag far behind their international counterparts. Long plagued by approaches that focused on coverage, such as "two years of Spanish" or "three years of French," American students have failed to achieve what matters most: real fluency. New global schooling companies will commit to true fluency as an academic outcome and will design their programs accordingly, including launching language instruction in the earliest grades, committing to excellence in one or two languages (versus offering a wide but shallow variety of choices), employing immersion techniques, and outsourcing language education to highly skilled providers often used by companies and governments.

Another central feature of these new designs will be ensuring that each student graduates with a worldview. These new programs will feature larger helpings of world history and world geography. They will strive to provide their graduates with a greater working knowledge of the world's leading countries and their cultures. Domestic schools understandably skew their social studies curriculum to their locale and country. New designs will continue to provide an appropriate level of focus on the host country, but the balance will shift, ensuring that graduates are more grounded in world matters. These schools will be ideal settings for global issues courses, such as those now found in the International Baccalaureate program, that cover topics crossing national boundaries, such as conflict and violence, world poverty, and environmental concerns.

Because their network of campuses around the world will be supportive, international exchange programs will move to another level in both the number and frequency of opportunities provided. Students will be encouraged to spend time on multiple campuses and continents within the network and will be able to do so without disrupting a clearly articulated curriculum, as these new schooling companies will use one core curriculum worldwide. Far from interrupting the normal flow of a curriculum, time abroad will actually enhance instruction. Imagine a student spending time on four or five continents over the course of middle and high school. Well-planned experiences that include both pretravel prep time and posttravel debriefing will become a dramatic extension of the concept of *teachable moments*. A three-month stint in China will ensure that a student cares more about Chinese history both before and after the trip. A student who spends time in Mexico will take Spanish a bit more seriously before and after the trip.

Finally, these new designs will necessarily push the boundaries of how technology is utilized in instruction, professional development, and system-to-school and school-to-school communications. Often separated by thousands of miles, these campuses will communicate with their headquarters in advanced technological ways. Well-designed video conferencing will be standard fare. Online courses will stretch across the system and be enhanced by certain centers of excellence that feed the entire network of schools. For example, a U.S.-based school within the network will be the natural staging area or bureau for U.S. history for the entire worldwide system, as will a China-based school for Chinese history. In-school social networks will take on new meaning, with students communicating from across the globe about their courses and their experiences, often after having met one another during extended exchange programs.

THE NEW MELTING POTS

Each year, Atlantic College, a United World College campus in Wales that serves 350 students at the junior and senior high school level, typically admits 170 students from more than seventy-five countries.[15] It is not unusual for major international schools to host students from a hundred-plus countries on one campus. While this degree of cultural diversity can be found in some public schools around the world, it is certainly not the norm, and particularly not so outside of large internationally oriented cities.

As global systems of schools spring up, they will expand and accelerate the growth of an already established practice in leading international schools: cultural interaction. At Atlantic College, four-student dorm rooms are occupied by students from four different countries. During evening events, students present their countries to the student body. Programs such as these encourage greater understanding and tolerance as well as increase a student's knowledge of various parts of the world. In global systems of the future, this will happen not only among students but also with the school staff. These new schools will encourage faculty members to teach in multiple locations throughout the system.

THE FIRST MAJOR K–12 SCHOOLING COMPANIES

As any Wall Street investment banker knows, education is a hot sector that outperformed virtually all segments of the U.S. stock market during the recent financial crisis. On the world level, education is huge—second only to health care. Education is growing both in the total number of students and in the amount of money countries apply to it. And it is noncyclical.

In terms of market value, today's education sector is dominated by postsecondary companies such as Education Management, the University of Phoenix, Devry, and Corinthian Colleges. In the United States alone, more than half a dozen postsecondary companies sport market values of $2 billion to $10 billion. Conspicuously absent from the list of high-value education stocks are K–12 schooling companies. Although there are K–12 schooling entities with hundreds of millions in revenues (including K12 Inc., the virtual schooling company, and EdisonLearning), the K–12 sector has yet to rival its postsecondary counterpart.

That may be changing soon—and in two ways. First, governments will increasingly reach out to Western-based K–12 companies to import designs and best practices for their public school systems. This should drive revenues and market capitalizations of the private managers of public schools in the decades ahead. Second, as demand for English-speaking schools continues to rise around the world (with hundreds of thousands of additional seats added in English-speaking international schools in just the past decade), the new global networks of private international schools will become financially important entities. As an indication of potential scale, the International School of Geneva is an enterprise with three campuses enrolling four thousand students at a per-student tuition of up to $25,000. Imagine a company with a network of twenty or so of those types of sites around the world.

The importance of the emergence of such entities goes far beyond shareholder reward. As noted above, these new entities will be important funders of research and development and, equally important, of *scalable* research and development. It is one thing to study a problem or create a new technique; it is quite another to think about how to bring it to life with tens of thousands or hundreds of thousands of students.

PLATFORMS FOR GLOBAL VIRTUAL SCHOOLS

A study by the American Academy of Arts and Sciences estimates that, worldwide, 323 million school-age children are not in school.[16] For perspective, that means the equivalent of six times the total number of school-age children in the United States are not in school. Although multiple factors contribute to this alarming statistic, a leading cause is that the cost of providing a traditional, in-school, brick-and-mortar education is simply too great for some underdeveloped countries to bear. Even India, with its booming economy, is a case in point. In 2007, UNESCO said India's central government spending on higher education was only $400 per pupil, in contrast to $9,600 in the United States.[17]

One solution to this educational crisis is for underdeveloped countries to abandon the brick-and-mortar era of education and move directly to virtual, online delivery— just as some countries that were unable to develop the costly infrastructure required in the land line–only era of telecommunications moved directly to the cellular world.

The new systems and networks of global schools will be uniquely positioned to provide these new virtual schools. First, parents are attracted to virtual schools that are associated with or spring from brick-and-mortar institutions. Some of the largest and most successful online, postsecondary educational institutions in the United States were first physical campuses, the University of Phoenix being the most notable. Second, schooling companies that have a brick-and-mortar site have a substantial *sunk cost*—faculty in place—that can be exported to the virtual world. A terrific third-grade math teacher can be broadcast to thousands of students beyond her eighteen-student classroom. And her students play an important role, too. Like live studio audiences, they inspire their teacher to do her best work both for them and for their online counterparts. Third, brick-and-mortar educational institutions can serve as the administrative and creative hearts of these new virtual entities. Finally, a global system of brick-and-mortar campuses is much more important than, say, one individual campus. Each campus will contribute something special to a global virtual school, similar to the way an individual computer contributes to a cloud of computer capability.

CONCLUSION

Counterintuitively, domestic schools may be the greatest beneficiary of the rise of global schools, and particularly of global private schooling entities. These new entities will be excellent models to follow. Located initially in the world's largest, most international cities, which typically house the media nerve centers of all countries, global schooling entities will be widely reported on and will thus inspire many to follow their lead.

Pressed by parents and students demanding a more modern and worldly education, global schools will jump beyond parochial, country-oriented views to become important forces in showing schools how to bring cultures together. Inspired by best practices they will see from all parts of the world, global schools will have the opportunity to incorporate elements from around the world into school designs of the future.

Anchored by brick-and-mortar campuses around the globe, these entities will spawn country-specific virtual schools soon to be followed by global ones. Similar to worldwide news networks, their campuses will act as educational bureaus, feeding and enriching their own networks first and then surrounding public schools. And freed of difficult political constraints, they will be able to focus on the exploration of innovative techniques of teaching and learning and the development of new curriculum.

Fueled by higher per-pupil revenues, these new global entities will have the resources to invest in research and development. The breakthroughs made by global schools and global, private schooling entities will flow—sometimes freely and sometimes at a cost—to their domestic counterparts. Local schools will be able to use the examples of these new strategies as wedges to lift or improve legislation that restrains them from progress. While students in global schooling entities will certainly benefit from their services, it is clear that such institutions will have a widespread impact on the entire educational community.

4

Multiple Pathways to Graduation

Tamara Battaglino and JoEllen Lynch

THROUGHOUT OUR ECONOMY and across industries, companies supply a wide variety of products and services to meet the broad diversity of demands from the customers they serve. Consumers have come to expect the almost infinite combination of car features or credit card offerings available. But K–12 education is different. For most students, our public schools offer a one-size-fits-all model. This homogenous approach to education has caused particularly severe problems at the high school level, as many students disengage and opt out of the system entirely. This chapter explores a range of proven solutions that are working, at scale, to offer differentiated solutions to significantly increase graduation rates for student populations with historically high dropout rates. While the chapter will address in detail the specifics of the school models that have delivered these results, our approach of using data and an understanding of student populations to build a student-centric portfolio of school options is broadly applicable across K–12 reform.

The notion of a common four-year high school experience underlies a significant and urgent national crisis. Graduation rates in many leading urban school districts are below 60 percent. The average graduation rate among the country's fifty largest cities is 52 percent.[1] In other struggling urban school districts, fewer than 35 percent of students graduate. College readiness measures are even worse, ranging from 5 to 30 percent for many urban districts.

When a student drops out of school, it is rarely a sudden event. Typically, the actual moment of dropout is foreshadowed by years of struggle, often characterized by the student falling further and further behind academically as the school system fails to recognize the increasingly differentiated needs of students as they progress within high school. Over the course of a number of years, a student may transition from being on-track with his or her peers and progressing through school, to beginning to demonstrate risk factors such as low attendance, to actually falling behind in reaching graduation requirements—all before the moment when that student fully disengages and drops out of school. Understanding the nature of the dropout problem, therefore, requires understanding this progression, which is aided by the definition of two student segments:

1. *At-risk students:* students most likely to fall off-track toward high school graduation and who can be identified by early indicators evident no later than the student's first year of high school
2. *Off-track students:* students who are not earning credits at a pace that would allow a four-year high school graduation

Approximately half of all students become off-track during their high school career, and a student is all but destined to drop out of high school once falling off-track.[2] Graduation rates for off-track students in large urban school districts are alarmingly often below 25 percent. The at-risk and off-track students in large urban school districts represent more than 90 percent of eventual high school dropouts.

A common misperception is that students who fall off-track in high school do so because of academic deficits stemming from poor preparation in elementary and middle schools. While this is certainly a factor for many students, it cannot sufficiently explain the dropout crisis. In New York, for example, one-quarter of all off-track students enter high school with on-track academic preparation, as measured by eighth-grade ELA scores. Solutions for off-track youth, therefore, require addressing unmet academic needs as well as youth development and social supports. Both are critical to serving the needs of at-risk and off-track youth.

Off-track student populations represent America's dropouts of today and tomorrow. The off-track challenge also perpetuates the persistent achievement gap in the United States. Exacerbating these challenges is the fact that most districts lack the scale and quality to adequately address our district's most underserved youth who, even today, have not been provided adequate academic support, school options, and other critical social-emotional services.

Why have districts failed to serve these populations? One reason is their overall lack of strategic focus on and investment in differentiated school models and programs to specifically address the needs of students who are off-track or who have dropped out of school. Where differentiated school models do exist, they have often been stratified as alternative schools that are undermanaged and underresourced and that lack clear and high expectations for the students' and schools' performance. Also, existing systems are too often enrolling and serving students who fall across multiple off-track student segments in one school or program rather than ensuring that students are matched with the specific model that addresses their individual needs. Lastly, inadequate investment affects both the total number of diploma-granting seats in targeted schools and programs as well as student and community supports that address the youth development and college- and career-ready skills of students.

The New York City (NYC) Department of Education (DOE) has pioneered innovative strategies to serve off-track youth, and the district offers particularly compelling evidence of the power of a differentiated portfolio approach. With the creation of a dedicated Office of Multiple Pathways and a portfolio of options designed to support at-risk and off-track youth, the city has identified, codified, and scaled specific school models for these historically underserved student populations. In particular, the Transfer Schools and Young Adult Borough Centers have delivered student outcomes that have exceeded overall system graduation rates by two to three times, meeting the same diploma standards as all other New York City graduates since there is no alternative diploma for these schools.

While the results of these focused school models have been exciting, the per-pupil cost of the schools is higher than the average comprehensive high school. For a district that must meet annual budgets, short-term pressures may create significant obstacles to building long-term investments. However, an analysis of the return on investment (ROI) demonstrates that these schools actually generate new graduates for the district in an efficient manner and at a lower cost than many other alternatives. The use of ROI analysis, therefore, can be a powerful and essential tool to inform critical resource allocation decisions not just in this case but with broader applications as well. Allowing district leaders to rely on data rather than anecdote in distributing scarce funds, the ROI approach focuses the district organization on the cost-results trade-off, helping to build an internal culture of accountability.

The Parthenon Group has partnered with the New York City DOE and a number of other urban school districts, foundations, and local school reform partners across the country to develop actionable strategies to improve the identification of and solutions available for urban off-track youth. Projects have typically involved a two-phase approach, beginning with the comprehensive Situation Assessment, which includes an in-depth quantitative profile of a district's student populations as well as performance and cost assessments of high schools that enroll at-risk and off-track students. A second phase, Strategy Development, concentrates on the articulation of specific recommendations and a proposed strategy to make drastic and measurable improvements in how a district serves its at-risk and off-track student populations. In all cases, the ultimate strategic goal is to significantly increase the district's overall graduation rate. Through such partnerships, a number of salient themes have emerged.

First, early identification of youth who are most at-risk of dropping out is feasible. Across districts, over 75 percent of eventual dropouts can be identified by eighth or ninth grade (and typically no later than the end of their first year of high school) in both a predictive and comprehensive manner. Earlier methods for identification, before eighth grade, for example, can be useful but are less comprehensive and generally do not capture as many of the district's eventual dropouts. Many common early indicators exist across districts (including risk factors such as eighth-grade attendance, middle school course failures, and being overage), and where indicators vary across districts, it is often the result of different student demographics (e.g., higher concentration of English language learners [ELLs]). Early-indicator segments have very low graduation rates, often below 35 percent. They are the at-risk groups. Focused investments at this stage can have a high ROI for some groups of students, as students who are just slightly off-track are brought back on-track before falling significantly behind.

Second, ninth grade matters—a lot—and can be readily tracked and translated into action. Research from a number of sources across the field consistently finds that credit accumulation in ninth grade (both number of courses and specific course content) is highly predictive of eventual high school graduation.[3] Across districts there is strong evidence of the power of intervention in the different trajectories of students who fail multiple core courses in ninth grade. Closely monitoring ninth grade progression (or lack thereof) presents opportunity for action.

Third, focusing on prevention is not a sufficient strategy, as the number of students who have already fallen off-track is staggering and prevention alone is unlikely to work for all students in the near future. When the populations of in-school and out-of-school youth are combined, the total number of off-track students in large urban districts typically ranges from 40 to 60 percent of all school-age youth. These students need recuperative options to accelerate credit achievement, as well as social-emotional supports, to mitigate the developmental consequences of school failure. As the district portfolio increases the supply of high schools with high engagement and on-track high school achievement, the proportional need for recuperative strategies will decrease in the long term.

Fourth, at-risk and off-track populations are distinct and not homogenous. Nationwide patterns are emerging that identify consistent segments of students that, when combined, represent the majority of the off-track population in a district. Individual off-track segments require differentiated strategies and solutions based on variables such as reading level, high school credit achievement, and reason for non-attendance, all of which require different school designs. For example, an eighteen-year-old with three years of credits, reading on grade level, and with family and/or work obligations has very different social-emotional and scheduling needs than a sixteen-year-old who has not completed ninth grade credits and has a reading level below seventh grade. Too often these students would be offered the same solutions or would simply be served in a traditional comprehensive high school that fails to provide the specific school engagement strategies and services that they require.

Finally, successful proof points exist across the country with many common design elements. There are school models that have been designed with the customer—the student—in mind. They share common elements and flexible designs that are able to meet the needs and strengths of students. Organizing these models into a portfolio of different solutions across schools, rather than school by school, can be effective in providing the diversity of supply that matches the diversity in demand. While the focus of this chapter is secondary reform, these same design principles can be applied to broader K–12 reform.

This chapter draws on Parthenon's experience and explores how districts can employ strategic approaches to develop comprehensive portfolios of schools that best address the needs of all students, with a focus on historically underserved populations. It identifies core components for effective school models as well as resource requirements and key considerations regarding the relative return on investment based on student outcomes—the latter being a critical requirement for districts to ensure the most effective allocation of its resources to areas of great need.

Growing local, state, and national awareness of the dropout crisis presents a window of opportunity for reform. A strong potential exists to stem the rising tide of dropouts and close persistent gaps in student performance—especially relative to high school graduation and an enduring achievement gap—and the United States cannot afford to miss this opportunity for change.

RIGOROUS FACT-BASED APPROACH WITH COLLABORATIVE STRATEGY DEVELOPMENT

School design must begin with the customer—in this case, students—in mind. Despite the best intentions of many school systems across the country, few districts apply truly student-focused strategies to K–12 reform. However, data exists to inform deep and meaningful strategic planning across districts, which can facilitate the most leveraged investment decisions across K–12 education reform efforts.

Recent investments in understanding the national dropout crisis have been significant. Unprecedented partnerships between public district leadership and foundations and private-sector entities (e.g., the Michael and Susan Dell Foundation, the Broad Foundation, the Bill and Melinda Gates Foundation, consulting partners, and others) have supported rigorous, objective, fact-based, and collaborative strategy development.

This section will explore a two-phased approach to addressing the dropout crisis in individual districts. In the first phase, a comprehensive *situation assessment* creates a fact base for district leadership, while the second phase uses the same analytic assessment of students as the basis for *strategic planning*.

Phase 1: Situation Assessment:
Overview of Student Population and Existing Programs

A detailed and analytic situation assessment helps district decision makers establish a common set of facts before embarking on new strategies and can be a tool to move away from historic reliance on anecdotes about what works. The detail that follows outlines three stages of analysis that focus on secondary reform, but a similar approach could be employed for a K–12 strategy.

Define, size, and profile the at-risk and off-track populations and understand their progression through high school.   This stage begins by defining *off-track,* which differs by district depending on the specific graduation requirements for a four-year high school progression as well as on the priorities of the district leadership. For instance, New York City defines its "overage and under-credited" (OA-UC) students as those who are two or more years behind graduation requirements relative to their age and years in school. In Chicago, students are off-track if they complete ninth grade for the first time with fewer than five credits and more than one semester of a failing grade (twenty-four total credits, averaging six per year, are required for graduation).

Once defined, the off-track population can be sized and the progression of off-track students in high school can be studied. This analysis benefits from both a snapshot view and also a cohort analysis. The snapshot view allows the district to understand how many students are off-track at any given point in time and where they are in the system. Depending on the definition of *off-track,* the total number of off-track students typically ranges from 20 to 40 percent of the total student population.

Cohort analysis, however, allows districts to determine what percent of all students fall off-track during high school and at what specific point in their high school career this occurs. The percent that falls off-track is highly correlated with a district's total number of eventual dropouts, and in representative districts such as New York, Chicago, and Boston, the off-track population represents *more than half* of a district's total school-aged population. The cohort analysis also allows the district to analyze the progression of off-track youth and thereby better understand the timing of when students fall off-track, the patterns and outcomes once students fall off-track, and the final outcome for all off-track students (e.g., graduation rates and type of diploma earned). In Chicago, for instance, the majority of students who drop out fall off-track during their first year of high school, with only one in five students who fall off-track eventually graduating.

The situation assessment may also include measuring basic demographic characteristics of the populations (e.g., race, gender, students with IEPs and special needs, and ELLs). Populations differ by district, but sample urban districts included in this work have off-track populations that are approximately 40 percent African

American, 45 percent Hispanic, 60 percent male, 30-plus percent with IEPs or special needs, and 15-plus percent ELLs, demonstrating that the off-track population mirrors the gender and racial achievement gap also evident in high school graduation patterns.

In addition, in this first stage of the situation assessment, the district can determine the relationship between incoming skill levels and becoming off-track, quantifying the proportion of students who enter high school on-track but fall off-track as they progress through high school. Throughout this type of work, a frequently asked question is, Were students prepared when they started high school? Of course, academic preparation is important, and students with higher levels of proficiency in middle school are more likely to graduate high school. However, the data also reveal some surprises. In New York City, for instance, a full quarter of all off-track students entered high school with high Level 2 eighth-grade ELA scores (see figure 4.1). So while academic preparation does matter, it is not the only issue affecting the dropout population.

The differences among the population of off-track students can be further understood by examining each student's age and level of credit attainment relative to graduation requirements. As demonstrated in figure 4.2, the majority of off-track students in New York City have completed less than one-quarter of credits required for graduation, despite having spent more than two years in the high school system.

FIGURE 4.1

Academic preparation of off-track students in New York City, June 2005

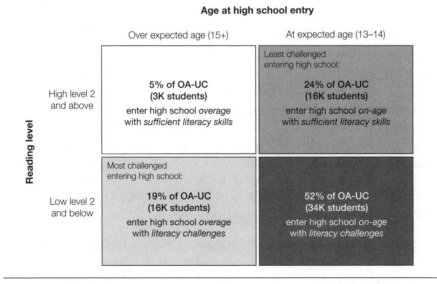

FIGURE 4.2

Age and credit accumulation of New York City off-track high school students

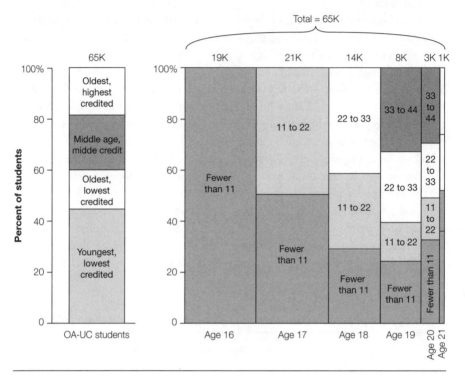

The off-track population is not homogenous; it includes students along a spectrum, from just slightly off-track to severely off-track.

Develop early indicators and segment the at-risk and off-track populations.   As the district develops a more nuanced understanding of its at-risk and off-track populations, it may also create early indicators to identify and segment these populations, recognizing that this group of students is not homogenous but includes students with significantly different academic and social-emotional needs. Early indicators of at-risk and off-track youth should meet two critical criteria:

1. *Are they predictive of dropping out?* What is the graduation rate of students with a certain risk factor and/or within a specific off-track segment? Students with predictive risk factors would typically have graduation rates significantly below the dis-

trict average (e.g., 15–35 percent versus 60 percent in the district overall). In other words, a more predictive indicator would have relatively fewer false positives.

2. *Are they comprehensive in identifying many dropouts?* What percent of total dropouts can be accounted for by any given early-indicator and/or off-track segment? Can we identify the majority of eventual dropouts across this group of early indicators (e.g., over 70 percent)? A set of comprehensive indicators would have a relatively low level of false negatives.

These two criteria are often in conflict with each other, with highly predictive risk factors typically being less comprehensive and vice versa. For instance, extremely low scores on eighth-grade standardized tests are highly predictive of a student eventually dropping out but not very comprehensive, since a relatively small group of students fits in this category. Therefore, designing useful indicators often requires balancing these criteria while ensuring that the indicators are also easy to communicate to schools, parents, and students. By designing strategies around factors that are both predictive and comprehensive, the district can be assured of making efficient, targeted investments that also address a large enough portion of the dropout problem to fundamentally shift existing trends in student outcomes.

Segmenting student subpopulations can be useful in tailoring both prevention and recuperation strategies. A district may even employ two different student segments, the first for prevention by identifying segments of at-risk students and the second for recuperation by segmenting off-track students by their distinct needs.

A sample at-risk segmentation from a large urban school district included the following four representative student segments, which account for three out of four eventual dropouts. Most can be identified before ninth grade, and all can be identified by the end of a student's first year in high school.

- *Late-entrant ELL:* ELLs who enter the district for the first time during high school (approximately 35 percent systemwide graduation rate)
- *High-need students with disabilities or IEPs:* Substantially separate special education students (approximately 25 percent systemwide graduation rate)
- *Students with eighth-grade risk factors:* students with low attendance or multiple eighth-grade course failures or who are two or more years overage (approximately 35 percent systemwide graduation rate)
- *Students with ninth-grade course failures:* first-time ninth graders who fail one or more core courses and who are not captured in the above categories (approximately 30 percent systemwide graduation rate)

These factors are both comprehensive (accounting for three-quarters of all eventual dropouts) and predictive (student segments have graduation rates half that of the system overall). Early intervention strategies targeted at these groups and tailored to their specific needs have the potential to prevent some students from falling off-track and dropping out.

Later in the high school experience, as students fall off-track and recuperative strategies become necessary, segmenting along different lines becomes useful in order to tailor the most appropriate school or program to that student's specific needs. Across multiple districts, the following segmentation has been meaningful:

- *"Young and far" from graduation:* sixteen- or seventeen-year-old students who are two or more years off-track toward completing graduation requirements (on average, 10–20 percent systemwide graduation rate)
- *"Old and far" from graduation:* students eighteen years or older who are two or more years off-track toward completing graduation requirements (on average, approximately 20 percent systemwide graduation rate, many through GED programs)
- *"Old and close" to graduation:* students eighteen years or older with less than one year of completion requirements toward graduation (on average, 40–50 percent systemwide graduation rate)
- *Overage late-entrant ELLs:* ELL students new to the district and who are overage relative to expected grade level (on average, 20–30 percent systemwide graduation rate)

Measure the power of existing options to keep students on-track and identify options with strong recuperative power.   Armed with a deep understanding of the at-risk and off-track populations, the final stage of analysis focuses on evaluating the district's current options to serve these youth. The majority of existing schools likely follow a traditional model, accepting incoming first-time ninth graders from eighth grade. For these schools, a simple calculation of the on-track rates and graduation rates across the district is a useful starting point, but it should be followed with an evaluation of the schools' performance in the context of the needs of incoming students. One way of accomplishing this is through different forms of regression analysis, which can compare performance of schools while adjusting for the composition of the incoming student population. This lens is critical for finding options that work for high-risk populations. Otherwise, schools and programs with high concentrations of high-need students and strong results with those populations may simply appear average relative to the rest of the district, when in fact their results may be significantly above average when compared to schools serving similar student groups.

In addition to reviewing school performance, the district may also choose to study the effectiveness of specific programs that are offered districtwide or at a select number of sites. Rigorous program evaluation is often challenging because a true control sample is rarely available, so districts may need to rely on the best available proxies.

While programs in the context of traditional schools have not typically demonstrated significant recuperative power with severely off-track youth, examples do exist of effective targeted programs that can help at-risk students or students who are just slightly off-track.

Lastly, but importantly, is the search for options that have recuperative power with off-track youth—specifically, the ability to reengage students, accelerate credit recovery and course completion in a meaningful way, and graduate students who have fallen off-track. Some districts may not have any schools dedicated to this effort, while others may have an existing network of schools and programs. Some districts may find pockets of success within traditional high schools, while others do not. This final stage of analysis includes determining the current enrollment patterns of at-risk and off-track students, assessing the population served by differentiated school models, and identifying articulated high school models that demonstrate higher graduation rates with similar populations.

Phase 2: Develop a Strategic Plan for Future Investment and Capacity Building

With a common analytic fact base as a foundation, district leadership can use an improved understanding of student needs to develop a comprehensive strategy to increase graduation rates. By leveraging the analysis of the first phase of work, the strategy can include detailed financial and student performance targets. This stage of work may vary significantly depending on the district's priorities and the existing schools and programs in the district. Some districts may choose to focus on prevention, others on recuperation, and still others on a comprehensive strategy that spans the spectrum of interventions and supports.

Regardless of the district's area of focus, a rigorous strategy process should start with an estimate of the graduation rate lift afforded by both existing and potential new schools and programs. This may require using the relationship between credit accumulation in early high school years and eventual graduation outcomes to make projections and forecast future results, including graduation rates. Benchmarks from other districts may also inform forecasts where the district does not currently have programs or school models in place.

Districts may then combine the graduation rate impact with the cost per pupil of various schools and programmatic options in order to calculate the ROI for different investment options. A key metric for the ROI analysis is the annual operating cost per point of graduation rate increase. Faced with a number of different potential investment opportunities to serve at-risk and off-track students, the district can prioritize among different program and school options based on a number of potential factors, including ROI, as well as the potential scale of the specific strategy (the number of new graduates that could be generated), implementation challenges (e.g., considering if a program or school model already exists in the district or would be imported or created), and the specific needs of students and existing options available to serve such student segment. Once the set of strategies is chosen and an implementation plan is created, the underlying data allow for the calculation of the total cost per year, the annual number of new graduates from each strategy, and the yearly impact on systemwide graduation rates.

SOLUTIONS EXIST, WITH DEMONSTRATED IMPACT AT SCALE

The New York City Department of Education and the Chicago Public Schools have pursued distinct but complementary strategies to serve off-track youth more effectively. While Chicago's efforts are in earlier stages, New York's work is mature enough to provide concrete and exciting results at a scale that can be a model for districts of any size. It's outcomes are encouraging for two simple reasons: (1) significantly positive graduation results among off-track students were found in a 2006 study at significant scale; and (2) the district has continued to successfully scale those school models while maintaining the quality of outcomes.

Demonstrated Impact

New York City's DOE has developed and implemented a portfolio of schools and programs designed to explicitly and intentionally serve different segments of the off-track population. In doing so, it has dramatically improved student outcomes relative to the typical performance of off-track students. Indeed, the Multiple Pathways Schools graduate overage and undercredited students at two to three times the rate of the city's large comprehensive high schools. Based on research done in 2006, Transfer Schools demonstrated an average graduation rate of 56 percent, compared to 19 percent in traditional schools for overage and undercredited students. Young Adult Borough Centers (YABCs) converted 44 percent of overage and undercredited students into high school graduates. These results were not at just a single school. In 2006, there were twenty-five Transfer Schools and twenty YABCs. At the highest performing Transfer School, 69 percent of students graduated.

Appreciating the power of these school models requires an appropriate set of comparisons. If these schools were compared to traditional high schools, the results of many schools would simply look consistent with the system average graduation rates (though some schools well-exceeded the system average despite serving some of the highest-need student segments). The key is to compare similar students, as defined by age and credit accumulation. In 2006, 16 percent of overage and undercredited students were enrolled in Multiple Pathways Schools (including GED programs). Yet, if these models were further scaled, would outcomes hold?

Successfully Scaling the Models

As New York has further grown its network of Multiple Pathways Schools, results are quite promising. Since the fall of 2006, the district has opened an additional sixteen Transfer Schools with a seat capacity of 3,400 and six additional YABCs with another 1,500 seats. The new Transfer Schools have focused their enrollment on the largest segment of the overage and undercredited population, which is the youngest, lowest-credited group (the "young and far" group). This segment historically has extremely low graduation rates, but early results from growth efforts have been strong. For the 2007–2008 school year, one of the new transfers school models, West Brooklyn Community High School, posted a six-year graduation rate of 72 percent. Other new models (which do not yet have a sizeable six-year cohort) have posted credit accumulation rates of over eight credits a year. Transfer Schools with this level of credit accumulation have historically had six-year graduation rates of over 60 percent. The data are summarized in figure 4.3.

FIGURE 4.3

Graduation rates of overage and undercredited students in New York City

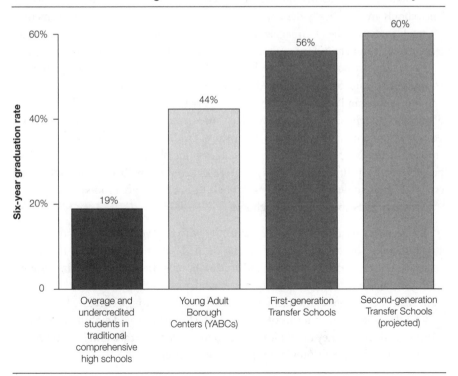

The increase in graduates generated by Multiple Pathways Schools has contributed to New York's overall system improvement, where graduation rates increased from 51 percent to 66 percent between 2002 and 2008 (using the city's traditional calculation of graduation rates). Transfer Schools contributed to four-year graduation rate increases, while a broader portfolio of Transfer Schools and YABCs supported increases in five- and six-year graduation rates systemwide.

The NYC Multiple Pathways Models

The Multiple Pathways Schools and programs are deliberate models that address youth development and academic needs while accelerating credit recovery necessary for students to earn a high school diploma.

NYC's Office of Multiple Pathways to Graduation manages the strategic planning, school development, and implementation of a portfolio of diploma-granting high schools and programs.

Transfer Schools.   These small, academically rigorous, full-time high schools are designed to re-engage students who are off-track or who have dropped out of high school. The schools are specifically designed for the needs of the "young and far" segment of off-track students. The essential elements of a Transfer School include a personalized learning environment, rigorous academic standards, student-centered pedagogy, support to meet instructional and developmental goals, and a focus on connections to college. All Transfer Schools designed as a result of this data have the essential element of opportunities and supports of Learning to Work (LTW), which offers additional academic and student support, postsecondary and career exploration, work preparation skills development, and subsidized internships. Students must have been previously enrolled in an NYC public high school for at least one year and be far from grade-level promotion; most students enter at age sixteen or seventeen with less than ninth-grade credits. Eligible students enroll in these schools through a choice process.

A few key facts about Transfer Schools:

- Transfer Schools typically are most effective with the "young and far" student population (those with time to catch up through effective literacy and numeracy strategies across the curriculum and acceleration before aging out of the system in June of the year of their twenty-first birthday).
- Transfer School populations mirror that of their large comprehensive high school counterparts in terms of age, credit accumulation, and eighth-grade ELA and math scores (they are typically two to four years off-track and have been disengaged from their previous high school experience).

- Transfer Schools significantly increase student engagement, with a nearly twofold increase in student attendance (from 40 percent to 78 percent), and they also improve student progression, where the number of credits earned per year increase from 4.9 to 8.9.
- Across every level of eighth-grade reading preparation, graduation rates of off-track students in Multiple Pathways Schools have more than doubled that of the same populations in comprehensive high schools. The most powerful outcomes appear among students with the highest need (e.g., students with the lowest eighth-grade preparation and fewest high school credits).

Young Adult Borough Centers (YABCs). These small learning environments offer full-time customized evening academic programs and comprehensive youth development strategies through community-based practice for students who have been in high school for at least four years and have attained a minimum of seventeen credits, comparable to sophomore standing. These schools are designed to meet the needs of high school students who might be considering dropping out because they are behind or have adult responsibilities that make attending school in the daytime difficult. These programs are specifically designed for the "old and close" student population.

YABCs stand out as effective solutions for this population for several reasons:

- YABCs have Learning to Work as a key design element, which offers additional academic and student support, postsecondary and career exploration, work preparation, and skills development. The elements of LTW are designed to enhance and complement the academic component of YABCs.
- Many YABCs also include the LTW internship component, in which students can gain valuable work experience and earn money at the same time.
- Students graduate with a diploma from their home school after they have earned all of their credits and passed all of the required exams while attending a YABC. Students who are registered in a YABC program remain assigned, for all accountability measures, to their sending school. This ensures that accountability remains with the school that initially failed to meet the student needs.

The comprehensive approach of YABCs, combining academic rigor with comprehensive youth development services, is a critical differentiator versus prior evening high school models.

Access GED Program. This newly created program for off-track youth and dropouts is particularly relevant for the "old and far" segment. Intentionally designed through a district-supported research and development process by practitioners and subject experts, this model was developed to meet the specific academic and developmental needs of students in a full time GED school setting. With the principle that GED students must do more than pass the GED exam to be successful in today's economy, the program is structured so that every Access student uses the GED as a springboard to training, college, and /or employment. GED programs are viable, college-ready options when rigorous programmatic elements are in place to serve a select student population that, due to age and circumstance, cannot attend high school on a full-time basis. NYC policy was amended to limit enrollment in GED programs to students eighteen years or older, with exceptions granted on a case-by-case basis. The full-time model is designed to assist students to reach a college-ready score on the GED test without remediation at the college level. Essential components include:

- Age- and culturally appropriate, research-based curriculum
- Contextualized learning experiences and student portfolio process
- LTW partnership, which provides opportunities to participate in the workforce
- Explicit pathways to postsecondary training and employment
- An orientation phase that encourages students to reinvent their identities as learners and achievers before they begin class work
- Student support services, which start at enrollment and continue for one year after graduation

New York City's Department of Education, like most districts across the country, faces persistent challenges in serving the "old and far" student population given the academic gaps and time pressures that face students aging out of the system. The district's focus remains on revamping GED programs and allowing for proficiency-based progression, seeing it as relevant and meaningful. An innovation challenge exists to ensure that appropriate focus, as well as opportunity, is provided to currently underserved student populations. Ideally, these students would be identified earlier, when they fall into the "young and far" segment and could be served by the Transfer School model.

EARLY INTERVENTION EFFORTS IN CHICAGO

Chicago's Office of Graduation Pathways has included in its portfolio a range of prevention and early intervention strategies targeted toward at-risk students earlier in their high school careers. These programs take place in the context of existing comprehensive and new small schools.

Use and communication of data has been a cornerstone of the work in Chicago, serving two critical purposes: (1) focusing school-level personnel on early intervention, and (2) ensuring accountability for both schools and the district. The Consortium on Chicago School Research, in partnership with the Chicago Public Schools (CPS), developed the freshman on-track indicator, which for a number of years has been part of every school's publicly published school report card. Recently, as Chicago has built out its data dashboard for principals and school personnel, new elements have been added and refined so that schools can flag incoming ninth graders in at-risk categories and track all students' progress regularly throughout the freshman year. In addition, by including the ninth-grade on-track rate in school report cards, the district has focused schools on ninth-grade performance.

CPS has also used a number of programs to help keep students on-track. Focusing efforts on the key eighth-to-ninth-grade transition, CPS has revised its student placement process; improved timely communications about placement with students, parents, and schools; and broadly extended a special summer program called Step-Up, which provides both academic and social-emotional supports to students before starting ninth grade.

During ninth grade, the district provides a dedicated credit recovery program targeted specifically at students who are just slightly off-track (e.g., those who would have finished the year with four or five credits rather than the required six). Entry requirements for the program ensure that the program is targeted at these specific students. Credit recovery is a strategy with limited reach (it is not relevant for all students), but it has the potential for significant impact and a high ROI. For instance, for a student who is two years behind in credit accumulation, earning one additional credit is statistically unlikely to increase the student's chance of graduating. Schools that routinely send all off-track students to evening classes or summer school may actually do a disservice to those students, who put forth effort but do not get significantly closer to graduation while at the same time consume resources that might have helped other students reach graduation. A student who is just one credit short of being promoted or being on-track, however, can receive tremendous benefit from such programs. The impact of one additional credit is especially powerful early in high school, in the first or second year.

Virtual classes offer a nascent but exciting opportunity within the realm of credit recovery. These online courses allow scheduling flexibility for both the school and the student, as well as important economic benefits for the district. Even with in-person teacher supervision of virtual credit recovery, a school can consolidate a full classroom of students who may need to be studying half a dozen different subject areas. Credit recovery in traditional classroom environments can be prohibitively expensive (with just a few students to a room, especially in smaller schools) as well as a scheduling problem for high schools already juggling complex flows of students, teachers, and classrooms.

Chicago developed and implemented these strategies beginning in 2008. Efficacy is still to be determined, but leading indicators suggest traction is occurring in the field.

CORE OPERATING PRINCIPLES FOR NYC'S MULTIPLE PATHWAYS

The NYC Office for Multiple Pathways to Graduation has outlined five core operating principles that guide its work across school models.

1. The district focuses on *Leadership, Faculty and Management,* empowering their school leaders with flexibility over matters that support school design, including hiring, scheduling, budgeting, and curriculum decisions. They insist that their teams have a commitment to students who will succeed nowhere else and a universal focus on youth development, often in partnership with community partners.
2. A *Culture of High Expectations, Rigorous and Engaging Instruction* includes strength-based instructional approaches that emphasize youth development embedded in curriculum, environment, and school design elements. Backwards curriculum mapping also emphasizes literacy and numeracy across the curriculum.
3. A focus on *Student Support and Engagement* incorporates transformational developmental strategies to engage older students, engagement efforts and counseling for at-risk youth, core attendance outreach, and a structured competency approach related to real-world experience.
4. *Career Exploration and Reflection* has proven vital in engaging youth in the relevancy of the high school experience. This includes subsidized opportunities to participate in real life roles and reflective information gathering used for career exploration.
5. *Assessment and Accountability* includes ongoing assessments of student progress at the school level to inform curriculum and individual student programming needs. Students are also represented in all accountability and reporting systems.

The Multiple Pathways schools tend to be small schools that optimize the application of these operating principles while increasing intensity and personalization. Ideally, program enrollment ranges between 200 and 250 students, to ensure scale efficiency within a school size that fosters a personalized environment. Schools also operate in adolescent-friendly spaces—that is, at a single site versus on a campus—and include extended academic calendars and flexible scheduling to enable accelerated course completion and credit recovery. Lastly, these schools all operate with choice-based enrollment, combined with specific intake criteria, to ensure fidelity to each school's specific target population and the related school model design.

KEY PROGRAM DESIGN ELEMENTS IN NEW YORK CITY

School systems often lack the ability to serve all students through effective teaching, schools, and supports that meet a range of individual academic and social-emotional needs. Specifically, most traditional comprehensive high schools have failed to incorporate school elements that increase graduation rates for students who fall off-track. However, programmatic design can matter significantly, and the differences in outcomes and student perceptions vary substantially based on the school arrangement. Large comprehensive high school environments too often trigger conscious disengagement. Due to their size and frequent overcrowding, large schools present challenges for students to build meaningful relationships with school staff and peers. "I hated my old school because it was so big," we might hear students complain. "I didn't know anyone. I didn't want to know anyone. I kept to myself. I never asked for help." We would hear another student noting that "school is so big that it is easy to skip, and no one notices when you're not in class. I cut school so much that my teacher asked, *Are you in this class?* when I showed up."

Students also report notable discouragement by teachers once they go off-track. Student testimonials such as the following underscore this unfortunate pattern: "Teachers would tell the group of students who got good grades that they were going to go to college. They would say it in front of everyone, and it made me feel bad."

Multiple pathways programs, however, demonstrate clear evidence of recuperative powers with previously disengaged students. Personalized attendance outreach and repercussions are significant disincentives to absenteeism, as many students note, since there are often swift and direct measures taken for missing school. Staff dedication to integrated youth development also helps affirm student strengths and reinforce achievement. "Our advocate counselors [and teachers] really care," students noted. "We can talk to them about anything." In addition to zeroing in on preexisting student strengths, teachers also focus on engaging instruction to reset student interest levels and enforce cultures of high expectations. Both of these actions are supported by frequent assessments that demonstrate the link between student effort and progress. "Our biweeklies are one of the biggest differences between my old school and new school. Every two weeks you get graded on everything possible—homework, participation—so if you're behind you can fix it."

RETURN ON INVESTMENT

Sadly, too many district administrators are forced to make enormous financial decisions based on scant data or simple anecdote. Here we explore an approach for calculating ROI, which measures the impact on student outcomes relative to the financial cost—defined in this case as the incremental cost to the system to graduate students who otherwise would not have graduated. In addition, we address the wide range of returns possible from different strategies as well as funding policy issues that can help or hinder effective implementation of a portfolio approach.

Multiple benefits exist to pursuing ROI calculations for superintendents and their leadership teams. Most importantly, this approach enables well-informed trade-offs among different investment opportunities for district leadership. In addition, the expectation of measurement of costs relative to results establishes a culture of accountability for district managers to track and be able to justify reforms as they are implemented and brought to scale. This helps the ongoing review and decision-making process regarding reform efforts that should be sustained, merit additional investment, or be discontinued. This lens provides a framework for more disciplined strategic planning and implementation to help avoid reform overload.

An Approach to Calculating ROI

Calculating ROI requires defining an end goal. In business, that goal is profit. For the purposes of this work, the goal has been defined as high school graduation. In Parthenon's work with districts, ROI has been a measure of the incremental money that must be invested in order to generate new graduates. This approach has allowed superintendents to ask questions such as, If I invest a million dollars, how many new graduates could I expect from different program and school models? The basic approach to answering this includes answering four key questions:

1. *What is the graduation rate of target populations in the core system today?* This provides a sense of the baseline performance that can be expected without further investment. In establishing this baseline, it is critical to be specific about target student populations. For instance, in a program targeted at late-entrant ELL students, comparing results versus the system overall or even all ELL students could significantly understate the effect of the program.

2. *What graduation rate can be reliably forecast for new schools and programs?* The strength of the NYC experience was that existing programs offered clear benchmarks for performance across the system. Other districts may or may not have clear success stories against which to benchmark. If this is the case, district planning would likely include importing new models. This introduces an implementation risk to forecasting expected impact on graduation rates, but it does not preclude using the ROI approach.

3. *How much will it cost to bring these programs to scale?* To calculate meaningful ROI for schools and programs, estimates must include start-up expenses, school operating costs, and the funds spent on the central supports and youth development services that are often critical in differentiating the most successful schools and programs

4. *How much of this spending would have happened anyway?* To the extent that opportunities exist to refocus/reallocate existing spending on eventual drop-outs toward more strategic and results-oriented programmatic options, there is opportunity for efficiency. Per-pupil funding policies are critical components of effective resource management.

The Extent of Return Variation

The variation in ROI is striking. Within a single district, it is not uncommon for the ROI of existing schools or programs to vary by a multiple of 5 to 10. In one district, the cost to graduate at-risk students was one and a half to two times their non-risk student counterparts, while the cost to graduate substantially separate SPED students was between four to six times the system average. In another district, targeted early intervention programs generated incremental graduates for one-tenth the cost of programs to serve severely off-track students.

For the school models designed for off-track youth, specific costs vary by district, and the true incremental cost of the schools is affected by the district's particular funding formula. On average, the cost of these models has ranged from 10 to 50 percent more than traditional comprehensive schools, depending on the specific model and the district. The incremental cost per new graduate has ranged from $10,000 to $40,000 in districts that can achieve some repurposing of existing dollars toward the new schools. The cost would be higher for districts that cannot repurpose funds. In general, lower cost options tend to be targeted at early intervention programs that help at-risk youth stay on-track. Higher cost options typically reflect more comprehensive school models for students more severely off-track.

ROI analysis can yield surprising results. For instance, in New York City the Transfer School model targeted at off-track youth was known to have a high per-pupil cost, with graduation rates close to the district average. One might imagine this to be an inefficient way to generate new graduates. However, the ROI analysis demonstrated that the probability that these off-track students would graduate in a traditional high school was very slim, so raising their graduation rate to the district average actually represented a very significant increase in the number of high school graduates. Therefore, the high cost per-pupil was spread over a large number of new graduates, generating an attractive ROI for Transfer Schools compared to less expensive programs that had smaller incremental benefits.

Districts, unlike businesses, may not choose to make ROI their sole investment criteria. Districts may also factor in equity considerations, wanting to ensure that at least some options are available to all student groups, even if they cannot provide a sufficient number of seats to meet the total demand. In the face of academic, equity, and economic considerations, superintendents and their leadership teams should seek to arm themselves with the most robust fact base available in order to decide between options in an informed manner. ROI analysis is a vital part of this process, helping to ensure optimal use of limited resources.

Investment Coordination of New and Old

One of the great challenges for any superintendent or CFO is the typical fragmentation that characterizes a district budget. The fragmentation is often a result of the myriad funding streams that generate one-off programs, as well as the legacy of years of different reform efforts. All too often the creation of a new reform effort comes on top of everything that has been tried before. District cultures are simply not oriented toward stopping activity but instead focus on starting new activity. This orientation is natural. Stopping an activity requires removing resources from schools and students, which is painful and difficult even when data demonstrate that those resources are not having an impact. But the work that we have outlined here is expensive work, and funding it requires significant incremental funding and/or the redirecting of resources to areas elsewhere in the district that cannot demonstrate their ROI for students.

In addition, districts can reduce the timeline necessary to evaluate new investments. Graduation may take up to six years, but because ninth grade is so predictive of graduation (and tenth grade even more so), reasonably accurate forecasts can be made many years earlier. Any new program or school with one to two semesters of data is ready for at least a preliminary review. One district adopted a mantra to continuously reduce the cycle time across three key activities: *innovate, evaluate, and adjust.*

The Role of Weighted Student Funding

If a district chooses to create a portfolio of options for its at-risk and off-track youth, it must also help connect students with the right seats, ensuring that students are counseled regarding schools and programs that fit their individual needs. Of course, this implies that students will move around the district, not just between eighth and ninth grades but also at other points in their high school careers. The movement of students can cause the portfolio approach to become prohibitively expensive for districts that do not use some form of weighted student funding or per-pupil funding formula. While these types of models have advantages in allowing for a school's portfolio approach, there are, of course, many complex considerations that are part of the decision to change funding formulas.

A clear advantage of weighted student funding is that most of the resources move with the student. When the enrollment at High School A declines by one, and the enrollment at High School B increases by one, there is little or no impact on the total district budget. By contrast, in a district with staffing formulas and other centrally dictated funding approaches, the budget of High School A (the "sending school") would likely remain unchanged. If many schools lose just a few students each in order for a new school to open serving off-track students, the cost of the new school may be almost entirely incremental to the district.

Obviously, the move to weighted student funding is complex and requires additional considerations on the part of the district. For instance, this approach puts additional responsibility on already-burdened principals. However, without this policy, the ROI calculation cannot include the costs saved from reduced enrollment from the original school, and the total cost of generating new graduates can increase 20 to 50 percent.

Wider Policy Challenges

The costs associated with dropouts are real. Societal costs associated with the dropout crisis have been well-documented, with estimates placed at over $200,000 as well as lost earnings for the individual estimated at $260,000.[4] While such data are helpful and powerful in focusing public attention on the urgency of the issue, they do not always speak directly to the decision-making criteria of district leaders, who cannot tap into the long-term savings of dropout prevention and find themselves instead resource-constrained and facing numerous proposals for how to spend the incremental dollars they do control. Successful investments in dropout prevention could recoup substantial resources for state and local governments over time.

Unfortunately, the relatively short political life cycle for most elected officials—and perhaps the time horizon considered by most taxpayers—makes it difficult to invest more money now in education in order to save money later on prisons. Sadly, therefore, we are left with investment opportunities that would have a significant positive return for taxpayers over the long term (and, of course, a benefit for students) and yet cannot be pursued. With Race to the Top and the focus on turnarounds and School Improvement Grants, thoughtful and analytic planning with a student-centered approach can ensure that those funds are well-used. A portfolio approach, with differentiated models for specific student segments, can help serve the populations targeted by those federal initiatives.

REFLECTIONS AND CONSIDERATIONS

Despite significant progress by districts in both understanding student needs and mapping solutions to such needs, the fact remains that the needs of at-risk and off-track students remain largely unmet due to strategic pressures, lack of capacity in the field, and financial constraints. Following are some reflections on elements that increase a district's ability to raise graduation rates.

Increase internal capacity to "do the work."   Internal capacity requirements span multiple levels. First, this work requires cultural change, including establishing and communicating high and clear expectations while providing the supports to teachers to deliver instructional strategies aligned with youth development principles and supports. Second, dedicated capacity at the central office has proved necessary across districts to develop new school and program models, oversee the startup phase, support capacity in the field, advocate for the schools and programs internally, and be accountable for ultimate results. This group also typically becomes active in student placement, though that capacity may officially reside elsewhere in the organization.

Bolster external partner capacity.   External capacity through intermediaries has also been central to success in large districts like NYC, where they are able to help the district in providing youth development and operational supports. However, few intermediaries are experienced in serving and educating the off-track youth population, and resource constraints to fund development and support of new program models are severe. Reluctance to support aggressive expansion efforts is common, given the difficulty of work and limited incentives. Districts ideally seek to identify and groom strong intermediaries to partner with expansion efforts, though short-term capacity limitations may exist. In some cities, private philanthropy has proven an important partner is developing external intermediaries.

Ensure intentionality of multiple pathways school and program offerings.   Successful schools and programs tend to create deliberate models that are designed to address the differentiated academic and youth development needs of overage and off-track youth and that typically have explicit entrance requirements.

Adopt a portfolio approach across broader K–12 strategies.   The Multiple Pathways work in NYC originated as a way to differentiate models for a specific group of underserved and off-track students, but at the core of the work is a process and an approach to reform, rather than a specific set of school models. As such, this process and approach can be extrapolated for a district to pursue a broader portfolio strategy for reform, one that is focused on understanding student need and innovating around school organization and structure for all schools.

Policy considerations given No Child Left Behind (NCLB) and state accountability.   NCLB accountability rules are misaligned with successful multiple pathways outcomes. Clear accountability is needed for schools that generate off-track youth. Current measures punish effective schools that focus on serving off-track youth, as students are assigned to cohorts after spending multiple unproductive years in other schools. In addition, given NCLB's sole focus on four-year graduation outcomes, schools do not receive credit for students who graduate after four years, which is often the case in multiple pathways schools.

In New York City, for instance, the average Transfer School student spent 2.7 years in a traditional comprehensive school prior to enrolling in the Transfer School. The average enrollment in the Transfer School lasts 1.9 years, and 90 percent of all students have a final outcome (either graduating or dropping out) by the end of the sixth year from which they first entered high school. In this system, however, cohorts for accountability purposes are created at the start of the fourth year of high school, 0.3 years after the average enrollment in the Transfer School and at a point when those students are typically far off-track from a traditional four-year progression.

The traditional comprehensive school from which the student transferred has no accountability for that student's disengagement, despite the fact that these students had attendance below 50 percent and are severely off-track toward graduation on leaving the original school. Meanwhile, the Transfer School that accepts this student is held accountable for results within a window of time that makes it almost impossible to achieve a four-year graduation rate. This system can also be an impediment to attracting strong leaders to these schools. Six-year graduation rates are the appropriate performance metric for schools and programs serving off-track youth. Use of a six-year graduation rate to measure outcomes with overage and off-track students continues to be an important policy consideration for local, state, and national forums.

State accountability metrics are varied across the alternative accountability system. The choice of many possible metrics prohibits comparative evaluation across the transfer school network, and the creation of a more uniform set of metrics would allow for important comparisons. Metrics should be aligned with assessments of whether students are on-track for graduation and incorporate value-added metrics in order not to punish schools that accept the most challenged students. Ultimately, the ideal system of incentives motivates school leaders to match students with the most effective school option for them, given their needs and circumstances, in time for them to be successful.

Policy considerations given competency based progression. In order to meet the needs of older, lower-credit students, transfer school models need to incorporate strategies for credit acceleration and personalized programming. Opportunity exists for the state to allow transfer schools to award credit based on demonstrated competence aligned with state standards, not seat time. This strategy can be pursued while maintaining high school exit requirements, such as the Regents exams in New York State.

CONCLUSION

The work with off-track youth across urban districts has generated two broad observations. The first relates specifically to the dropout crisis in America, which is driven primarily by students who fall off-track toward completing graduation requirements.

The off-track youth population represents the face of dropouts. This is a population that is knowable; our schools can identify the students before dropout occurs. While the challenge is significant, solutions do exist. Schools and districts can learn from the experience of Chicago Public Schools' innovative strategies to address at-risk students and from the NYC Department of Education regarding off-track youth intervention and recuperative reforms.

As a nation, we cannot afford to ignore the dropout crisis, as it disproportionately affects our most vulnerable youth and perpetuates the achievement gap, especially in large urban areas. With appropriate strategic alignment and integration, organizational focus and discipline, and thoughtful resource reallocation, powerful programs can be designed, supported, and scaled to improve student outcomes in the short, medium, and long term.

With almost half of all urban students not graduating from high school, districts must recognize that programs and schools targeted to off-track youth must be as integral to the secondary strategy as anything else. The investment requirements to develop and sustain meaningful strategies for at-risk and off-track youth are significant and require reflection relative to other district priorities. If prioritized, recuperative options present opportunities to drive significant measureable results in the short term. Dramatic systemwide increases in graduation rates are realistic and should be pursued.

The second major observation from this chapter relates more broadly to education reform. Within the construct of our current basic district educational system, this chapter demonstrates that it is possible to meet the diversity of needs that exist among students. District administrations can use data to deeply understand student need, looking not just at the average student but also identifying distinct segments that can be targeted directly with differentiated school models. In other words, our districts are capable of creating the diversity of supply to meet the diversity of demand that clearly exists among students. This approach, however, does require a shift in mentality under which many districts have traditionally operated.

This approach to reform has succeeded because it invests heavily in understanding student need, identifying distinct segments that can be targeted directly, and then being flexible about the basic building blocks of a school in order to rethink what will work for high-need populations. This differs from traditional approaches, which often focus on the average student and work within the basic organizational constraints of the traditional school to try to improve achievement. Recuperative options are just one example, and an important place to start, given how critically linked the population is to unlocking the dropout problem. But the ultimate value for a district pursuing this path may lie in building a platform for how to approach broader reform with a more nuanced view of student need and greater flexibility in school design.

There are, of course, a number of unresolved issues that remain specific to the work with off-track youth. First, while most of these models meet the same standards for a high school diploma as all other high schools in the district, they struggle, as do many urban high schools, to ensure that their diploma represents college-readiness. Second, innovation challenges still exist to serve some of the highest-need student segments, in particular the "old and far" students and the students with IEPs who are served in substantially separate classroom environments. While there are no easy answers to these issues, continued investment, resources, and attention to the efforts to serve off-track youth may help drive innovation and progress.

Lastly, this work has raised questions that pertain to school choice. As the analysis demonstrates, districts may sometimes be in a position to "know what is best" for a student. Specifically, a data-driven district may be able to predict that a student has a 10 percent chance of graduating from one school but a 60 percent chance at another school. In that situation, what is the district's obligation to the student, and how should it balance the value of student choice, and the associated benefits of student engagement and empowerment, with efforts to connect the student with the best possible chance for graduation success?

Businesses in our economy face similar questions, believing that their products or services offer value to customers. As a result, most businesses invest in advertising and marketing in order to help inform the purchasing behavior of prospective customers. While there are obvious differences in our public education system, there are lessons that can be learned from the business approach. Within the construct of our current district structure, a district can offer a diversity of supply (school models) to its customers (students and parents) while ensuring that appropriate structures and information flows are in place so that customers can make informed decisions. Our districts have the ability to create a market mechanism, complete with choice among a diverse supply of schools to meet the diverse demands of its customers.

5

The Evolution of Parental School Choice

Thomas Stewart and Patrick J. Wolf

OVER THE PAST DECADE, we have been involved, individually and collectively, with various aspects of education reform in America. In particular, we have conducted extensive research and evaluations of school choice programs, which has provided us with direct access to the low-income parents and students who have participated in some of the newest school reform initiatives in the country.[1] Our interactions with low-income families have provided us with an extraordinary perspective on a unique aspect of contemporary education reform—the evolution of parental school choice. In our view, "Parental choice is a term commonly used to describe the opportunity for all families to pursue educational options that are in the best interests of their children. Parental school choice, specifically, begins when families have access to multiple school options."[2]

In the District of Columbia, we conducted a five-year longitudinal qualitative study involving 110 families and 180 students participating in the Opportunity Scholarship Program (OSP), the first federally funded school voucher program in the United States. We used a phenomenological research approach to capture the lived experiences of the participants. This included using focus groups, personal interviews, and keypad polling information gathering techniques. This study provided us valuable insights into the ability of low-income families to participate effectively in parental school choice given the challenges they face.

As education policy in the United States continues to expand school options, we as a nation must consider whether all Americans are fully prepared to assume the responsibilities associated with the effective exercise of parental school choice. We argue that the move from residentially assigning schools to parental school choice is a dramatic shift for many low-income families. We use the transition from shopping at a corner store to shopping at a mall as metaphor for school choice. Our research with the low-income participants in the OSP indicates that their ability to manage the demands of shopping mall school choice varies substantially in understandable ways. The success of urban parents in effectively exercising widespread parental school choice appears to be linked to the family-based and programmatic resources available to them. Family-based resources, such as a two-adult family or extensive personal support system, enhance the ability of families to navigate the school choice process. Access to accurate comparative school information from a reliable independent source—much like a site map for the mall—appears to be a key programmatic resource for urban school choosers. Parents in our qualitative study who lacked such resources, though eager and excited, were unable to act as effective consumers on their own, often needing considerable support to manage fundamental aspects of school choice.

This study is placed in the context of a small body of previous research that has examined the impact of service delivery on the political and consumer behavior of program participants, specifically low-income families. We offer in this chapter recommendations on how policy makers, philanthropists, and other stakeholders can better support efforts to provide low-income students and families with the transitional support many of them need to take full advantage of the growing number of educational options available to them.

THE DEMAND SIDE OF SCHOOL REFORM

Urban education is undergoing a major transformation, particularly as it relates to public schools. The U.S. Department of Education's Race to the Top (RTT) funding program is fueling an unprecedented set of investments in new methods of teacher recruitment and professional development, merit pay, and numerous other areas of school reform. This is occurring in the context of an ongoing expansion of school choice throughout the country, particularly involving the choice mechanisms external to public school systems, such as charter schools and vouchers. In response, many traditional public school systems are moving from assigning students to neighborhood schools to the internal choice mechanisms of open enrollment within or across school district boundaries. The unprecedented expansion of school options on the educational supply side has created an increasingly complex school marketplace, particularly for low-income urban families, to whom many of these reforms are targeted.

The demand side of education, which involves the attempts of families to gain access to quality educational services, is a matter that has received less attention and fewer resources than the supply side of educational choice. As Erin Dillon writes, "Discussions about quality in markets often focus on the supply-side—how to build high-quality options. But equally important is building high-quality demand—the ability of consumers to identify and select good options."[3]

RTT is the most recent example of a comprehensive education reform initiative that either overlooks or assumes the vital role that families play in the demand side of school reform. Of the many items mentioned as essential to accelerating educational transformation, there is no explicit reference to parents and families.[4]

Families, of course, have a vital role to play in educational improvement. As Chester Finn and Eric Osberg argue in chapter 2 of this volume, students and parents must be placed higher on the national educational agenda, especially regarding their role in school choice reforms. They note that "an education system responsive to—and guided by—the priorities of parents and children would have many merits." Similarly, chapter 1 authors Kim Smith and Julie Petersen also stress that the private sector must play a larger role: "The road toward such responsive supply in public education begins with a serious commitment to placing students, parents, and educators at the center of our [education entrepreneurs'] efforts and making a significant investment in what the business community calls *market segmentation*."

As America moves deeper into school choice and expanded school options, we must examine the extent to which the people targeted by school choice expansions are adequately prepared to assume the full responsibilities associated with exercising parental school choice effectively. Much of the literature on school choice assumes that parents are either born with school selection consumer skills or develop them naturally in the course of becoming adults.[5] Once given the opportunity, they are then expected to initiate a "stampede to quality" and away from educational dysfunction and neglect. This anticipated demand-side response would subsequently result in the expansion of quality schools and the elimination of bad schools.

Our research indicates that stampedes to quality by new parental consumers of education tend to include only part of the herd. Real consumerism entails not just the provision of choices regarding service providers but also fostering the ability of customers to make well-informed choices. Policy makers and other concerned stakeholders cannot assume that most new school choosers have experience developing and accessing the skills and knowledge necessary to seek, recognize, and obtain a quality educational environment for their child.[6] Some do, but many do not. School choice programs likely would be more effective in the future if concerned stakeholders are attentive to the demand side of parental school choice.

THE CORNER STORE VERSUS THE SHOPPING MALL

A useful heuristic for understanding the challenges that low-income urban parents face in exercising school choice can be drawn from the contrast between a corner store and a shopping mall. Traditionally, public schools in the United States have been like corner stores. The corner store is conveniently located within a certain neighbor-hood and managed by shopkeepers who frequently help you find what you seek to purchase. Corner stores are relatively small, however, and sometimes do not stock the specific product that you need or only carry an inferior brand. "Do you want Puffs? Well, we only carry Kleenex. That will have to do." Consumers sometimes leave the corner store having purchased the product that they sought; other times, they leave empty-handed or with a product that will simply have to suffice. Still, it is easy to shop at a corner store. People know where to find them and generally know what to expect once they are there. There is a reason why corner stores are now referred to as convenience stores.

Neighborhood public schools share many features with corner stores—convenient locations, trained staff who can try to "get you what you need," and a supply of goods limited by staff decisions regarding what is best. There is a shared element of pater-nalism surrounding both corner stores and neighborhood public schools. Of course, neighborhood public schools have the added consumer benefit that the service they provide is free, at least to the consumer.

Early experiments with parental school choice did not necessarily seek to replace the educational corner store. Instead, they essentially provided families with an alter-native corner store from which to purchase educational goods. Magnet schools are an excellent example of alternative corner stores as opposed to alternatives *to* corner stores in education. The motivation behind magnet schools was to get consumers from far away to shop at a particular corner store in an urban neighborhood. The goods stocked by the urban corner store were designed to appeal to the tastes of consumers outside of the urban market and thereby entice them to come and shop alongside a specific group of locals in a particular place. Similarly, the Milwaukee Pa-rental Choice Program (MPCP), America's first urban school voucher program, op-erates in a way that resembles magnet schools. Students enroll in the MPCP through their chosen private school, and parents participating in the program report visiting an average of just 1.3 private schools before making their selection.[7] Parents in the MPCP might be attracted to the High Education Standards or Religious Items aisles of the alternative educational corner stores in their neighborhoods. Still, their shop-ping remains easy and surprisingly limited.

Recently, school choice expansions have moved beyond simply providing an al-ternative educational corner store and have made the jump to the equivalent of edu-cational shopping malls. Urban areas such as New Orleans, Washington, DC, and Dayton, Ohio, offer dozens of highly variegated public charter schools that enroll more than a third of the K–12 students in their respective cities. Such choice-rich environments represent a qualitative change from the alternative corner store model of educational choice. If transportation is easily available, such systems provide the equivalent to educational shopping malls to parent consumers of education.

Anyone who has visited a shopping mall for the first time knows that they can be difficult to navigate. It is highly likely that one or more stores in the mall will have exactly what you want to purchase—but how do you find it? New mall shoppers can visit various stores and ask for specific products and services. The first store to assure them that they have what they want is likely to get the shopper's business, as it can be a long and tiring walk all the way to the opposite wing of the mall. Other shoppers will have done their homework and know which store has the product that they seek. For them, a clear and comprehensive store map is all they need to navigate their shopping excursion. Finally, some parents will do a complete mall crawl, checking every possible store for the highest-quality product at the lowest possible price. These shoppers, referred to as *active* or *marginal choosers* (or picky parents) in the education literature, are likely to acquire the best product available for their family.[8] Research suggests that only about 15 percent of school choosers perform the full mall crawl in acquiring comprehensive schooling information before making their school choices.[9]

The exhaustive search of the few mall crawlers improves the quality of educational services for even passive consumers of education due to the pressure it puts on providers.[10] Yet, to the extent that schools differ in their educational environments and offerings and students differ in their educational needs, we would expect that students would be better matched to schools if more new education consumers were able to effectively navigate the education shopping mall. Some students might need the services of a particular boutique or a high-quality brand to succeed educationally. It likely requires a committed educational shopper to find the best school fit for their child and, more importantly, to know when to call off the search because they have found what they need.

We do not decry the move from corner store to shopping mall school choice. To the contrary, we think it opens up the possibility for many more low-income urban families to match their children to a school environment that effectively serves their needs, a view that was echoed by parents throughout our study. Moreover, our research indicates that the added responsibility of choosing a child's school from among many distinct options appears to inspire some parents to become more active consumers and involved citizens.[11] These parents rise to the challenge of higher expectations and greater responsibilities regarding their children's education. The shortcoming we see in shopping mall school choice policies is that they often are launched with inadequate supports for parents largely unaccustomed to making high-impact consumer decisions. As Finn and Osberg write in chapter 2, "Choosing a school is more like buying a car than buying jeans, so it's important that parents have every opportunity to make the best possible decision." The reality is that many families who qualify for contemporary school choice programs have never even bought a car.

Our central argument is a play on the biblical adage that from those to whom much is given, much is expected. In the field of parental school choice, *to those from whom much is expected, much needs to be given.* We expect a lot from parents involved in shopping mall school choice programs. Policy makers, philanthropists, and community leaders need to be attentive to the informational and support needs of choosing families in order to maximize the likelihood that they will choose well for their children. We have seen this need close up in our qualitative research with families participating in the District of Columbia's Opportunity Scholarship Program.

AN OVERVIEW OF THE OPPORTUNITY
SCHOLARSHIP PROGRAM

Policy makers have proposed a school voucher program for the District of Columbia for decades.[12] One clear motivation for increased parental school choice in the nation's capital has been the widespread dissatisfaction with the performance of the DC Public Schools (DCPS). Fewer than 60 percent of DCPS eighth graders eventually graduate from high school.[13] An astounding 85 percent of DCPS students who do graduate and enroll in the University of the District of Columbia require remediation.[14] These dismal results have led observers to wonder if parental school choice might offer a better way to move students forward.

The first attempt to enact a school voucher program in the District took place in 1981, when the Committee for Improved Education placed a voucher initiative on the ballot.[15] That initiative failed in the subsequent election, as almost all contentious initiatives and referenda do. The District of Columbia school voucher debate then moved to the halls of the U.S. Congress, since the federal government possesses the ultimate responsibility for funding and overseeing education in the District. Throughout the 1990s and early 2000s, Congressman Richard Armey (R-TX) annually proposed a school voucher program for the District, only to see his efforts fail on largely partisan votes. With fellow Republicans in control of both houses of Congress in 1998, Armey's voucher bill passed but was vetoed by President Clinton.

The school choice policy breakthrough took place with the District of Columbia School Choice Incentive Act of 2003. The initiative, signed into law by President Bush on January 22, 2004, established the first federally funded school voucher program in the United States. The legislation was packaged as part of a three-sector strategy to improve education in the nation's capital. The $40 million annual appropriation attached to the bill included an extra $13 million for educational improvements in DCPS, $13 million to increase the availability of facilities appropriate for public charter schools, $13 million for a school voucher initiative (OSP), and $1 million for administration and evaluation of the voucher initiative.

The purpose of the OSP was to provide low-income students with "expanded opportunities to attend higher performing schools in the District of Columbia."[16] According to the statute, the key components of the program dictate that eligibility is limited to students entering grades K–12 who reside in the District and have a family income at or below 185 percent of the federal poverty line (about $36,000 for a family of four in 2006). Participating students receive scholarships of up to $7,500 to cover the costs of tuition, school fees, and transportation to a participating private school in the District. Scholarships are renewable for up to five years (as funds are appropriated) as long as students remain eligible for the program and remain in good academic standing at the private school they are attending.[17] In a given year, if there are more eligible applicants than available scholarships or open slots in private schools, applicants are to be awarded scholarships by lottery. In awarding scholarships, priority is given to students attending public schools identified as "schools in need of improvement" (SINI) under the No Child Left Behind Act (NCLB) and to families that lack the resources to take advantage of school choice options.

Private schools participating in the program must be located in the District and must agree to requirements regarding nondiscrimination in admissions, fiscal accountability, and cooperation with the government-sponsored evaluation of the program.[18] A total of sixty-eight of the eighty-eight general service private schools in the District participated in the OSP in 2005–2006, the program's first year operating with a full complement of students.[19] Participating schools were religiously diverse: 34 percent were Catholic, 22 percent were non-Catholic faith-based, 24 percent were independent private schools (many of which have a religious tradition), and 21 percent were secular private schools.[20] The independent private schools participating in the voucher program included many of DC's elite preparatory academies, including Sidwell Friends School, which has educated the children of Presidents Clinton and Obama.

The OSP was designed to initiate access to shopping mall school choice primarily for new school choosers. About 81 percent of public school applicants in the first year were attending traditional, residentially assigned District public schools, with the remainder attending charter schools.[21] For the parents of students previously receiving their education from the corner store, receiving an Opportunity Scholarship suddenly opened the doors of sixty-eight distinctive private schools to their children. Although the doors to some of those private schools, as well as applications to the program itself, have been closed recently due to actions taken by Congress and the Obama administration to phase out the program, we were able to capture the experiences of more than 110 families representing 180 students who were provided with shopping mall school choice in Washington, DC, from 2004 to 2008.[22]

OUR RESEARCH DESIGN

Our observations regarding the evolution of parental school choice from the corner store to the shopping mall are based on a longitudinal qualitative study of families participating in the OSP. We invited sixty families from the 2004 cohort of program participants (Cohort 1) and fifty families from the 2005 cohort (Cohort 2) to join in our study of how they experienced the OSP. This study is rooted in phenomenology, which seeks to understand the essence of the lived experiences of distinctive groups of people.[23] Study participants joined us for up to four interactive focus group discussions, two semi-structured interviews, and one keypad polling session in order to share with us their perspectives on what it is like to be a school chooser, in many cases for the first time. We recorded and transcribed their remarks and analyzed the transcripts using both formal (e.g., NVivo) and informal (e.g., comparative team charting) methods.[24] We present our results in the form of general impressions we developed based on consistent responses by multiple parents as well as in actual quotes from respondents that illuminate critical insights.

OUR FINDINGS

Although participation in the OSP offered their children access to some of the best private schools in the country, the parents in our study were also being presented with new responsibilities that challenged them to assume more demanding roles in the education marketplace. To an extent, the families in the OSP had already demonstrated their ability to act as consumers in that they had applied for the program and selected a school for their children. The practical steps they took to gain initial access to the program, such as making visits to several schools and consulting various sources of information before making their choice, should not be underestimated. Most of them checked out the educational shopping mall before making their purchase.

As we interacted with these families through interviews and focus groups, however, we found that many of them faced unanticipated challenges that complicated their school choice experience. We found evidence that many families had chosen schools on the basis of immediate concerns and objectives, such as school safety and improved discipline, rather than consideration of their likely effectiveness in producing longer term positive educational outcomes. As one parent said, "I think security is an issue . . . It's useless if a school has a great academic program but there are shootings outside the school."[25]

Given the resource constraints faced by low-income families such as those in the OSP, services like mentors and tutors, meals and afterschool programs, and other products and services may have to be part of the educational support they need to succeed.[26] Without these resources in place, many students and their families may be unable to take full advantage of the educational opportunities that school choice programs make available. At a minimum, parents need to make difficult trade-offs between schools that offer the academic environment they desire and schools that provide the support services they think their child needs.

We did notice a shift from focusing on short-term to long-term student outcomes as the families gained more experience with the program and participating schools. During the second year of focus groups, for example, we asked parents how they determined whether things were going well academically for their children. Their responses provided signs that they were not thinking about or measuring academic progress in formal or conventional terms. They mainly focused on immediate outcomes, such as their child's improved attitude toward school and their studies, behavioral changes, and the work that they were producing. One parent indicated how she measured educational progress: "As far as attitude, my children's attitude has changed . . . They have so much involvement in school where, by the time they get home, all they have time to do is study then get ready to go to bed."[27]

Over time, other aspects of the school environment, such as the standard of teaching, became more important to many of the parents. And if their expectations were not being met, they were more likely to voice their concerns or offer recommendations to improve the situation.

By the fourth and final year of the study, a larger number of parents across the whole sample began expressing interest in longer-term outcomes. They began to place a greater emphasis on student academic development or progress as well as on their student's interest in pursuing college. As one parent related, "She's doing good in school, and she says, 'Mommy I want to continue . . . and when I finish I want to go to a university.' She's very interested in college. I don't have to tell her you have to do your homework . . . She starts to do her homework, and she's doing it on the computer . . . she's learning, learning, learning!"[28]

There was emerging evidence, therefore, that participation in the OSP was transforming many parents from merely passive recipients of services, or clients, into more discerning consumers. The development of observable consumer behavior among parents began from the outset of their involvement with the program and appeared to improve each year. From the application process in the first year on, parents refined their consumer skills as they assessed annually whether to remain with the school they initially selected, transfer to a different school within the OSP, or exit the program. By the end of the second year of data collection, it became clear that the vast majority of the families were moving in very practical ways away from a marginal role as passive recipients of school assignments to a role of active participants in the school selection process. For example, they were being challenged to collect information about several schools, review this information and use it to refine their choices, and eventually visit schools and engage teachers and administrators in a completely new fashion. Even the minority of families that decided to transfer schools or leave the program due to dissatisfaction with their experiences, which sometimes occurred when expectations of a school were not met, used their newly developed or refined consumer skills to identify and visit alternative schools, meet administrators, sit in on classes, and consult other parents.

However, we also found that some families were unable to complete the transition to fully effective consumers, exhibiting some aspects of consumerism but also elements of a client mentality. On one end of the spectrum, many OSP parents jumped in and fully embraced this new school marketplace by visiting numerous schools, asking many questions, and setting clear expectations of the schools that they ultimately chose for their children. On the other end of the continuum, some parents appeared to remain relatively passive participants in the school search process and in relation to the school that their children entered. These parents only considered a small number of schools or a single school, and they did not conduct school visits. They tended to defer accountability to others—for example, recommending that the Washington Scholarship Fund (WSF) provide more oversight and quality control of the schools in the program, making it virtually impossible for parents to choose a "bad" school for their child. These new school choosers were engaging in corner store consumer behavior in the midst of a shopping mall school choice program.

Many of the families who did not fully make the transition to effective consumers consistently expressed the view that the OSP needed an independent entity that could verify the information provided to them by participating schools and that would also be responsible for monitoring the schools during the academic year. Many of the elementary school parents in particular were concerned about school quality and thought the program could be improved if participating schools were evaluated to ensure that they met a minimum set of quality standards. Generally speaking, these types of recommendations suggest that the parents realized that the process of thoroughly assessing and monitoring schools exceeded their individual and collective capacity and could be better managed by individuals or an organization that was more skilled in these areas. They were not up to a full mall crawl. They still wanted access to the complete set of schools in a shopping mall choice system; they just wanted a map with reliable information about which mall stores, located where, offered which products and of what quality.

As administrator of the program, WSF also specifically noted a need for wraparound services for some of the families. WSF interviews confirmed that some families had needs that transcended the statutory scope of the program. In particular, WSF representatives stressed the importance of assisting families with the hidden and unanticipated costs (time, energy, and money) that may be associated with enrollment in a private school. For example, the costs of field trips and school meals are not covered by the scholarship. In addition to nonacademic or social support services, WSF staff quickly realized that high school students needed a variety of academic and social supports. Because some schools did not provide tutors or allow private tutors on their campus, WSF had to facilitate efforts to provide tutorial services and other resources near students' homes. It formed partnerships with a variety of organizations in an attempt to connect families with the resources they needed.

TYPOLOGY OF PARTICIPATING FAMILIES

Although the data generated from this study did not allow us to fully investigate why some families were more empowered by the OSP than others, or why some needed considerably more support in order to participate effectively, it is possible that preexisting experiences and levels of family resources may have contributed to their different experiences of the program.

It appears that the ability of families to benefit from the OSP is influenced by their family structure and the associated levels of resources available to them. Since the OSP targeted low-income families, all had relatively low levels of resources in a strictly financial sense. What emerged quite clearly as we became familiar with the participant families, however, was that there was considerable variation among them in terms of nonfinancial family-based resources. We define family-based resources broadly in terms of time, existing knowledge, and practical support from their social networks. Our three identified family types have varying levels of resources available to them, and each family type is associated with a focus on particular levels of student outcomes: immediate, intermediate, and long-term.

Type 1: Underresourced Families.   These families are typically headed by a single parent (often a mother) who has weak or very limited extended family support. In many cases, she must focus primarily on providing her family with the basic necessities. When this parent is focused on finding the best school for her child, a safe and convenient location—the corner store—most likely will be her first priority. Her limited resources and family support will make it very difficult for her to be as active as she would like to be in both a school search and in her child's formal academic development. She is most interested in her child's immediate outcomes, which include good attendance, safety, and staying in school. We estimate that roughly 50–60 percent of all urban low-income families fall into this category.

Type 2: Modestly Resourced Families.   These families are also typically headed by a single parent who is most likely a mother. She has a relatively strong support structure around her, however, and lives in a stable environment and has viable employment. Her modest level of resources and support network allow her to consider a wider range of school options outside of her immediate surroundings. She has the time to be more hands-on and active with her child at home and attends most events related to her child. She consulted with friends and visited several nearby private schools before making her school selections. Time and other commitments do not allow her to participate in parent organization meetings and other school-based activities that are not directly related to her child as often as she might like. She demands that her child do well in school, and she is more likely to discuss student outcomes that include postsecondary possibilities. We estimate that nearly 20–30 percent of all urban low-income families fall into this category.

Type 3: Well-Resourced Families.   These families have either two parents or a single parent with an extremely strong social support network. Although these families have roughly the same level of financial resources as Types 1 and 2, at least one parent or caregiver is able to devote considerably more time to supporting the child. These families are very ambitious when selecting schools and often consider the very best options regardless of where they might be located and without considering factors that might deter other low-income families. They perform the full mall crawl. They are very involved in their child's development and are more likely to participate in school-based activities. They take graduation from high school as a given and are most likely to discuss student outcomes from a long-term perspective that includes a discussion about what the child will one day contribute to the family or broader community. We estimate that roughly 10–20 percent of all urban low-income families fall into this category.

EMPOWERMENT AS A STEPPING STONE TOWARD MORE EFFECTIVE PARENTAL SCHOOL CHOICE

During our examination of the experiences of families in DC's Opportunity Scholarship Program, we identified patterns of refined and growing consumer behavior among the parent participants that led us to tentatively theorize that certain aspects of the program had an empowering effect on families. We were also struck by the reported levels of satisfaction with the program, which seemed unusually high for a means-tested social program. These findings triggered our curiosity about which aspects of the program were contributing to these high satisfaction levels, and we also began to wonder whether the participants' positive experiences with the OSP were influencing their consumer and citizenship behaviors.

There is very little previous research that examines schools from a service delivery standpoint. However, a small body of previous research has examined the impact of service delivery on the political and consumer behavior of program participants, specifically low-income families. Previous studies of low-income participants in social programs have shown that programs that are well-designed and effectively delivered often provide recipients not only with tangible resources but also with the attitudes and skills needed to become more astute consumers and empowered citizens who can promote their own interests in society.[29] This often happens when participants have positive rather than negative experiences of participating in a program and interacting with program personnel and when they are provided with accurate information and helpful support.

Anne Schneider and Helen Ingram explained this in terms of the ways that the design and delivery of social policies result in the formation of social constructions of target populations. For example, the intended recipients of such policies are seen by policy officials and the general public as either deserving or nondeserving and as either able to take care of themselves or needing active government intervention in order to do so.[30] Programs such as Social Security and Medicare, which are based on universal principles, usually target people who are seen as deserving of them or able to take care of themselves under normal circumstances.[31] Most Americans view means-tested programs, such as Aid to Families with Dependent Children (AFDC) and Medicaid, as primarily serving the nondeserving, or individuals who have been unable to support themselves. In general, universal programs are associated with high levels of benefits and relatively few burdens on their participants, while means-tested programs bestow low levels of benefits and impose high demands on recipients. Participants in means-tested government programs are expected to divulge a great deal about their personal lives and make their homes available for random inspections from social workers or other service delivery agents. As a result, it is argued, the recipients of the public services internalize these social constructions, with significant impacts on their self-image as well as their orientation toward government and the likelihood of their political participation.[32] As Amber Wichowsky and Donald Moynihan observe, the experience of participating in social programs influences both "internal political efficacy," or the extent to which individuals believe they have the skills and abilities to be politically active, and "external political efficacy," or the extent to which they believe they will be able to influence political outcomes.[33]

A number of qualitative studies have provided important insights into the ways in which experiences of social program participation influence participants' attitudes and beliefs about government and their own efficacy. For example, Joe Soss conducted a comparative study, based on in-depth interviews, of the experiences of participants in a Social Security Disability Insurance (SSDI) program and the AFDC program.[34] He explained that the SSDI did not involve mandatory reviews, and contact with the agency was infrequent and mostly initiated by the participant. He found that SSDI recipients developed a stronger sense of their ability to play an active role in the program and a positive image of the responsiveness of the agency. In contrast, participants in the AFDC were means-tested, subjected to regular case reviews, and involved in casework relationships and frequent interactions of a supervisory nature. They rarely initiated contact with the agency themselves, simply complied with requests for attendance and information, and often experienced disrespectful or condescending attitudes and behavior. Participants were often summoned to the agency with the threat of termination of support if they did not comply. Soss found that the AFDC recipients developed a set of beliefs in which the agency in general and the individual officials in it were powerful forces in their lives over which they had little or no control.[35]

It can be inferred from this body of research that experiences with service delivery, which can be extended to include school choice programs, may also have an impact on consumer efficacy, as supported by the findings of our own research. Given the lessons learned from previous studies of citizenship in general and the influence of government programs on civic efficacy in particular, we might expect to see cross-cutting forces affecting the participants in school choice programs. Voucher programs in the United States, which enable parents to select private schools for their children to attend at government expense, tend to be targeted to disadvantaged students and families. The school voucher programs in major cities such as Milwaukee, Cleveland, New Orleans, and the District of Columbia are all means-tested and limited to those families with levels of income that would qualify their children for the federal lunch program. As initiatives targeted to low-income families, these urban school voucher programs might, on the one hand, be expected to foster the spirit-killing paternalism demonstrated in many of the means-tested programs discussed above. On the other hand, school choice programs are designed to rely on the effective participation of parents to make them work. Parents are expected to seek out information about their child's newly available schooling options and to find an available school that is a good fit for their child's needs.

It appeared that the high levels of satisfaction parents expressed throughout their involvement with the OSP stemmed in larger part from their sense of empowerment, in terms of being able to make an important choice about their child's education and to participate in the process that could yield the types of outcomes they envision for their children, than from aspects of the schools themselves. Parents repeatedly expressed that the scholarship represented an "opportunity" to pursue what they perceived were better schools or schools that were more conducive to providing the type of learning environment most appropriate for their children. This helps explain the consistently high levels of satisfaction with the program itself, despite criticisms of or concerns about specific schools or aspects of them. Parents appreciated what the educational shopping mall had to offer, even if they had a bad experience in the first store they visited.

The provision of more extensive programmatic supports to OSP families after the initial program launch was central to the high levels of participant satisfaction with the program. In 2004, the first year of partial program implementation, WSF provided minimal assistance and guidance to families regarding selecting private schools and managing relationships with school officials. This hands-off approach of program administrators was partly driven by circumstances (the program was launched late in the spring, with just weeks before participating schools closed their enrollments) and partly due to the common view that parents will figure out on their own how to manage school choice. In 2005, when the program was filled with a large second co-hort, WSF pivoted to a position of providing clearer guidance and more counseling to parents about how to navigate the school choice shopping mall. This administrative change was at least partly in response to our initial study findings that some families felt lost and confused during their initial school choice experience.[36] In the first year, WSF simply opened the doors of the school choice shopping mall to new education consumers. In the second year, the administrators provided the shoppers with mall guides and shopping tips, supports that were greatly appreciated by participants.

HOW CAN INTERESTED STAKEHOLDERS BETTER SUPPORT LOW-INCOME FAMILIES?

What have we learned from this research that can help low-income families, espe-cially those with very low levels of family-based resources available to them, become more effective school consumers? Assuming that good school consumers are made or evolve as a result of their direct experiences with parental school choice, what support do parents need based on their location along an experiential and family resource continuum?

Simply opening up the educational shopping mall to low-income families appears to be a problematic approach. Based on the experiences of the families we engaged in our qualitative study, there are few resources that are specifically designed for low-income families seeking to exercise parental school choice. There are some promis-ing advances being made that are closing the gap for parents in general, such as the *Picky Parent Guide* and *My School Chooser Guide*.[37] However, early versions of these literacy-based products and services were not sufficiently customized for low-income families living in many urban communities across the country. Literacy, technology, and limited social networks are major barriers to effective parental school choice. For example, according to a study commissioned by the District of Columbia State Education Agency, 40 percent (or approximately 130,000) of adults residing in the nation's capital are functionally illiterate.[38] So even highly accessible school guides will be of limited use to some of the most disadvantaged families participating in a school choice program.

Although published guides can help, our research suggests that there is no substi-tute for people. It is essential that every child have at least one adult in their life who can help them navigate the preK–12 educational system. In cases where children do not have someone who meets this criterion, interested stakeholders should make ad-ditional support services like education advocates or family education coaches avail-able to families that need them. At the macro level, this might include establishing an independent education oversight body that would make information about schools and other education options more accessible and user friendly, as well as coordinate the activities associated with the education coaches and advocates.

Finally, we think that more precise market segmentation of low-income families is needed. Administrators of school choice programs should be encouraged to hold an initial meeting with each participating family to assess its level of family-based resources and ability to navigate the emerging school choice process. Engagement strategies based on family type and other unique demographic and psychographic factors could then be customized for each family, providing encouragement but minimal support to the best-prepared families and much more extensive direction and support for those that otherwise would be overwhelmed by the perceived chaos and other challenges associated with crowded educational shopping malls. For example, given the large number of single mothers who are involved in choice programs, more care and attention should be devoted to providing customized resources and transitional support services to them.

To those who might say that we are prescribing the disease of paternalism as a cure, we acknowledge that implementers would need to be careful not to fall into that trap. The goal would be to hit the "sweet spot," whereby families are appropriately supported so that their school choice experiences can be highly successful but to the minimal extent possible, so that their opportunities for free choice and empowerment are maximized. Where that sweet spot is for a given family and a particular program will be a matter of judgment. However, the OSP families provided insights that can inform those judgments. They clearly do not want the educational shopping mall to be closed to them, but they do seek a more rewarding shopping experience, particularly as it pertains to outcomes for their children.

6

Education Tools in an Incomplete Market

Douglas Lynch and Michael Gottfried

MUCH HAS BEEN SAID about the potential of innovation to reform education. But given the zeitgeist, it seems to be rather a moot point.

Educational entrepreneurship combines the sexiness of dot-com with good old American "can do" spirit. But the focus has rested squarely on innovators changing the production of schooling. This book rightly notes that for change to occur, we need a market with both suppliers and consumers willing and able to interact. This interaction is what elicits an eventual economic equilibrium where suppliers and consumers interact in a way in which each has maximized its benefit. However, without distinguishing between the sides of the equation in the nation's analyses of what does and does not work in educational reform, all we are left with is the old story of the tree falling in the woods: without anyone around to consume the sound of the fall, the tree's crash is essentially meaningless. Without an evaluation of the demand side of the market equation, resting our analyses entirely on supply is also meaningless.

In this chapter, we evaluate what ought to be a fairly benign subsector—educational tools that support schooling—and use economic theory to reason through the potential value of using these tools to reform schooling. One can already infer from the title that we are telegraphing what we perceive as thwarted innovation; we have an utter lack of hope in the potential of tools to significantly impact schooling unless policy makers take certain steps to fix the demand side of the equation.

WHAT IS AN EDUCATIONAL TOOL?

We examine the use of educational tools not only in terms of how they might impact learning but also, more broadly, as a litmus for educational entrepreneurship. We use the lens of economic theory (since this is a book on demand) as well as some evidence to support our analysis and conclusions. However, some structure and caveats are needed. In terms of a structure, we first define an educational tool and what a demand for educational tools might be and then use two examples of educational tools to illustrate our analysis and highlight potential problems in the current direction of the reform movement.

To start, we define an educational tool and its uses and reason through what economic demand for it might be. One can think of a tool in its most fundamental sense as something that aids in the process of producing a good or service. For example, in the car industry, the assembly line may be considered a tool. A tool is perhaps also something that facilitates the bringing to market of the product or service. In other words, a tool may not necessarily be important in the construction of a good or service, but it is crucial in the postproduction process. For instance, a company's Web site may be a tool, as it links production to purchase.

In terms of economics, the production function models a firm's input-output process. The function asserts that materials enter the firm (i.e., the inputs) and the result is a product based on having these inputs (i.e., the output). In the model, a tool is what aids in the transformation of these inputs into outputs. In essence, the tool is the technology eliciting interactions and synergies among the various inputs. Because we are examining K–12 schooling, we can also define tools in terms of the educational realm. For this purpose, a tool is specifically any process or instrument that facilitates the development or delivery of education (i.e., the output) based on a series of inputs (i.e., students, teachers, classrooms, schools, etc).

This is an appropriate general definition for an educational tool. It will allow us to identify those aspects that change (and hopefully enhance) the educational experience in some capacity. This general definition is also reflected in the education production function, implemented by economists and sociologists alike. The education production function, then, is based on the standard, aforementioned economic production function. In this case, the tool is a change in the learning process, turning educational inputs (i.e., students, teachers, classrooms) into academic outputs (i.e., achievement, graduation).

While such a pragmatic definition may be useful, it still may feel vague to practitioners and policy makers. Consequently, before we delve deeper into exploring some of the tensions that exist in applying educational tools to schools, it might be useful to provide a framework, a taxonomy, that might help us categorize tools so that we are comparing apples to apples in terms of function. As educators, we are used to taxonomies. Lexicons are common among subspecialties, and libraries use the Dewey system to organize their shelves. Education professors have even created taxonomies of learning (Bloom being the one most commonly mentioned). In terms of educational tools, though, perhaps because of the nature of the space, the taxonomies either tend to be quite technical, relating to the underlying programming or to the underlying pedagogy of the approach. We suggest a more straightforward set of axes that might help us categorize the various tools available to educators. A taxonomy and associated questions for market purposes might include:

- *Instructional focus:* Is the tool designed to support instruction directly or more to support systems? Some tools, such as textbooks, are designed to directly support instruction, whereas other tools may be designed to facilitate things such as tracking attendance. Typically, investors simply divide the education market between K–12 and higher education. But since we are looking at the market for all educational tools, it would be appropriate to have some way of describing the tool's purpose.
- *User base:* Who uses the tool? Is it designed for the student, the teacher, or the administrator? Even when looking solely at instruction tools, there are certain tools that students use directly to support their learning, others that teachers use to augment their instruction, and still others that administrators use to support instruction.
- *Unit of user:* Is the tool for a single individual, or is it team- or cohort-based? Instructional tools such as virtual tutors or data systems can be classified in terms of user unit: is it employed by the teacher to use on an individual student or in the teacher's class or for an administrator to assess a school's efficacy?
- *Timing:* Is the tool time-bound, or is it asynchronous? There are certain tools that require synchronicity—such as a virtual classroom or voice-over IP professional development—while other tools are utterly self-paced.
- *Space constraint:* Some tools that perform similar tasks are space constrained. Imagine an assessment delivered on a computer in a classroom versus on the Internet at home or versus an application on an iPhone.
- *Ease of use:* How much training is required in order to use the tool? How intuitive is it? Is technical support a prerequisite?
- *Multimodality:* How many media are presented? Is it text only, or are there sounds and images associated with it? For example, does a report for parents include audio, video, graphs, and text, or is the information simply presented in text?
- *Costs:* Is the tool free, such as Google Wave? Is it a relatively inexpensive system that can be downloaded, or is it more capital intensive, such as a higher-end SMART Board?
- *Other technological constraints:* Does the tool require access to the Internet, electricity, or social networking capabilities?

We propose this framework around which to initiate useful conversations among entrepreneurs and policy people about categorizing the efficacy of educational tools. However, within the universe of educational tools as we have defined them, there are some processes and instruments that, for various reasons, will complicate any potential analysis. We believe that if we were to use such examples, it would lead us overall to the same conclusions, but it would obfuscate the more obvious lessons. So, we are going to advocate that we further narrow the field of educational tools.

One example that is fundamentally problematic is online learning. While companies may provide these online educational services to enhance learning, there are several online service providers that supply both individual schools and/or districts with supplemental materials or individual classes (e.g., Educere, which sells empty seats in college online courses to high schools to meet dual enrollment requirements). However, there are also organizations that could be viewed as not only supplying tools or even individual courses to schools and districts but as also actually competing with schools and districts in the delivery of schooling. The e-learning company K12 Inc. is an example of this type of organization.[1]

K12 Inc. has contracts with, and often manages, many public schools throughout the country, reaching a total of 55,000 students. It is an entirely online group of schools with an online, student-focused, individuated curriculum. Unlike a typical school in a district, students in K12 Inc. interact with teachers online and submit homework online. Students can also learn offline; however, all offline material is also provided by K12 Inc. rather than a district school. For example, it sends pedagogical materials to students' homes, where, with the help and guidance of their parents, students engage in activities and homework assignments. Thus, in competing with a school district, K12 Inc. attempts to use a technological medium to provide student-directed learning. It does so by drawing on the expertise of content area experts in science and math who offer an integrated content training approach in which scientists train the developers who create the curriculum. In this fashion, K12 Inc. is not only directly competing with a school district on learning styles (online versus offline) but also on curriculum development.

We argue that our analysis also captures challenges these organizations face when it comes to consumer demand. However, in the specific case of online learning, the analysis becomes too muddled to include in this chapter. This is so because the service these companies provide can be two-pronged. It can be complementary to the school's educational environment and therefore considered a tool. However, in the case of K12 Inc., the same educational tool could also appear to be a substitute for the district's education. In this regard, the same tool now is framed as being a competitor in the market rather than as an educational enhancer to the district. The fact that the tools of online learning can be seen from these two perspectives implies that the analysis becomes complicated. As such, we recognize that these online companies do exist, though we choose not to focus our energies on tools that can be viewed as both complements and substitutes for schooling in the eyes of a district administrator.

The second constraint we want to put on our parameter is one of scale. We recently held a summit of educational entrepreneurs, and in one of the presentations,

Larry Berger, from Wireless Generation, observed that the educational tool sector does not follow the typical Pareto curve, which is convex and holds that in any given industry there ought to exist a smaller number of very large and very small producers and a much larger number of midsize firms. Visually, this would appear like a bell curve with a normal distribution. Instead, Berger noted a different shape in the education market. When it comes to providers of educational tools, various subsectors can have an almost infinite number of very small providers (think of retired principals as consultants), a few very large providers, but also only a few midsize firms. This stands in sharp contrast to the Pareto curve. We decided to label this concave function the Berger Education Pareto Curve. We will return to Berger's hypothesis later in this chapter, but for now we suggest that it is not useful to look at examples of industries that are described by the Berger Education Pareto Curve. For instance, the textbook industry (which provides a very concrete notion of education tool due to the tangibility of a book as well as the ease of construction of its market valuation) has attributes that would be characterized as firms possessing market power. Following the same logic as with the online learning companies, we will not focus our analysis on the textbook industry or on the scores of small educational tool providers that serve only one district.

This leaves us with several poignant alternatives to use as examples for our analysis. We focus on Wireless Generation and SchoolNet because they are generally perceived as both good businesses and educationally minded social endeavors, and each provides what seem to be regarded as high-quality, effective educational tools that support schooling.

Wireless Generation is known for its mobile assessment software. In 2000, two Rhodes Scholars founded the organization. They were interested in pinpointing where technology could make a meaningful improvement in the interactions between students and teachers. They first invented the mClass System, a platform that enables teachers in grades K–6 to efficiently give assessments using a handheld computer instead of paper, receive real-time data on students' needs, and access both mobile and Web-based tools for using data to improve teaching and learning. With this mobile assessment software, among others, the company has built its mission around improving teachers' classroom assessments and allowing them to make data-based instructional decisions. As such, Wireless Generation has allowed for growth in the educational environment by providing technology that analyzes student data and provides curriculum customized to individual learning needs. The company currently serves more than two hundred thousand educators and three million students.

SchoolNet is a provider of data-driven education software that helps align student assessment, curriculum and instruction, and operational efficiency. It was founded in 1998 by experts interested in how technology could improve educational reform. The founders initially developed tools to streamline education technology and generate online programs that were easily understood by educators. According to company rhetoric, the purpose of every product is to improve teachers' capacities for student assessment, the development of curriculum, and the improvement of instruction. Thus, these tools aim to guide collaborative, data-informed discussion and to enable targeted instruction for all students in the classroom. The solutions are used by many of the nation's largest school districts, including Chicago Public Schools and the School District of Philadelphia.

In the scope of this discussion, these two companies provide us with benign and uncontroversial educational tools to evaluate. They are first and foremost considered tools because they enhance the inputs to education. Further, they are benign because the suppliers of these tools are not in direct competition with the district (i.e., they are not substitutes), nor are they monopolists. To be clear, we are simply using these organizations as examples of applying economic theory. We did not evaluate the performance of these companies vis-à-vis educational reform in any analytical way.

WHAT IS DEMAND FOR AN EDUCATIONAL TOOL?

Now that we have clarified what can be categorized as an educational tool and have focused our analysis on which educational tools we consider benign, it makes sense to develop an operating definition of the demand for such tools. In its most basic form, what we call demand for an educational tool (or any product for that matter) is actually the aggregation of each individual consumer's desire for the tool given the constraints of the price of the tool and the budget of the consumer. The process of aggregating each individual demand curve leads to what is known as market demand. Consumers will make choices based on these preferences within the constraints that exist. Within this context, the value of educational tools becomes fairly easy to assess; namely, it is their ability to add value in the educational process versus how much they cost.

One question for our analysis is, *Who is the consumer?* If the suppliers are Wireless Generation and SchoolNet (i.e., those agents delivering the educational tools), it is crucial to know to whom they are providing services. Only with the identification of supply and demand do we have a market. We think it is beneficial to look at two different consumers' points of view; first, the district as the entity that is responsible for the schooling; and second, the parents who make the choice of where to live and/ or where to send their children to school. We suggest looking at consumers in this dualistic way because of the nature of how tools are marketed in a final product. An example might be to see how both a car manufacturer (analogous to the school district) and a car purchaser (analogous to a parent) think about the car stereo in the car. The producer of the overall product, such as a car manufacturer, certainly has preferences based on considerations like cost and compatibility. However, the manufacturer also recognizes that additional car attributes, like the brand of car stereo, also matter to the end-consumer. Thus, the inclusion of a Bose car stereo boosts the marketability of the car and increases intermediate demand by the car manufacturer for the stereo. Or we can think of computer microprocessors, such as Intel, as being the tool demanded by the final consumer (i.e., the individual) but intermediately demanded by the laptop manufacturer. Based on the evaluation of benefits and costs, an intermediate consumer, like Dell or IBM, may find Intel to add value to the final product. They may find this particular attribute invaluable to the marketability of the computer because the end-consumer desires it so.

So it is not uncommon to see producers of the larger product leveraging the brand of the attribute to help differentiate the larger product in the market. In the framework of education, we reason through how both parents and districts, as consumers, could demonstrate preferences for these two educational tools, Wireless Generation and SchoolNet.

WHAT IS AN APPROPRIATE CONCEPTUAL MODEL?

In economics, there is a popular quip regarding demand. Two economists are looking at a Ferrari. Economist 1 says, "I want one of those." Economist 2 says, "Obviously not."

To understand this punch line, it is necessary to know a little bit about revealed preference. This concept, first described by Samuelson in 1938, states that what you want is revealed by what you do and not by what you say.[2] As the adage goes, actions speak louder than words. If the first economist had really demanded a Ferrari, he would have already bought one—if he didn't already own one.

Economists have three main approaches to modeling demand. The first is the cardinal approach. In this framework, an economist asks consumers how much utility they would receive from consuming a particular good. The economist then aggregates all goods and services and subsequently calculates demand based on the assumption that people consume the combination of goods and services that maximizes total utility.

A second approach, the ordinal approach, does not require consumers to determine how much utility they would receive from a particular good. Instead, an economist evaluates how much relative utility consumers receive from consuming one item compared with another. An economist is interested if consumers prefer one basket of goods to another or are indifferent.

There is a setback when using these two first approaches to understanding consumer demand. Notably, both cardinal and ordinal demand estimations are based on the notion of utility. While utility may have its utility (for lack of a better word) in economic theory, its policy implications are questionable. This is so because measures of utility are empirically unobservable. In the case of cardinal utility, for instance, it is impossible to construct a quantifiable measure of the satisfaction a consumer receives from a particular good or service. Although it is possible to assert theoretically that consumers maximize utility when choosing a particular bundle of goods and services, there is no empirical proof. As for ordinal utility, an economist has difficulty observing the infinite choice-sets and pathways that led a consumer to choose a particular good and service. Thus, finding the relative value of a consumer's choice seems dubious.

While the first two approaches are based on this nebulous concept of utility, it is not utility itself that is so controversial in the public policy arena. Rather, it is the idea that utility forms the basis of demand (and hence the demand curve in economics); for, it is in demand in which we describe consumer behavior. However, if the basis of demand is this notion of utility, and if the concept of utility itself remains so vague, then it seems nearly impossible to truly describe why consumers act as they do under these theories. In reality, no one has ever seen a demand curve.

A third approach attempts to evade the theoretical issues of cardinal and ordinal utility. This method of understanding consumer demand is known as revealed preference. To model demand in this scenario, it is only necessary to be able to compare an individual's consumption decisions in situations with different prices and/or incomes and to assume that consumers are consistent in their decisions over time (that is, if they prefer good A to B in one period they will still prefer A in the next). In other words, the goods and services that a consumer has selected in the market represent the best possible option for that consumer. Empirically, revealed preferences imply that preferences of consumers are revealed by their purchasing habits.

As a brief example, assume a consumer selects a first bundle of goods even though a second bundle of goods is more affordable. Empirically, the first bundle of goods is revealed to be preferred to the second. It is then assumed that the first bundle of goods will always be preferred to the second. Because of the consumer's actions in the market (which can be demonstrated by the fact that he or she physically selected the first bundle over the second), preferences have been revealed. In this way, all selections that consumers make are then part of the revealed preferences framework.

This revealed preference system of demand has the potential to provide critical information about the ways in which consumers select goods and services in reality without the reliance on vague measures of utility. In policy, it may be possible for empiricists to develop a rubric by which demand can be described and tested based on the choices that consumers tend to make, rather than having to rely on hypothetical decisions. Therefore, if patterns of revealed preferences are made evident, then suppliers may be able to tap into a particular market to satisfy demand more effectively. This can be true of any market, including education.

APPLYING THE THEORY

Looking at market innovations without considering the impact of demand is a pointless exercise, and revealed preference may be the most prudent way within economic theory of evaluating the demand for innovation within education. In applying the scenario to SchoolNet and Wireless Generation, we expect the tools to be ubiquitous among districts and to see the tools branded as value added attributes to parents and policy makers. Yet, neither company has been able to penetrate the market to the extent that one would expect. To be clear, they are both very successful companies in the fact that they serve millions of students and upwards of a thousand districts—but that is still less than 10 percent of the market—and if they are suppliers in the largest districts in the nation, then they are (or at least have the potential to be) the "best of brand," so to speak.

The reason for the lack of total market penetration exists due to a poorly functioning market. While there is the apparent availability of educational tools by these two companies, their supply is nevertheless not satisfying demand if only 10 percent of the market has been penetrated. Something has gone awry in the educational market. We argue that consumers have not been able to reveal their preferences. Thus, the supply side has no gauge or empirical evidence of full demand (from both parents and districts) for their products and no outlet.

If, for the moment, we assume that the supply side has created the adequate technology to meet demand theoretically and is not meeting demand in reality, then it seems clear that a further evaluation of the consumer side is in order. Our diagnosis, then, is that perhaps the market failure has arisen because the educational market has not sufficiently focused on who or what is doing the demanding. There is simply a market failure.

For demand (in our case, revealed preferences) to function properly, the market must exhibit the following five characteristics: *widespread availability of information; ease of market entry and exit; absence of significant monopoly power; achievement of public interest objectives;* and *absence of market externalities.* We are going to suggest that none of these characteristics are present, at least for organizations like Wireless Generation and SchoolNet and in all probability for all educational tool providers.

To help inform policy makers, let us spend a little time reasoning through whether, prima facie, the characteristics requisite for a market are present in the educational setting. We will again telegraph our finding: using a very blunt anecdotal approach quickly leads us to the conclusion that, indeed, the market is incomplete.

We begin with the market assumption of the widespread availability of information. In theory, all parties in the market, both firms and consumers, must be well-informed in order to make effective decisions. Timely and relevant information must be easily accessible to both parties in order to achieve what economists refer to as Pareto efficiency. However, barriers to information weaken the ability of parties in these markets to function efficiently.

A quick scan of some of the professional literature reinforces our perception that both SchoolNet and Wireless Generation are well-regarded by education professionals. In addition, on each company's Web site there are a significant number of laudatory testimonials by important districts. There are, in fact, testimonials from school districts in fifteen states from teachers, directors of instruction, principals, and reading specialists. This was the first set of consumers. None, interestingly, were from parents or students. There is an absence of movement from our second set of consumers.

Our first assumption, then, is that much like a computer company that advertises "Intel Inside," it seems to be the provider (the district) of the final product that markets the tool to the final consumer (the parent). Thus, we looked for evidence of how districts themselves frame their provision of education around these two organizations. More deeply, we wanted to investigate if the districts advertise their own versions of Intel Inside in their own markets, in this case to parents and students.

We began by selecting the ten largest districts that both companies claim to serve. A perusal of these ten districts' Web sites turns up no reference at all to any partnership and/or vendor relationship with either SchoolNet or Wireless Generation. In addition, for at least one of the companies, there is evidence to the contrary: it appears that several districts have obfuscated their relationships with SchoolNet. From what we can tell, some of the districts that selected SchoolNet have rebranded the educational tool. Examples include Philadelphia (IMS, FamilyNet), Denver (Teacher Portal), Atlanta (INSIGHT), and Albuquerque (AIMS).

We wanted to explore this obfuscation further. A brief survey that we conducted using social networking tools to elicit participants yielded a group of 452 respondents to a list of questions, among them: Do you know the brand of car stereo in your car? If you own a PC, do you know if you have an Intel processor as a component? Have you ever heard of either of these two software companies: Wireless Generation or SchoolNet? Of the overall sample, 96 percent of respondents knew if they had an Intel processor in their computer, and 74 percent knew the make of their car stereo; only 16 percent had heard of either Wireless Generation or SchoolNet. Given additional questions in the survey, we can identify two subgroups among our respondents (noting that there are potential biases in the responses because of the nonrandom selection process by which we solicited respondents) that correspond reasonably well to our two types of consumers: parents and educators.

If we look at the professional education group as those who work within the ten largest districts served by both SchoolNet and Wireless Generation, we have a sample of 77 respondents (we listed the districts in our survey). Of this group, 53 percent had heard of either company, while only 47 percent knew the make of their car stereo.

However, fully 100 percent knew if they had an Intel processor in their computer. In other words, of those who work in districts that Wireless Generation and SchoolNet supply, and thus who ought to be encountering the tools on a frequent basis, only a little more than half had heard of either educational tool.

Among the broader group of respondents who self-identified as educators (66 percent, or 298) but who lived all over the country, only 23 percent had heard of either Wireless Generation or SchoolNet. Yet, within this same group, 98 percent knew if they had an Intel processor and 63 percent knew the make of their car stereo. So, among professionals who ought to have some sense of either a competitor's attribute or a potential tool to help them provide a service, less than a quarter had heard of the tools.

If we focus the survey on the noneducators and examine the general public, the news gets bleaker. Among the noneducators, 63 percent of the respondents were parents (97), and of that, 64 lived in one of the districts we identified as being served by both SchoolNet and Wireless Generation. Among this latter group, only 4 percent had heard of either company. So among parents within districts using the tool, only 4 percent were aware of the tool. That is, direct consumers of education had no notion of the attributes that compose their final products. In our minds, this is analogous to having a PC and not knowing whether or not your processor was made by Intel. But this is not the case for the computer market. If one expands to our sample's broad group of 154 noneducators, only 2 percent had heard of Wireless Generation or SchoolNet, yet 92 percent knew if they had an Intel processor and 95 percent knew the make of their car stereo. Given the import of school choice as a strategy for educational reform, these anecdotal results do not bode well for reformers.

It is striking how unknown these two educational tools are given that they are generally believed, among experts, to be incredibly useful to the educational endeavor. Moreover, these educational tools do not seem to have any negative image associated with them but instead—as the Web site testimonials demonstrate—actually enhance the educational product. In other words, they have nothing to hide. Thus, given the supposed synergistic relationship that exists between districts and Wireless Generation or SchoolNet, we would expect districts to brand themselves, both within the professional world and the world of parents, as users of these tools in the same way we see high-end automobile manufacturers marketing their stereo systems as product attributes. Yet, at least from our brief survey, the exact opposite seems to be occurring.

The consequence, we believe, is that there is a significant market failure in terms of access to information about these education tools that affects both professional educators and parents. The lack of available information leads to an asymmetrically designed market in which one group (namely the district) has more information than the other (parents and students). To reel this discussion back into revealed preferences: it is not possible for parents or students to reveal their educational preferences because there is simply no outlet through which their preferences can be revealed. They do not know if they prefer good A over good B because good B (Wireless Generation or SchoolNet) is never presented to them as an option.

The problem, then, is that this incomplete market cannot be replicated in new ventures, which explains why these companies have only penetrated less than 10 percent of total districts, even though their products are seemingly so successful. With a lack of information on the entire landscape of demand, there is simply no demand for the suppliers to evaluate. As a consequence, the supply of effective educational tools remains limited. In the case of Intel, both Intel and Dell both know its consumers' revealed preferences; they have analysts who know exactly how much a consumer is willing to pay for a laptop with Intel processing. Thus, in designing new technology and sparking innovation, the market for laptops can adjust to both supply and demand, making transactions readily—and globally—available.

In the case of an educational tool such as Wireless Generation or SchoolNet, such replication is not possible simply because we do not know the demand schedule for consumers of the products. Educators seem to "like" the products, according to the testimonials, but there is no information on how the final customer enjoys the product. Thus, there is no way to access current demand in education or hypothesize about future demand in other, currently unserved markets. Without transparency of information, it would appear that widespread innovation is not possible.

There are other challenges to the efficiency of the market when it comes to demand for these education tools. We will next quickly discuss two other requirements: the ability to enter into and exit a market and whether there are tendencies towards monopolies.

We have already mentioned the idea of the Berger Education Pareto Curve. In a well-functioning, competitive market, no firm has the power to dominate the market. From a supply-side perspective, the existence of significant monopoly power in a market restricts the participation opportunities of smaller competitors and potential new market entrants. The market pressure for competitive efficiency and innovation is reduced. This change in the market is extremely detrimental because consumer choice is weakened.

Within K–12 education, this challenge to market efficiency is most evident in the textbook market. The structure of the market lends itself to tendencies toward monopolies; there are really only a very small number of textbook publishers in the United States. Some of this may be due to efficiencies in production (e.g., it may not be feasible to make a different history text book for each of the country's approximate fourteen thousand districts), and this can be thought of as a tendency toward a natural monopoly and may be regulated as such.

That being said, we posit that part of the tendency toward monopolies can be a trifecta of monopsony, a highly regulated market, and a long sales cycle complicated by turnover in school leadership. Specifically, it is again the skewed nature of the demand side of the equation that forces the market to consolidate into a few large producers that look to contain costs while permitting relatively little disruptive innovation through new entrants.

A monopsony exists when there is, for all intents and purposes, only one buyer of a good or service. The educational system in this country has, in effect, not one market but thousands of smaller markets, each of which can be characterized as a monopsony; each district, by law, is in essence the sole consumer of educational tools. The consequence of having our school systems be monopsonies is that they tend to drive down the price of a service, for the producer of the product only has one option for a consumer and is subject to their demands—the same way in which consumers are subject to the prices placed on the market by monopolies. As a consequence of these educational monopsonies, innovators are less likely to enter into a market since there is no incentive if firms cannot maximize profit. Thus, the empirical evidence of the school district markets is what we would expect: little innovation and few providers of educational tools.

Having free entry and exit allows for markets to function efficiently. However, when barriers to entry exist, such as monopsonies, restrictive licenses, and very large investment requirements, there is a reduction in firm potential for participation in the market by suppliers. This has the negative effect of limiting the extent of supplier competition and thereby market efficiency. With the lack of competition, consumers may not be able to make their preferred choices and thereby have to select a less efficient bundle of goods and services due to affordability not prompted by a properly functioning market. In essence, their revealed preferences are somewhat skewed.

A final challenge in this area can be thought of as selling entropy. According to the Council of Great City Schools, the average tenure of a superintendent is three and a half years. One recent estimate of school districts' cycles is eighteen months for major purchases, such as software systems. This suggests that there is a large probability of entropy, or having to resell to a new superintendent because of turnover. The problem here is two-fold and is in essence a downward spiral. First, because of the monopsony characterization of the education market (in which, at bottom, the superintendent has full market power), it becomes extremely difficult for suppliers to evaluate the preferences of their markets because their often sole consumers are so frequently changing. This makes innovation difficult. Since the current superintendent may reveal different preferences than the new superintendent three years down the line, it makes firm research and development an extremely risky endeavor. As such, firms have less incentive to innovate or even enter the market, leaving consumers with little choice in their educational tools. And this little choice in tools implies that preferences may not be fully revealed to begin with. Thus, the suppliers in the educational markets are working under the constraints of skewed demand preferences, thereby further inhibiting the incentive to innovate.

There are two other requirements for efficient markets on the demand side that also seem to be absent for schools: a lack of externalities and achievement of public interest objectives. If all the costs of producing a good or service are not borne by the firms supplying it, the additional social costs (e.g., pollution) are external to the market. If the benefits to society are not all captured in the prices that consumers pay and the revenues the firms collect, the social benefits (e.g., public health and safety) are external to the market. In a well-functioning market, the social costs and benefits are fully recognized within the market. There are no spill-over effects of consequence. When the market achieves its goals of efficiency, innovation, and consumer protection, it will at the same time achieve any special public interest objectives as well. There are no special public interest objectives to satisfy (e.g., universal coverage) that go beyond the capabilities of a well-functioning market. There are certainly a host of positive externalities and public interest objectives in education (e.g., increased housing prices, tax bases, reduction in crime). For educational tools, these could be captured in a way similar to how insurance companies reduce premiums for drivers who have cars with safety features in them. One could envision a given district getting a funding premium for using certain technologies that add value to learning.

POLICY IMPLICATIONS

Using Wireless Generation and SchoolNet as examples, we argue that the K–12 education industry has a number of characteristics that prevent consumers from revealing their true preferences, whether the consumer is a parent or a district leader. If we accepts this premise, then it stands to reason that, for all intents and purposes, there is no market or, at best, a very poorly performing market. This means that the most well-intentioned efforts to foster innovation will fail because there will be little incentive for producers to continue to innovate. Even those innovations that seem to hold promise and yield results will not be able to become ubiquitous in a system that has no system and no ability to disseminate information.

Furthermore, if educational markets are monsponies, as deemed by the market structure of individual districts, then firms inspired to create new educational tools are actually inhibited from generating new growth, since there are barriers to entry and exit based on the price set by consumers. If there are no profit-maximizing incentives for firms to enter the market, then monopsonistic consumers begin to face monopolistic suppliers (i.e., what we experience in the textbook industry). As a result, market inefficiencies spurred by demand may allow for further inefficiencies on the supply side.

One potential implication of this analysis, then, is that there is simply not enough information in the market for reform. While Wireless Generation, SchoolNet, and the districts they serve are in full communiqué, the same cannot be said about parents— the true consumers of the educational tool. Although we cannot make any causal claims in this analysis, there seems to be a high association between lack of knowledge on the part of parents and the lack of market penetration. The crux of this problem, then, is that even if educational innovators have created an effective tool, it cannot be fully realized in the market, since the final consumers cannot reveal their preferences. It is analogous to Intel not truly knowing if Dell's customers prefer a particular processing chip. Without such insight, it seems unrealistic that Intel (or Dell, for that matter) would invest heavily in research and development. Thus, without a full evaluation of the demand landscape, it becomes difficult to plan for future educational opportunities on the horizon.

Our analysis also suggests that the current public policies directed at fostering changes to market power might also be effective, given scarce resources, for facilitating the creation of a true market with all of the characteristics described above. At a minimum, dealing with issues of monopsony and monopoly and the utter lack of efficient mechanisms to disseminate information in these markets would be the most fruitful policies to undertake if one truly wants to foster an entrepreneurial culture. For as the market currently stands, there is a lack of educational innovation due to the fact that monopsonists dominate and that the tenures of these monopsonists are quite short. The fact that preferences are shifting every few years is compounded by the fact that there is little incentive to innovate or even enter the market, thereby inhibiting the reveal of true preferences of educational consumers and limiting future growth and reform. Thus, while the etymological origins of entrepreneurship suggest *champion,* few would hold up Don Quixote's jousting at windmills as the most salient example of a successful endeavor.

7

A Typology of Demand Responders in K–12 Education

Joe Williams

A SCIENCE LAB INSIDE a loft on 28th and Broadway in New York City is packed with lizards, tarantulas, a white boa snake, a rabbit, and a host of other creatures. The animals are joined by slightly irreverent props, including a skeleton wearing a pink dress, solar system models, butterfly specimens, a cow skull, and model volcanoes ready to explode. Each day in the lab—including holidays and many weekends— a steady stream of elementary school children work their way through a series of hands-on experiments designed to make science education fun.

The lab is the scene for some messy experiments (the children are instructed to "dress for a mess," and one Sunday lab session is titled Grossology 101), but the independent classroom also serves as the backdrop for one of the more successful entrepreneurial efforts in K–12 education today. Sarah Corning, a former public school teacher known to her excited students as Science Teacher Sarah, has created a one-woman cottage industry to meet multiple forms of demand from New York City parent-consumers. Corning is certainly not the first educator to combine her love for teaching with proprietary savvy to meet the needs of a relatively untapped market, but she certainly stands out in a K–12 education culture that often expresses outward disdain for all things businesslike.

But for educators like Corning, and for the students and families she serves, these types of privately run afterschool and holiday science programs provide a safe and educational environment for young scholars whose parents are working. Her hands-on experiments, deep scientific knowledge, and ability to connect with her enthusiastic students allow students to walk away with a considerably stronger grounding in science than they get in their regular schools, public or private. The demand for Corning's product has even spilled over to birthday parties, for which she charges more than $500 for "1.5 hours of thrilling science entertainment, decorations, helium balloons, snacks, birthday cake, juice, party bags with home science experiments, set-up and clean-up and an assistant," according to one of her colorful promotional brochures.

In short, Corning has created her own mini-empire of science education for Manhattan elementary school students. In doing so, she is somewhat unique within an education industry (including both private and public schools) that tends to be far more comfortable with making demands of students and parents than in responding to demand from an actual educational marketplace.

But Corning is hardly alone. In the last several decades, demand for specific educational services has intensified along with growing pressure on parents, schools, and districts to meet a host of social and academic challenges, and entrepreneurs have emerged to meet this growing demand.

Where is the demand coming from? Various levels of demand origination can be traced, starting with concerned parents and moving up to state and federal governments.

- Parent demand for safe schools in which a high level of student learning takes place
- Civil rights and education activist group demand for equity and adequacy
- Business and civic group demand for graduates capable of joining the workforce and making positive contributions to the community
- State and federal government demand for student proficiency and academic growth across all subgroups

Because all of these levels of demand have the potential to serve as pressures on public school districts, district leaders have increasingly found themselves looking for help from entrepreneurial ventures in eliminating one or multiple demand pressures. As pressure from demand builds around them, districts are finding themselves playing the role of the needy customer and creating a new level of demand that can be satisfied by effective entrepreneurial organizations.

For purposes of this discussion, I divide the types of demand responders into five somewhat distinct (but sometimes overlapping) categories: demand corresponders, demand enablers, demand commandos, demand nurturers, and demand surfers. Each category recognizes demand in different ways and reacts accordingly.

DEMAND CORRESPONDERS

Educational entrepreneurs like Sarah Corning develop products, services, and programs that respond to very clear demand from the marketplace—in this case a private marketplace where parents are willing to pay piecemeal for intellectually stimulating science instruction after school. Corning was an education major at New York University who discovered she had a marketable talent as an überbabysitter when she chaperoned a preschool class trip to the Central Park Zoo. She found herself telling the young children more about the animals than the group's tour guide was able to articulate, and soon the Village Pre-School Center had found its new science teacher. Corning led hands-on experiments at the preschool and then expanded to create an afterschool program. The expansion came after she began to field a slew of requests from older elementary school students who wanted to come back and participate in her preschool science experiments.

Corning's science classes are offered within an afterschool culture in New York City, where it is commonplace for well-heeled parents to pay significant fees for tutoring and athletics programs to compensate for perceived weaknesses in what their children's schools are providing during the typical school day. Her work also takes place within a hypercompetitive schooling environment where Manhattan elementary and middle school students compete for coveted spots in the borough's best public middle and high schools, many of which require students to perform well on entrance exams in order to secure a seat. Tutoring programs at places like Kumon Math and Reading Learning Centers see a steady stream of Manhattan parents who supplement their children's education at their own personal expense, because those parents believe that the math and reading instruction provided during the traditional school day is lacking. Kumon, another demand corresponder, was started a half-century ago in Japan by Toru Kumon, a teacher and parent who wanted to help his son do better in school. The company's promotional literature claims that Kumon's methods were so successful that his son was able to do calculus by the time he was in sixth grade. Today there are more than fifteen hundred Kumon centers in North America alone

In Corning's case, the Science Teacher Sarah classes are sold as fun, hands-on activities that would otherwise be elusive to students in traditional school science classes. So the students are attracted to the enjoyable aspects of the classes, and the parents are sold on the academic and intellectual enrichment they sneak in along the way.

The key ingredient to the success of Science Teacher Sarah is Corning herself. Her enthusiasm, knowledge, and ability to draw children directly into the classroom experiments are essentially the product she provides. The entire operation revolves around her talent. One could reasonably presume that if all Corning did was teach science in a typical Manhattan elementary school, she would be a successful teacher in her own right. However, it is unlikely that she would have the resources (time and materials) to run her in-school science classes the way she does in a system that has so many other conflicting priorities.

DEMAND ENABLERS

The field of public education has long been a place where outside consultants have been able to convince state and local school boards and superintendents that they possess levels of expertise and outside validation to either bail out these school leaders from

pressure-cooker situations or pave the way for school leaders to promote controversial or expensive programs or policies that would be difficult for school leaders to advance on their own. Because public school systems have so many built-in
constituencies and bureaucracies, school leaders often face fierce resistance if they
emerge on their own with plans that either threaten entrenched interests within
the system or result in tremendous outside political pressure on their school board
bosses. One school leader going up against a billion-dollar bureaucracy can be the
education management equivalent of Don Quixote tilting at windmills, especially if
it is not abundantly clear that real demand truly exists for the changes or reforms
that the school leader is proposing. Demand enablers make it easier for demand to
break out from the confines of public school institutions so that school leaders can
act in ways that respond to calls for change rather than stir up a political hornet's
nest on their own.

Imagine the school superintendent, hired by a school board (which itself is under
pressure to control skyrocketing costs), who privately determines that a $100 mil-
lion capital plan for school construction and renovation is necessary in order for the
district to accommodate a surge in student enrollment in one part of town where
the existing elementary school is bursting at the seams. At the same time, significant
retrofitting and other renovations are needed in existing school buildings in order
to comply with federal requirements for serving students with disabilities and to allow for widespread electrical upgrades so that millions of dollars worth of computer
equipment could be used in seventy-five-year-old school buildings.

The superintendent and his team feel they have no choice but to embark on a
bond referendum in their community, but they are worried that a split school board
(several members were elected on an antitax, antispending platform) will go after
their professional scalps if they even bring it up, especially since the previous year's
school operating budget increases caused so much commotion at the board level.

Enter the big-city management consulting firm that, as part of an external assessment of the school system's capital needs (at the request of the superintendent and
his facilities team), determines on its own that the district and taxpayers will be facing
serious challenges unless a $100 million school construction and renovation bond is
approved by voters in the next year. The outside report by and large matches the recommendations that the superintendent privately concocted on his own.

The firm, which does work for major corporations worldwide and hires only
the best and brightest business school graduates, makes a flashy presentation to the
school board with charts and arrows and circles and conveys the impression that
its proven methods of analysis have determined that what the district needs will
cost no less than $100 million in additional taxpayer funding. In press accounts,
the recommendation for the construction and renovation work is tied directly to
the consulting firm, which is treated as expert and all-knowing, and only indirectly

to the superintendent and his team. Essentially, the superintendent's own opinion has been validated.

In this hypothetical case, we see several layers of demand piled atop one another. There is demand from families in the suddenly overcrowded part of town to meet the needs of students; demand from the federal government to provide facilities that are accessible to students with various disabilities, as well as demand from the students with those disabilities themselves; demand from the public to bring the district's classrooms into the modern era by upgrading electrical systems so they can accommodate an influx of new computerized equipment; demand from the school board to meet all of these needs in a way that appears to be fiscally responsible; and, finally, demand from the superintendent and his team to deal with all of these previously mentioned demands in ways that do not cost them their jobs.

It is this outermost layer of demand—the one where the local superintendent is feeling all sorts of heat emanating from the other layers—that demand enablers tend to satisfy. In this case, the consultant's job is to tell the superintendent what he wants to hear. More precisely, it is to tell the school board and taxpayers what the superintendent wants them to hear. The consultant's job is to provide cover for the administration and provide external validation for what had covertly originated as the superintendent's plan.

By providing cover for the superintendent, the demand enablers allow for all of the other layers of demand to be satisfied. For purposes of this discussion, we assume that the intentions of both the superintendent and the consultant are pure. Local politics being what it is, demand enablers serve as an important tool for school leaders who are looking to navigate through a maze of complex considerations in order to meet the various demands they are facing. They are a tool that can help bolster the case that school leaders are making for change. And because they often are tasked by the leadership to find solutions to problems that interests within the system would be content to let fester, demand enablers often end up poking around in places where district employees are simply not supposed to poke.

The consulting firm Alvarez and Marsal, to cite one prominent example, was hired by New York City Schools chancellor Joel Klein in 2006 to redirect $200 million from the central bureaucracy to the city's fifteen hundred schools. It is easy to understand why someone from outside the bureaucracy would be brought in to help with this kind of cost shifting, since it is unlikely that anyone within the bureaucracy would volunteer to eliminate or otherwise disrupt their own department or program. And Alvarez and Marsal had some experience in the public school finance sector. In 2003, the firm's vice president, Bill Roberti, was hired by the St. Louis Public Schools to come in as superintendent for one year and clean house. In St. Louis, the outsider Roberti closed sixteen schools, sold forty properties, slashed inefficient bus routes, and streamlined services like maintenance and food service. As Roberti told journalist John Merrow in

2004, "St. Louis brought in a firm from outside to do this work because no one inside the city of St. Louis could get away with some of the things that have to be done and live here without suffering the consequences."[1]

In two years of work in New York City, Alvarez helped redirect $290 million from the central bureaucracy by consolidating departments, minimizing service overlap, and making it easier for schools to pay for the services they most needed. For example, the firm recommended merging the Office of Youth Development and School Community Services with the Office of Student Placement, Youth and Family Services. The end result was a new, streamlined, and unified Office of Youth Development and a savings of $4.7 million. The consultants also reorganized the city's special education delivery system, helped create new school support organizations, and reorganized the city's complicated bus transportation system, among other cost-saving measures. One seemingly simple task, the creation of a night shift for facility repair work in schools, reduced the need for outside contractors (saving nearly $10 million) and, at the same time, addressed the historic backlog in repairs to broken windows, light fixtures, and other disrepairs in schools across the city.

These were not just cuts for the sake of saving money. Chancellor Joel Klein hired the firm to help better align the school system's resources with his push for greater autonomy, accountability, and leadership for individual schools, and the cost-cutting work coincided with a shift of school supports from one centralized bureaucracy to multiple school support organizations that sell their services to schools. At the end of their review, the consultants reported to the city that they had redirected more than $290 million of these cumulative cost savings to schools (or $166,000 per school). In addition, they freed up $20 million for the chancellor's centralized Children First reform initiative and $40 million to support the operating growth of special education classroom services.

Alvarez and Marsal helped Klein achieve what he needed, and they even took the hits for making suggestions that proved to be unpopular within the school system. The firm was the subject of frequent negative press, seemingly initiated by parts of the bureaucracy that were not thrilled with the outsider's suggestions. (The reorganization of school bus routes in the middle of the year caused considerable confusion, and the firm was widely blamed in the press for leaving students stranded at bus stops in the cold.) Over time, however, the controversial cost-saving measures kicked in, and Klein was significantly closer to achieving his vision of more autonomous schools.

Demand enablers also sometimes provide valuable managerial services for districts whose specific needs have been highlighted by demands from federal and state accountability systems. In the 1990s, when state-level testing and accountability systems were becoming more commonplace, companies like Evans Newton, Inc., marketed their curriculum alignment services directly to superintendents and school boards "with a problem." According to the company's publicly accessible Web site in

1998, "No matter how much you stress excellence, no matter what new teaching technique you try, your students are performing poorly on state or standardized exams. Welcome to the proven solution for improving your students' test scores."[2]

Evans Newton is in the business of helping schools and districts alter and align their teaching and curriculum with existing standards and testing so that students are taught skills and content that are expected to have been mastered on state exams. The company's Web site in 2010 marketed its services more broadly and highlighted its many successes around the country. But a decade ago, when many districts and schools were not only caught off-guard by the onset of new testing and accountability systems that were part of the "higher standards" era, the company marketed its services directly to school system administrators and school board members as a way to escape the heat. "As educational consultants, we work closely with your district on every level from school board to administration to the individual teacher helping you plan, implement and manage a concrete, point-for-point program that can improve achievement by 25% in one year," the company's Web site stated in 1998.[3] In the early days of the standards movement, companies like Evans Newton helped school districts reevaluate their courses and curriculum to make sure that what they were teaching matched what states were expecting to be taught.

As long as there are district and state education leaders who are feeling the impact of demand from above (federal and state accountability systems) and from below (parents and taxpayers who have more access to test score data than ever before), skilled demand enablers will be in high demand.

DEMAND COMMANDOS

If demand enablers tell school superintendents and school board members what they want to hear, demand commandos tackle problems from the opposite direction, often telling school leaders (their clients) things that are not particularly flattering. By dispensing advice and services considered taboo within school systems, these commandos end up working to solve problems that lurk beneath the more obvious demands that bring them to the table. (There is some overlap here with demand enablers if the school leader who brings in the demand commandos sees himself as a disruptor who needs to break some china within the school system organization in order to break longstanding practices within the bureaucracy. In this case, it is the rabble-rousing school leader who wants the demand commando to tell the entrenched system what it does not want to hear.)

One of the best examples of demand commandos in action is The New Teacher Project, a spunky organization founded in 1997 to address the growing issues of teacher shortages and teacher quality. The organization partners directly with school districts all over the country to oversee programs that allow alternative routes to the classroom for teachers and to work with school districts to improve their human resource systems.

The demand, in this case, comes from school districts that need more and better teachers. As a demand commando, however, The New Teacher Project meets that demand by acting far beyond the scope of a typical employment recruitment arrangement. Mere recruiters would scour the countryside in search of hidden pools of excellent teacher candidates to "fill the pipeline" for school district human resources departments. Demand commandos see their mission as being far beyond meeting the surface-level demand. They dig deep, acting as if the surface-level demand provides them with a mandate to push more lasting changes that will eliminate the root causes that lead to the strong demand in the first place. Tim Daly, president of the organization, put it this way: "One of the things that makes us different is that we're working on a problem (equitable access to effective teachers) rather than focusing on selling a service. This explains why we are willing to say difficult things to districts and policymakers; we know that the problem won't be solved otherwise, and selling services without solving the problem is uninteresting to us."[4]

The New Teacher Project, even while working in close collaboration with its district clients, takes the demand for new and better teachers and uses it as a mandate or justification for finding better ways for the district to conduct itself. It often aims at eliminating the root causes behind the scarcity of talent in schools. "We end up pushing the district to do things differently in ways they never asked us to do," Daly said. "Typically, the district wouldn't be looking to make the kinds of changes we are talking about because they aren't focused on it."

Unlike demand enablers, which meet demand by telling school leaders what they want to hear, demand commandos do the equivalent of telling a close friend that not only do her jeans make her look fat but that there is a step-aerobics class meeting the next morning and it has space for another participant. This advice, of course, is dispensed solely with the best interests of the friend at heart, and it is only received that way because of the preestablished relationship. "This sector is all about the need to push ourselves beyond the comfort zone," Daly said. "You have to be willing to break china every now and then. You have to be willing to take risks."

Daly also noted that the organization is unlike many consulting firms in that they remain focused on implementation even after their advice is dispensed. "Our general idea is to stay until the right outcomes have been attained—which again is due to our focus on a problem, as opposed to just selling advice," he said. "The biggest gains for school districts would probably come from executing what they already agree they should be doing, as opposed to coming up with new ideas or coming to a new consensus about what they should be doing."

The New Teacher Project, unlike typical recruiting agencies, has a sharp public policy and advocacy component to its work. The organization has published and publicized reports on teacher hiring timelines that caused districts to miss out on the best teachers, the adverse impacts of teacher transfer provisions in urban schools, the shift to mutual consent hiring in New York City schools, and the shortcomings of existing teacher evaluation systems. Not only does the organization urge its partner districts to take risks to improve their human resources systems, but it is also willing to walk the walk and take risks itself. For example, Daly and The New Teacher Project waded into the highly contentious battle in New York City over its reserve pool for teachers who have tenure but are rejected for assignments in individual schools. The organization issued a controversial report called *Mutual Benefits,* which quantified the pool of teachers who were not selected to work in schools and who were being paid millions of dollars to, essentially, not teach. Doing so meant that he and the organization became a very public target for the United Federation of Teachers, the teachers union in New York City, which felt management was maligning good teachers in a dispute over what to do with those teachers who were not hired for teaching slots. For The New Teacher Project, the larger issue revolved around raising serious questions about whether or not there was a better way to do human resources work within the district and under the existing teacher contract. "There's no reason to have the organization at all if we can't do that," Daly said.

Demand commandos call it like they see it, even when it ruffles the feathers of their clients. In 2009, The New Teacher Project ranked states that it felt had the best chance of winning federal grants under the Race to the Top contest created by Secretary of Education Arne Duncan. Several of the The New Teacher Project's clients were in states that did not fare well in their published rankings, and they complained. "We got calls appealing their rankings and urging us to change them," Daly said.

DEMAND NURTURERS

While the demand that enablers and commandos have satisfied tends to emanate from state and district leaders, demand nurturers tend to work directly with parent-consumers, who voice some of the most basic demands imaginable for their children: they want good, safe schools and educational programs for their children. Demand enablers understand that one parent, speaking alone, does not provide much leverage to issue demands or push change. They often work with large groups of parents to make a bold statement and to create the kinds of demand pangs that keep school leaders up at night.

Groups like Parent Revolution in Los Angeles work directly with parents to harness their desire for better schools so that the collective parent voice becomes a sharper instrument for promoting drastic change. Originally launched as a "parents union," with ties to the charter school management organization Green Dot, the organization in the fall of 2009 successfully pushed a rather novel guarantee to L.A.

parents: if 51 percent of parents at any school in the city sign the Parent Revolution petition, the organization will guarantee a better school in their neighborhood within three years, pledging to back up its guarantee one of three ways:

1. *Transforming the current school.* Parent Revolution will work with the parents at the school to demand that the Los Angeles Unified School District create a plan for how they are going to fix the school and turn it around. "Why will they listen to you? Why will they take you seriously?" the Parent Revolution Web site asks. "Because you have strength in numbers—hundreds of thousands of parents are standing together. And because you have leverage, and a credible threat: If they don't transform your school, you will put your child in a high-performing charter school, with the other two options we provide you."[5]
2. *Transformation of the current school into a charter school.* The model that Parent Revolution touts is the takeover of long-troubled Locke High School by Green Dot Public Schools, a charter management organization (CMO).
3. *Build new charter schools.* "If the District won't transform your school, and we can't turn your existing school into a charter, we will build new, high performing charter schools in your neighborhood," Parent Revolution promises. "Then you, the parent, will have choice. You can enroll your child in a high performing charter public school, or keep him or her in their current school. But the choice will be in your hands."

"This is not about wealthy philanthropists or smart academics coming up with the right way to reform schools," said Ben Austin, the executive director of the Parent Revolution. "This is simply about giving parents power. The trigger is not a recommendation, it's not advisory."[6]

Efforts like the Parent Revolution recognize that one of the elements typically lacking in major reform efforts is strong, articulated demand for change on the ground. Demand nurturers understand that while collectivizing the voices of large numbers of parent consumers is extremely difficult (and sometimes costly) work, the end result is some extremely powerful pressure that can be exerted on school systems from the outside.

Some demand nurturers go to great lengths to get into the hearts and minds of these parents so that they can most effectively understand what drives their thinking. The New York City group Harlem Parents United, originally formed by parents with students enrolled in the CMO Success Charter Network, benefits from information gleaned from extensive focus groups with parents—both parents who have chosen public charter schools for their children to learn more about why and parents who have opted to enroll their children in zoned neighborhood schools to learn more about why they did not select a charter school.

Founded by former New York City councilwoman Eva Moskowitz, the Success Charter Network has supported extensive recruitment efforts for elementary school students in Harlem and has organized a companion Parental Choice campaign for Harlem moms and dads, alerting them to the idea that they are allowed—even encouraged—to select a great school for their children. In addition to a comprehensive advertising campaign (including larger-than-life bus shelter ads), the network sponsors an annual school choice fair for Harlem parents that includes representatives from public, public charter, and private schools. Several thousand people attended the fair in 2009, leaving the event with Parental Choice Zone tote bags and buttons. All along the way, the Network uses messaging that it knows will connect with parent consumers.

Moskowitz said her work in city politics taught her that the emotional connection that a candidate makes with voters often carries more weight than specific policy platforms she supports. Extending that lesson to schooling was intentional: "We are looking to make an emotional connection with parents. It is mothers who tend to make the schooling decisions, so understanding the momma bear instinct—understanding that psychology—is important to us."[7]

Each parent focus group lasts approximately ninety minutes, and food and beverages are offered to the participants. As a trained facilitator guides the parents through a wide-ranging discussion, school leaders watch intently from behind a mirrored window. Similar sessions were held with New York City's public school teachers to help improve the network's teacher recruitment messaging. School leaders learned a lot from the parents in the focus groups about what kinds of advertisements worked for them, Moskowitz said. If the recruitment pieces were too hard-hitting, parents got defensive and took it personally. For instance, parents were scared off by too much emphasis on the word *lottery* to describe the enrollment process and were more motivated when the fairness of the process was emphasized.

"In the beginning we were talking about 'school choice,' but we learned [during parent focus groups] that parents thought that meant the school chooses them," Moskowitz said. "We decided to stay away from that." The messaging surrounding the network's student recruitment work did not change drastically as a result of the sessions, Moskowitz said. It was more like external validation and fine-tuning of some important concepts. "It validated a lot of the things we were already thinking about. It forces you to pick your horse when you go out there and sell your schools to parents. We settled on concepts of 'opportunity' and 'parent choice,' and we adopted a tunnel vision about those things."

When demand nurturers are effective, it sends a powerful message about the demand side to existing power structures. In the spring of 2009, approximately thirty-five hundred families entered a random lottery for just 475 seats in Harlem Success charter schools. The lottery itself, which attracted television and other press, included speeches from New York City Public Schools chancellor Joel Klein and even an important announcement from state senate president Malcolm Smith: $30 million in charter school funding had been restored in the state budget.

DEMAND SURFERS

What makes demand surfers unique is that they transition their approach as demand shifts direction. Demand surfers are nimble and are able to pick up on trends and seize new opportunities as they emerge. Of all of the demand types, this is the one most capable of capturing organizations and service providers that could easily be placed in one category or the other at various times in their evolutions.

When Mark Claypool founded Educational Services of America (ESA) in Nashville in 1999, the former social worker was simply filling what he saw was an obvious void. Claypool saw a tremendous need for schools that would provide services for special-needs students, particularly as public schools struggled to adequately manage caseloads and provide the right special education services for the students who needed them. The founding of ESA, interestingly, coincided with the passage of a small special education voucher pilot program in Florida, known as the McKay Scholarships. The scholarships, which originated in Sarasota County only, allow parents of special education students who are unsatisfied with their local public school to enroll in a private school.

The demand in many parts of the country at the time was clear: parents wanted quality special education programs for their kids, and they were not getting it in their local public schools. ESA was there to meet the demand. "Our purpose ten years ago was to get in and be agnostic about funding and labels and provide the best services to these students," Claypool said. "At the time, the lowest hanging fruit [from a business perspective] was to acquire smaller private schools that had served kids with learning disabilities."[8]

Florida's McKay Scholarship program was expanded beyond Sarasota to the entire state in 2000, and the demand grew, setting the stage for ESA to become the nation's largest provider of K–12 special education programs. Two things happened as a result of the increasing demand for ESA's services to parents: the company and its schools and programs learned a lot about dealing with students with special needs; and local school districts began to take notice that someone else was not only taking their students but doing a better job educating them. When it came to serving students with emotional disabilities, in particular, these two developments fueled each other and created a new, powerful demand pool in the form of local districts that wanted help from experts with a proven track record of success. "We began to focus on programs funded by public school districts," Claypool said. "We started acting not as a vendor but a collaborative partner."

The shift in demand emphasis from parents to school districts also coincided with increased pressure at the state and federal levels for districts to improve high school dropout rates. "We were seeing districts experience a lot of pain providing services for kids diagnosed with emotional handicaps," said Claypool. "When I started in my career as a social worker, these kids would have been institutionalized." Instead, those students today are part of accountability systems that determine whether or not school districts are successfully serving their communities. Claypool notes that ESA still very much views parents as customers for its private schools, but shifting political dynamics at the state and federal levels have created new demands that the company is looking to serve.

CONCLUSION

Case studies of educators like Science Teacher Sarah are rare, because lone educators tend not to move in worlds where startup capital is widely available and accessible and where professional risk is part of the culture. More often, demand is something that must be enabled, commanded, and nurtured.

The modern education reform scene is witnessing some significant changes that have been unleashed by demand responders. Envelope-pushing organizations like The New Teacher Project are getting hard-to-move human resources shops in school districts to rethink the way they do business, with an eye toward attracting and retaining the highest-quality teachers for students. Parent-organizing groups like Parent Revolution and Harlem Parents United are collectivizing the voices and frustrations of parents, creating a new political force for better schools that has been missing in the policy-making process for a generation. Together, these demand responders are helping move what can sometimes seem like an intractable public education sector.

Policy makers, philanthropists, and activists who wish to see public education evolve to become a sector that can be a home for dynamic, entrepreneurial educators like Science Teacher Sarah should pay particular attention to those demand responders who are working in creative ways to better harness and channel existing demand. Demand commandos and demand nurturers, because they work to prod schools and political systems from the outside, represent especially strong leverage points that have been largely untapped in an environment where intraschool district programs and initiatives benefit from much of the existing civic and philanthropic support.

Education is a sector that has been crying out for a revolution for years but instead has seen a long process of slow-moving evolution, caused in large part by bureaucratic inertia and a lack of incentives for demand responders to actually respond. Supporting those demand responders who work to reshape, refine, empower, and amplify existing demand would arguably help speed the pace of reform from the outside.

8

Price Competition and Course-Level Choice in K–12 Education

Burck Smith

EVER SINCE THE INTERNET exploded onto our global consciousness in the mid-1990s, technology evangelists have claimed that distance education could drive improvement in the three basic educational constraints at the K–12 and postsecondary levels. By removing geographic and temporal constraints, distance education could increase access to education for previously underserved groups. By reducing the overhead associated with buildings and by using digital technologies to drive down the cost of content production and delivery, distance education could dramatically reduce the cost of course delivery. And by taking advantage of cheap and ubiquitous communications infrastructure and sophisticated learning management systems, education quality could be maintained or even improved.

Indeed, over the last decade, distance learning has become an accepted and popular method of education in postsecondary and, increasingly, K–12 education. Over 3.9 million postsecondary students (about 20 percent) were taking at least one online course during the fall 2007 term, marking a 12 percent increase over the number reported the previous year. The 12 percent growth rate for online enrollments far exceeds the 1.2 percent growth of the overall higher education student population.[1] For K–12, the overall number of students engaged in online courses in 2007–2008 is estimated at 1.03 million. This represents a 47 percent increase since 2005–2006.[2] In higher education, the students taking distance education courses have tended to be nontraditional students who are older, have jobs, or have other commitments that would impede participation in a more traditional college program. K–12 students taking courses at a distance tend to choose electives that are not offered at their school or have nontraditional characteristics making enrollment in traditional school difficult.[3] It seems that the growth of distance education has practically eliminated the problem of access. Further, because all of these postsecondary and K–12 students are getting credit for their distance education courses from accredited entities, it is assumed that course quality is at least comparable to face-to-face course quality.[4] But what about cost?

By relying on servers instead of buildings, digital content instead of print textbooks, courseware instead of lectures, and remote instructors instead of in-person instructors, distance education reduces the cost of course delivery. By stripping nonacademic functions from the educational experience, it eliminates the built-in subsidies necessary to support athletic teams, school security, student centers, dormitories, cafeterias, some student support services, and other traditional academic functions. And by amortizing what infrastructure costs do exist across a much larger customer base, distance education can further reduce the cost per course delivered. Despite the dramatically lower cost structure of a distance-delivered course, the *price* of a distance education course—what an end-user actually pays as opposed to the course's cost of delivery—remains more or less unchanged in both higher education and K–12.

In an unregulated and unsubsidized market, this price versus cost difference would not last long, since new product choices from new or existing providers would drive the price down. However, in postsecondary and K–12 education, this dramatic difference between price and cost is maintained by a variety of regulatory, policy, and economic barriers that thwart the student-made course-level choices necessary for an effective course-level market mechanism. In postsecondary education, which has a longer history of online education than K–12, weak market forces are just now starting to create lower-priced options. For K–12, which has an even weaker market mechanism, lessons about how to create management structures to harness online education can be gleaned from higher education.

Policy makers for postsecondary and K–12 education are confronted with the same fundamental dilemma. How can the sudden and dramatic proliferation of course and service providers be harnessed so that the cost savings of this newly robust market are delivered to students and taxpayers? Although the dilemma is the same, regulatory structures and the paying customer for the two sectors are distinct. In higher education, the paying customer is an amalgam of student and taxpayer. In K–12, the payer is usually the taxpayer. Unlike K–12, postsecondary education is not compulsory, not free, and colleges must attract students who are more mobile and self-directed. This market dynamic, though tempered by a variety of restraints, means that higher education is closer to dramatic disruption and price competition. By learning from postsecondary education and adapting these lessons to its particular economic dynamics, K–12 education can also create policy and management structures to harness the savings of new technologies.

POSTSECONDARY BARRIERS TO COURSE-LEVEL CHOICE

Just how dramatic is the difference between price and cost in higher education? Astoundingly, there is little public data available about the per-student cost of course delivery by subject and institution. However, the National Center for Academic Transformation (NCAT)—a nonprofit group that has worked with hundreds of colleges to redesign high-enrollment courses to reduce costs and maintain or improve student outcomes—ran a grant program that required colleges to estimate the cost per student in specific courses before and after redesign. Using data from the thirty initial colleges (all of which were public), it cost on average $170 per student before redesign and $111 per student after redesign.[5] These colleges charge about $1,000 per course and receive state subsidies to boot. Unlike many colleges, the ones that participate in NCAT are proactively focused on improving course outcomes and course efficiency. While it is impressive that colleges are able to reduce their cost per student and, in almost all cases, improve performance, the difference between the cost to deliver a course and the price charged for these general education courses across all of higher education is extreme. Further, add in the cost benefits of online education, and the gap between cost and price is even more dramatic. The difference between price and cost is absorbed by administration, overhead, internal cross-subsidies, and net profit (for for-profit entities). Why does higher education pricing defy traditional economics? What barriers prevent effective market mechanisms? Start by following the money.

Higher education prices to students are subsidized by direct grants to schools from state governments, direct grants to students from federal governments, subsidized loans, and tax-favored status. Wisely, to reduce their prices, prospective students prefer to rely on some combination of these subsidies when enrolling in postsecondary education. Accordingly, access to these funding streams is critical to the success of most postsecondary providers. The only way students can get access to these grants and loans is to enroll in a nationally or regionally accredited institution. This system creates a variety of barriers to competition.

- *Increased start-up costs, start-up time, and regulatory burdens.* To receive accreditation, an applying college must offer a full degree program (as opposed to individual courses) and meet a variety of regulatory requirements designed to make a college look like other colleges. In addition, an applicant must have served students for several years before applying, and review takes an additional two to three years. This dramatically increases overhead and lengthens the time to a return on investment, thereby pushing prices up.
- *Lack of product interoperability.* Unlike K–12 education, course quality and performance standards are ambiguous from one college to the next, despite supposed oversight from accreditors. This allows colleges to justify ambiguous and byzantine articulation policies. According to a 2005 Government Accountability Office

study, "Institutions vary in how they evaluate credits, who makes the decisions to accept credits, and when credit transfer decisions are made. For example, some institutions evaluate transfer credits prior to student transfer, while others make final credit transfer decisions after student enrollment . . . A student's inability to transfer credit may result in longer enrollment, more tuition payments, and additional federal financial aid."[6] Without clear articulation policies, transferring courses taken from one provider to another is cumbersome and risky, holding students captive to the institutions in which they first enroll. To put it another way, colleges are neither open source nor interoperable.

- *Lack of financial interoperability.* Student financial aid is delivered by and to the school in which the student enrolls. A student wishing to take a course from another provider must typically pay for that course out of their own pocket or transfer enrollment completely.[7] By being able to apply government subsidies only at the institutional level, as opposed to the course level, course-level choice is discouraged.

- *Unequal competition.* New education providers wishing to compete on price must overcome the significant price subsidies enjoyed by public, nonprofit, and for-profit colleges. Composed of direct state funding, federal grants to students, and subsidized loans, this subsidy can be up to 70 percent or more.

Given the overhead required to start and maintain new colleges, the difficulty of transferring credits among schools, the barriers to using financial aid to choose competitive providers, the unlevel playing field, and the lack of performance information, it is not surprising that competitors who could deliver price reductions as a result of technological innovation are only now appearing.

Two new companies that are trying to take advantage of the dramatic price-versus-cost differential are Higher Ed Holdings and StraighterLine. Higher Ed Holdings, a for-profit company run by a successful education entrepreneur, partnered with Lamar University in Texas to offer graduate degrees in teacher education through Lamar at half the price of Lamar's existing program. Higher Ed Holdings provided the marketing expertise, student services, content, and other resources in exchange for a significant percentage of the tuition revenue. The partnership yielded record enrollment. However, a similar program at the University of Toledo generated enough opposition from the university faculty to prevent the program's implementation.

StraighterLine, a company I founded and run, offers general education courses that can be taken by students for $99 per month plus $39 per course and that can be transferred into any regionally accredited college that adheres to the credit recommendations of the American Council on Education (ACE). Further, a group of regionally accredited partner colleges has agreed to award credit for the courses directly. In both cases, partnerships with existing regionally accredited colleges were necessary to jump-start the companies. For Higher Ed Holdings, a partnership was required so that its students could receive financial aid. For StraighterLine, partnerships with accredited colleges were necessary because students needed a path to credit and StraighterLine needed to enroll enough students so that it could be reviewed by the ACE. Unlike other postsecondary competitors, StraighterLine has elected to forego financial aid in the hope that its prices are low enough that students will not need it. By forgoing financial aid, it avoids the overhead and startup costs required by traditional accreditation, but it also receives none of the governmental subsidies available to other education providers.

PUBLIC POSTSECONDARY ONLINE MANAGEMENT INITIATIVES

Higher education administrators are aware of many of these barriers to innovation. It is an annual rite to complain about the unpopular but unavoidable price escalation. They are aware that their ability to demonstrate and compare effectiveness is insufficient. Institutions spend a large and increasing amount of money on new technologies that they intend to use to save money and increase access to education. There are many, many efforts under way within higher education to address these problems.

Unfortunately, most of these efforts serve to perpetuate existing structures or to respond to critics. Like in less restricted markets, market disruption that dramatically changes product features and cost structures almost never originates from those who would be disrupted. Existing players tend to make incremental changes that will appeal to their individual customers. For instance, the addition of nonacademic amenities at a four-year college appeals to a particular subset of incoming students yet pushes the overall cost structure up. Here are some common postsecondary technology and distance education initiatives that are not likely to change the cost and accountability problems of higher education.

Statewide Collaborations.   In international trade, countries are happy to exchange the things that neither has. The United States is happy to import sushi, and the Japanese are happy to import hamburgers. However, when both Japan and the United States want to send the other its cars, negotiations get tense. Suddenly, tariffs, regulations, and motivated constituencies restrict trade. However, it is the trade in high-priced, ubiquitous goods that have the most beneficial impact on consumers. Similarly, colleges in collaborations are happy to accept courses and programs not provided at their own college but are much less likely to allow students to take courses already offered by the home institution. It is telling that many states have distance learning collaboratives, but most are structured as distance learning catalogs for the member institutions. Such an arrangement preserves college autonomy without creating price competition among individual departments or courses. Similarly, articulation agreements and coenrollment consortia are made by and among colleges that do not threaten the enrollments of the other members. Where there is a threat, regulations such as limitations on transferability or program distribution requirements are often created.

Voluntary Quality Assurance Programs.   In response to increased pressure on higher education to demonstrate accountability, several voluntary accountability programs that allow cross-institutional comparisons have emerged.[8] While these programs represent an improvement over the current lack of comparable data, they still suffer from several critical problems. First, these programs are voluntary. The participants are few in number and, presumably, are the ones with little to hide. Second, the information is usually self-provided, creating an incentive to provide biased information. Lastly, given the two previous problems, cross-institutional comparison remains difficult.

Content Collaboratives.   Classic economic theory states that the price of a good should equal its marginal cost of production. In other words, in a perfect market, the price of an item should equal the amount that it costs to produce one more unit of that item. Rightly, states have taken note of the fact that the marginal cost of electronic content is effectively zero. Therefore, electronic content produced by their institutions can be shared at almost no cost. In theory, this should reduce course development costs, textbook costs, and speed the development of new courses. Merlot is a collaboration of fifteen state college systems that contribute to a database of educational content objects, combinations of content, and software that provide a lesson or explanation. Unfortunately, while there are many states and individuals who are willing to contribute to Merlot, college governance structures, course development procedures, textbook adoption processes, and tuition policies conspire to limit the demand for free content.[9] For instance, a professor has limited incentive to develop a course more cheaply because none of the benefits accrue to the professor. Further, even if the professor does develop a course more cheaply, that savings will not be passed on to the student. Lastly, even if the savings were passed onto the student, the percentage of the price structure (as opposed to the cost structure) that online content represents is negligible.

OpenCourseWare.   In 2002, the Massachusetts Institute of Technology (MIT) made headlines by announcing that it intended to put all of its course materials online and make them available to anyone for free. In the last fifteen years, this evolved into the OpenCourseWare Consortium with well over one hundred members across the globe. With such materials available, everyone would be able to benefit from MIT's world-class educational content. By providing free materials, the cost of education should decline. However, while content may be available, the credentialing component and selectivity components of MIT are not. Further, new education providers wishing to take advantage of this material must still navigate the accreditation and regulatory barriers necessary to award bona fide credits. Accordingly, despite having free materials and very low startup costs for new course initiatives, prices to students have not budged. The lack of impact on prices from both content collaboratives and open courseware should be a red flag for those supporting the $500 million Online Skills Laboratory currently supported by the federal government.

Technology Adoption.   Colleges are eager to adopt new technologies. Most colleges offer some form of learning management system for both distance education and face-to-face classes. Most make extensive use of administrative tools to manage student data, grades, payments, and other necessary services. Overhead projectors, SMART Boards, clickers, and other in-classroom technologies are extremely common. Most colleges offer some form of distance education. However, despite the presence of all of these technologies, costs continue to rise. Without changes in the regulatory and financing structures in which these technologies are embedded, the potential for cost and quality improvements will not be realized.

WHAT DOES THIS MEAN FOR K–12?

Like postsecondary education, K–12 education, particularly at the high school level, suddenly has hundreds of course and service providers where just a few years ago there had been only a handful. Further, the proliferation of providers changes the existing and future set of education products and their price points. By aggregating students across a global service area, products that could only be used by a few students at each school can now serve thousands. Products that currently serve thousands can now serve millions more affordably by taking advantage of economies of scale. With a global service area, the speed with which students can complete courses, times in which they start courses, cost structures of offered courses, and elements of courses offered can vary dramatically and can be chosen by the student. Further, by aggregating the demand for services across a larger population, a wide variety of services—such as tutoring, college counseling, test preparation, career counseling, and countless others—can be provided at comparable or cheaper price points and with better service levels than that offered by a school or district. With newly viable markets for niche products and even larger markets for mainstream products, the potential product and price point permutations are dizzying.

For example, a quick Internet search reveals that the Michigan Virtual High School offers regular and Advanced Placement (AP) courses from $109 to $350 per seat. In addition, some of these courses are provided by a for-profit AP course provider called

Apex. Though not disclosed, Michigan Virtual High School must pay Apex a lower amount than they charge students directly.[10] The University of Oklahoma offers high school courses at $180 per course with a variety of fees that can be added in.[11] Dozens more classes, all with different price points, are listed. The prices might be subsidized if the courses come from in-state providers, might be market rate if it comes from private-sector providers, or might be the cost of building and maintaining the course if built by the local school district.

However, just because students can be aggregated to new levels, thereby creating new cost efficiencies and enabling a wide range of services, it does not mean that they will. These online offerings are not just competing with each other; they also present a viable and competitive alternative to the face-to-face instruction that is the core service offered by schools and districts. This increase in service providers can create competition between the various providers *and* between providers and the school districts themselves. Like with postsecondary education, schools will either close their borders to the most threatening competitive services, thereby protecting their existing institutional capacity, or they will create new management structures to harness the potential for quality improvement, cost reduction, and service innovation that are hallmarks of competitive markets. Early indications are that K–12 administrators will respond much as their higher education counterparts did a decade ago. When asked to rank the most and least important reasons for offering online courses, K–12 administrators said the three least important reasons out of ten were (1) students prefer online courses; (2) online and blended learning is more pedagogically beneficial; and (3) online and blended learning is financially beneficial.[12]

If K–12 public education chooses to embrace the competition created by online education, the policy structure and choice mechanisms that they will need to employ will be different than those of postsecondary education. Although characterized by significant barriers to innovation, higher education remains a market with a consumer choice mechanism. Colleges do tailor their offerings, experiences, and messages to attract students. Students do choose from a variety of institutions, courses, and, sometimes, the medium through which their coursework is delivered. Higher education students do move from school to school and do have the option to take classes at other colleges while enrolled at their home college, even if the class must be paid for out of their own pockets. As evidence, the numbers of swirlers, or students attending more than one institution prior to graduation, and coenrollments, students taking classes from one institution while enrolled at another, are growing. Also, students will pay more for program features like scheduling flexibility and tighter ties to employers. For instance, for-profit colleges typically charge tuition that is dramatically higher than that charged by community colleges for similar programs. Such willingness to pay signals at least a partially functioning market mechanism.

K–12, however, does not have the same market dynamic. The price of K–12 education is not just subsidized but is completely covered. Because the price to a student of a course provided by a local district is free, market entrants who might force price competition at the course level are at a severe handicap. Further, because K–12 students are far less mobile, enrollment alternatives are few. As in higher education, but with even fewer direct-to-consumer alternatives, K–12 third-party course and service providers must either sell their wares directly to schools, which then offer it to their students, or create their own charter schools that, by virtue of the charter approval process, will have a price structure that is the same as other schools.[13] Further, a weak market mechanism, like that found in higher education, is untenable because any kind of consumer payment for public education undermines the public, compulsory system that is a hallmark of the United States and other developed countries. Yet, K–12 education has done a far better job at defining educational outcomes at the course level. Simply having standards, even if there are fifty sets, allows far greater interoperability among schools and course providers. While K–12 education lacks an obvious course-level consumer choice mechanism, it has the potential to more quickly embrace additional course providers because of its open-source standards.

Because of these fundamental differences between postsecondary education and K–12 education, the solutions to harnessing student and taxpayer savings from the proliferation of third-party course and service providers are different. For postsecondary education, the levers to create course-level price competition are financial aid policy, accreditation, articulation, and the structure of government subsidies. Assuming policy barriers are removed or ameliorated, course-level price competition can be driven by consumers "voting with their feet," taking their education dollars to the provider who offers the best value for any given student and course. In K–12, students typically cannot vote with their feet. Individual schools or school districts will need to create internal structures that allow student choice at the course and service levels. What are the prerequisites for these structures? What might they look like? What might the impact be?

INTRASCHOOL CHOICE

Intraschool choice is the ability to choose from a wide variety of courses and services provided by a variety of providers, all to be offered and paid for as part of a standard public education offering. A prerequisite for intraschool choice is the availability of things to choose. Already, the growth of online learning has created many viable course providers. For instance, Clayton Christensen and Michael Horn, one a Harvard Business School professor noted for his research on market disruption and the other the executive director of an education-focused think tank, claim that predictive models of disruption in other industries suggest that 50 percent of high school courses will be delivered online by 2019.[14] To provide these courses and services, "school districts typically depend on multiple online learning providers, including postsecondary institutions, state virtual schools, and independent providers as well as developing and providing their own online courses."[15]

Other educational services, either traditionally provided by a school district or new services enabled by student aggregation, can be purchased and provided directly to students. These include online tutoring services, essay grading services, college counseling, career counseling, test preparation, and others. The power of student aggregation is evident in the growth of on-demand, online tutoring companies. Companies like SMARTHINKING, which I founded and ran for ten years, and Tutor.com aggregate the demand for instruction across educational institutions and the supply of tutors across the globe to create qualified, live academic help available twenty-four hours a day, seven days a week. A school simply does not have the scale to provide such a level of service at comparable price points. In some cases, such as Straighter-Line's college courses, these tutoring services can fulfill the teacher's role more affordably and with better levels of service for students.

In theory, now that cheaper and comparable courses and services are available, a savvy school district seeking to reduce its instructional and service expenditures should be willing to outsource a larger portion of its course delivery and service provision to the lowest-cost provider. In such a scenario, online course use would explode and the much-talked-about prediction of 50 percent of classes being delivered online within ten years would be realized. However, this scenario presumes that schools are only consumers of courses, not consumers *and* providers. Similarly, the predictive models used in *Disrupting Class* were derived from well-functioning markets. To the contrary, public education markets more closely resemble those of nation-states and international trade. Although students could have more educational options at a wider variety of price points than ever before, the likelihood of deriving dramatic quality improvements and cost savings is low because schools and districts control the delivery of courses to students and have incentives to prevent competition for the subjects and services that they already deliver. A nascent market of course and service providers exists, but its offerings and price points are determined by institutional purchasers, not students and families.

Even if a school does provide a list of options from which a student or family can choose, this by itself is not sufficient to create a course-level market. Student choices must be paired with real trade-offs and sufficient purchasing information. As with any other buying decision, *informed* would mean that information on features, performance, and price are easily available. Further, and more importantly, there must be consequences associated with a choice. These consequences must accrue to the person or family making the choice. For instance, if my son chooses an algebra course that is cheaper to provide than another algebra option, the cost savings should accrue to me and my son in some form. To create a market mechanism that delivers the efficiencies promised by educational technology, the benefits of choosing lower-cost offerings need to be passed on to those choosing, and those choosing should know what they are getting.

What might be the impact of intraschool choice? One of the tenets of economics is that in a well-functioning market, the price of a good is equal to its marginal cost, the cost to produce one more unit of that good. In a better-functioning market, the cost of content provision, content distribution, and remote communication would be dramatically lower and should be reflected in course price. Course cohorts could be comprised of students worldwide; therefore, start and stop dates can be chosen by the student. Students who finish courses more quickly consume fewer resources and could be charged less. Also, in addition to cost benefits, innovation in educational product construction and delivery would likely accelerate. Lastly, nonacademic components of an educational experience, like extracurricular activities and life experiences, could be better-valued and incorporated into our definition of education.

So, despite an explosion of educational choices that could dramatically improve the value (lower prices, more services, or both) of K–12 education, K–12's management, regulatory, and financial structures are not built in a way that allows the system and its taxpayers to take advantage of these benefits. Because K–12 education is free to students, there is no functioning market mechanism to make the most appropriate choices. Further, free K–12 education is a cherished feature of American education and is not likely to change. An intraschool choice model must allow a wide variety of courses, services, providers, and price points from which to choose; the cost benefits of choice to accrue to the chooser; the provision of useful information for making informed choices; and the maintenance of a single, public payer for public education. Is there a model that could fulfill these criteria?

ONE POSSIBLE MECHANISM: A CAFETERIA PLAN FOR SUBJECTS AND SERVICES

In unregulated markets, disruptive technological change is embraced by new market entrants who will eventually outperform old entrants by providing better prices, quality, or both to the consumer. For instance, Google harnessed the power of Internet searches to sell advertising. Google's growth dramatically reduced the revenue of other advertising outlets, such as newspapers, television, and radio, and increased the marketing value to companies needing advertisement. Apple's iTunes has replaced record stores and changed the unit of music sales from the album to the song, letting users purchase only the songs they want. The cell phone is replacing landline telephones. In industry after industry, new technologies give birth to new business models and new companies. In all of these industries, consumers are free to choose the product that provides them with the best value. This mechanism allows for the creative *destruction* of the marketplace.

In contrast, in education, where cost-saving technologies and products are integrated into school curricula, the benefits are not passed on to the student or family. More importantly, the school has little incentive to offer students third-party products that are more cost-effective than its own products. For instance, a school may spend $500 to enroll one of its students in an online algebra class, whereas it might have cost the school $1,000 to deliver the course itself. However, since all services to the student are free, the student has no incentive to enroll in the cheaper course. The school might have an incentive, but that would mean reducing the number of algebra courses taught and teachers employed at its own school. The lack of financial incentive for the student and the political disincentive for the school district are strong limiting factors in the demand and growth of new educational models. Because public education is free, the standard fee-for-service model does not apply.

Although society's multiple and varied demands on public education require a vast array of services to be offered, any single student may demand less or more of any single service. For instance, one student may need to focus on core math, writing, and reading skills but has no time for extracurriculars. Another student may be able to move through academic subjects at her own pace but would welcome the opportunity to participate in band or afterschool sports. It would better suit the first student's demands if the school could provide more academic instruction at the expense of extracurricular offerings. However, the second student would be better off if less expensive academic offerings could be provided and extracurricular activities could be bolstered.

Human resource providers have long known that each individual values different types and levels of employment benefits. For instance, one employee may value a lot of vacation time but does not want a dental plan. Another employee may want a robust dental and health plan but can live with less vacation time. Rather than provide a single plan to every employee, many companies use a "cafeteria" model to better allocate services while considering the services' respective prices. In these plans, employees are given a certain number of points that can be allocated toward different benefits of their choice. For education, students or parents could be given a predetermined number of points that could be allocated across different courses and services. A school could list courses from a variety of providers and set point values that reflect the true cost of providing each course or service. After fulfilling course distribution prerequisites as defined by the state, additional points could be used by a student to choose extracurricular activities or services that would also have a point value tied to cost of provision. As long as a student meets school-set academic standards, courses meet accepted standards of quality, and students choose courses according to a school-set curriculum distribution, such a model could allow the kinds of education and service recombinations that would truly harness the value of technology.

For instance, one student may excel in math but struggle in English. Therefore, an English tutor could be paid for by savings generated from math. An exceptional student may wish to push herself through her courses and allocate resources to music lessons, athletics, or a memorable summer experience. The cafeteria model will allow students and families to choose the curricular elements that best meet their needs. Further, such a model may instill a level of intrinsic motivation in the student who wants to play football but needs to fund it from savings in math.

By allowing students and parents to choose educational options according to the value that makes the most sense for the student, tremendous efficiencies can be generated. Using some of the price points found in a quick search on the Internet, a year of accredited coursework could be provided for less than $1,000. While a bare-bones academic plan might not appeal to most students, for some the savings could be tremendous and reinvested in extracurriculars and services.

The fictitious student academic profile in table 8.1 makes the cafeteria model more concrete. This model assumes that the per-pupil allocation is $8,000 per student and that 25 percent is reserved for school overhead and other fixed costs. It also assumes that this student is not strong in writing or math. The items in dark gray are the ones that the student is not allowed to take because past history has shown that weak students do not do well in this format. Items in light gray are the subjects that the student chose. After picking his educational subjects, formats and services, this student has three hundred points remaining.

It is important to note that this model makes no assumptions about what the school and district choose to include in overhead and what portion of points to allocate to it. It also assumes that students will be choosing from educational options offered by third parties as well as those offered by a school itself. Further, this model can accommodate a wide variety of educational options, subject distribution requirements, and option limitations.

An intraschool choice model combines educational service cost information with the multitude of newly available educational services, thereby creating a market mechanism to better judge the value of all educational offerings. Such a model should also result in a more efficient allocation of resources to students. For instance, in this model, a school does not need to offer college counseling to everyone, just those that sign up for it. Further, the school or district will have information on student course selections, service selections, student outcomes, price points, and student demographic data. Over time, such data will indicate which products and services are the best values and which ones are not. It also allows students to fund other experiences that have educational value but may not be part of a traditional academic curriculum, like summer camp or music lessons. Within broad parameters established by a school

TABLE 8.1
Sample student academic allocation profile

Per-Student Dollar Allocation	$8,000
Required Overhead Allocation	$2,000
"Points" Available for Distribution	6,000

HYPOTHETICAL STUDENT

Subjects	Math	Language Arts	Social Studies	Science	Electives
Self-paced	100	100	100	100	100
Online option 1	200	200	200	200	200
Online option 2	400	400	400	400	400
Face-to-face	1000	1000	1000	1000	1000
Hybrid	700	700	700	700	700

Other offerings	
Online tutoring	500
Face-to-face tutoring	1000
Test preparation	1000
College counseling	800
Sports	1500
Band	1000
Summer camp	3000

<-- Student not eligible
<-- Student choice

Total points used	5700
Remaining	300

or district, such a model allows students to define what is educationally meaningful to the student and family.

CONCLUSION

Every effective new technology—from the pencil to the wheel to the Internet—increases productivity. An increase in productivity means that more of the same should be able to be accomplished at the same cost, the same should be able to be accomplished at a reduced cost, or both. Computers and the Internet have become commonplace in all walks of life. Industry after industry has evolved and been disrupted by these new technologies—except education. In education, despite tremendous investments in technology at the post–secondary and K–12 levels, the price has gone up while quality seems to have gone down. Why? Because the market mechanism necessary to sift the good products from the bad *at the course and service* levels barely exists in higher education and does not exist at all in K–12 education.

Historically, such choice has not been possible because the range of choices has been relatively limited. Now, things are different. The explosion of online education and services brings options and competition. If embraced, this competition can drive tremendous cost reductions and product improvements. Further, it could more appropriately value the multitude of varied inputs that are part of a child's education. With a more accurate system of valuation, scarce resources can be allocated more efficiently across the entire educational enterprise—academics, services, extracurriculars, and formative experiences.

K–12 administrators and policy makers can look to postsecondary education's response to course-level competition to draw lessons about how it should respond. On the one hand, the state standards prevalent across the country make K–12 more interoperable than postsecondary education. Therefore, with the right choice structure, cost savings, and product improvements could accrue very rapidly. On the other hand, K–12 education is lacking the kind of consumer choice mechanism found in postsecondary education. Accordingly, K–12 administrators and policy makers will have to make a deliberate choice to open their borders, to embrace course- and service-level competition, or to close their borders to protect existing teaching and educational methods.

Which will be chosen?

9

The Data Challenge

Jon Fullerton

IN ORDER FOR A MORE individualized and choice-driven economy of education to develop, three prerequisites must be satisfied. Parents, teachers, and administrators need to understand the educational options from which they may choose. Potential providers must understand the needs of individual students and the other market segments they are intending to supply—that is, the needs of parents, teachers, and administrators. And tracking and information systems must be developed that can handle individualization and choice.

In theory, with these prerequisites in place, producers could organize to meet the demands of educational consumers and the market would function smoothly. Unfortunately, none of these information needs are met well now. The challenges involved in bringing the current, inadequate levels of data collection and management up to levels that could support decentralization and choice based on individual needs are substantial. Failure to meet data requirements could put a critical brake on the system's ability to separate the various components of education and provide robust, individualized educational programs. Indeed, for some of the more radical visions of choice, the data problems may prove insurmountable. While there are some promising efforts in this area, the jury is still out as to whether there will be any successful examples of actually implementing the kinds of data systems that will be needed.

This chapter argues that easily accessible and reliable data are critical to the success of individualized, choice-driven education. An educational model driven by the needs and choices of individual students and families would empower a wide range of agents, each with their own data needs. However, when potential data needs are assessed against current data capabilities, we find that current data capabilities fall short of what will be needed to guide intelligent choice. There are a number of steps that could be taken to move toward more adequate data systems, but the political and organizational challenges will be many.

WHY DATA ARE CRITICAL

Why should data be considered necessary for individualized, choice-driven education? Markets develop all the time in response to needs and without easily available
data. In fact, for proponents, this is one of the attractions of moving to a demand-
driven system. Student and family needs and preferences may be too complex to
know ahead of time, and simply by opening up the system to new players, innovators
will arise. Those that meet a sufficient number of families' felt needs will succeed;
those that do not will fail. A sorting will inevitably occur—not one driven by centrally
available data systems but by the type of sorting markets have been doing since time
immemorial: some enterprises will fail financially due to lack of demand.

Indeed, there is already a robust market for private schools, afterschool activities, and academic tutoring, and the unbiased, publicly available information on
all of these providers' performance is far less than that which exists for most public
schools. In fact, these schools and services are generally exempt from the test reporting requirements of public schools and allowed to select their own students, thereby
decreasing the meaningfulness of what little achievement information there is. Yet,
somehow parents interested in sending their children to these schools and services
both compete to get in and develop clear opinions of how these programs rank relative to one another.

While this is true, just because there is a demand-driven market does not mean
that services will be well-matched or well-delivered. In many ways, allowing schools
and parents choice in the education market without simultaneously ensuring that
better information is available to inform those choices risks creating a market similar
to that which exists today in health care. Right now, it is exceedingly hard for patients to
tell whether or not their doctor is particularly good or bad. Instead, patients tend to
focus on their doctor's interpersonal skills and subjective impressions of the doctor's
reaction to individual medical events. Although there are some sites (such as Angie's
List) that allow consumers to rate their doctors, it is unclear how such ratings compare to the underlying efficacy of those rated. In addition, as health-care consumers,
we are all bombarded with advertisements from pharmaceutical companies looking
to push their products for a variety of sometimes vague conditions. Unless one is
a medical professional, it is a challenge to understand the exact pros and cons of
one treatment versus another. Thus, while there is choice and a focus on individual
needs in health care, it is not at all clear that the system is optimized for either cost-
efficiency or health outcomes.

In a fully decoupled educational system, one with multiple choices of educational
services being made by parents, teachers, and students to meet individual needs, the
situation could well be worse. In health care, at least there is a strong, well-regulated set

of practices around determining the efficacy of particular treatments and of drugs. Most of the treatments available in education, however, have not gone through such rigorous, scientific review. Thus, without solving the above challenges, demand-driven education systems would be less like the health-care market in 2009 than the health care market in 1909.

WHOSE DEMAND FOR WHAT? THE SCOPE OF THE PROBLEM

The simplest vision of demand-driven education reform is that of a system in which families are allowed to select a student's school from a range of providers. For such an option to work well, families would need timely access to information about the schools available, how their instructional philosophies differ, how other aspects of the schools differ (e.g., the strength of the athletic program), and, ideally, how the outcomes of the schools differ. In this vision, the end-consumer and purchaser are the same (the student and his family) and the decision is unitary—which school does Johnny go to?

However, this volume rightly encourages us to consider that this approach is far too simple for best matching student instructional and developmental needs to educational offerings. First, it ignores the fact that many other layers of the system also can drive demand for educational goods and services, whether or not school choice is implemented. Schools could be (and often are) given the freedom to select the most appropriate professional development approach for their teachers. Districts could outsource more of their business operations. Thus, we should consider not only the information parents need but also what information is required in order for all levels of the system to become better purchasers of the goods and services they need to serve their students. Just as in the purchasing of health insurance for employees by employers, the purchaser is not necessarily identical with the end-consumer.

Second, in a truly demand-driven world, schooling could come to be seen as a network of services rather than a single activity. It is easy to see how this could be the case for schools themselves. Using charter schools as an example, the recruitment of many new teachers is already being outsourced to organizations such as Teach for America and The New Teacher Project; the training of teachers to new providers such as Teacher U; back-office operations to ExED; food services to Aramark; and so forth. Essentially, schools are becoming less discrete individual institutions and more bundles of different decisions about who will provide what services to the students and staff.

But this still assumes that a family needs to acquire all of its education for a child from one primary source: a school. We could imagine a world in which schools as aggregators of educational services are an option, but not the only option. Rather than thinking about choosing schools as packages, why not think about education for the individual student as a collection of choices? For instance, maybe I would like my daughter to get her writing instruction from the local high school and her physics instruction from the community college and to train with a private fencing club for her physical fitness. Needless to say, decoupling the various parts of schooling from one another would require not only that consumers have access to vastly more information than is currently available, but, as importantly, it would also require information technology (IT) systems capable of organizing data to enable the monitoring of student progress and the integration of information coming in from many different sources.

Before exploring the challenges of meeting the data needs of a more decoupled system, it is useful to highlight the key purchasing and decision-making levels that could exist in such a system and the types of demand they could generate: families and students; teachers and networks of teachers; schools; districts and school networks; and state and federal agencies.

Families and students are the most commonly thought-of consumers in the system. Whether we think of them as simply choosing schools or as assembling an educational program out of a more granulated set of offerings, their needs are critical to understanding what kind of information systems are needed.

Teachers and networks of teachers will also be key generators of demand in a world focused on individualized education programs. They will have both student- and self-focused needs. In trying to meet the individual needs of their students, they will want detailed, yet interpretable information about their students' needs; access to a wide range of materials, lesson plans, and strategies; and, as importantly, a means to navigate the plethora of options available to match offerings to students. Teachers will also have individual educational demands for themselves that are unlikely to be met by "one-size-fits-all" professional development programs being pushed down from districts or the state.

Schools themselves, whether or not they are subject to parental choice, will also play a critical role in demand-driven reforms. Currently, most public, noncharter schools must take whatever professional development, curriculum, and maintenance services their district has to offer, irrespective of whether the school's faculty actually have the needs the district professional development targets, whether the district curriculum is a good fit with the school's student population, or whether a local contractor could paint the school at a much lower rate.

One could imagine, however, districts simply being one service provider among many for district schools. An early and intriguing example of this approach has been undertaken by the New York City Department of Education. In New York City, each public school chooses its own school support organization (SSO). These SSOs provide support to school principals and staff, professional development, mentoring, curriculum development, and help with academic compliance issues. While the New York City DOE offers its own SSOs, it also allows schools to choose from a number of third-party support providers. Thus, the city has essentially created its own instructional support market for its schools.

District and school networks are, along with schools, the traditional purchasers of textbooks, food, and an array of educational goods and services. In addition, numerous districts outsource various parts of their operations (e.g., transportation, food services, and others). Very few districts, however, fully outsource core education functions such as the recruitment, placement, and management of teachers; provision of professional development and school support; and curriculum development. One could imagine much more activity here, with districts leveraging The New Teacher Project or a similar organization not only to recruit but also to place, manage, and evaluate teachers.

State and federal agencies currently serve as shapers of demand by regulating what textbooks districts and schools may purchase, how school monies may be spent, what accountability targets schools and districts have, and how students will be assessed for state accountability purposes. For demand-driven, individualized education programs to take off, states will likely need to become *less* important to the market for inputs. No longer will textbook publishers need to focus primarily on what they can push through the state selection processes of California, Florida, and Texas. Instead, they will need to focus their marketing efforts on newly "freed" teachers and students.

Allowing any of these levels of the system to generate and exercise more choice based on their identified needs will require radical upgrading of the capacities of the current command and control information systems that are designed to capture and provide simple administrative data in systems where all students are presumed to need the same basic educational services.

DATA CHALLENGES TO UNBUNDLING EDUCATION

Challenge 1: Limited Available Data on School Effectiveness

The first challenge to the development of robust demand-side school reform is getting useful data into the hands of key consumers and purchasers—families, teachers, and schools.

Currently the types of data available to families about public schools are extremely primitive. Parents can find basic demographic and test score data on potential schools for their children either through the state or nonprofit Web sites such as SchoolMatters.com or GreatSchools.org. In addition, trends in test scores tend to be easily available to parents. Some state report cards also include general information on teachers, such as how many are "highly qualified," and a grab bag of other items, such as disciplinary incidents. Finally, thanks to the impetus of No Child Left Behind (NCLB), test scores are often broken down by ethnicity and socioeconomic status, though not both at the same time.

This information is almost wholly inadequate for judging the quality of a school. First and foremost, the status data reported by schools are not very helpful. One generally cannot tell whether the percent of students proficient on state tests is the result of the school or the performance levels of the students when they entered the school. While some states, such as California, have alternate measures of school performance that adjust for basic student demographics, this is still not sufficient. There is more variation in performance within demographic groups than between them. Test trend data do not help either, as the trends could be caused either by changes in population mix or events at feeder schools.

At a minimum, parents should be able to tell whether and how much schools impact the academic growth of their students relative to other schools. In other words, the typical student growth or a school's value-added should be available to parents. For large schools, this information would be even more useful if broken down by ethnicity, grade, and socioeconomic status. Encouragingly, a number of states (e.g., North Carolina, Colorado, Massachusetts) have begun to provide publicly basic student growth information.

While better information about school impacts on student achievement is helpful, this information is only a small part of what the educated consumer in a demand-driven system would want. Presumably, parents would want to know who the most effective teachers are, how less-effective teachers are supported by the school, the quality of offerings outside of the tested grades and subjects, and, perhaps most importantly, the long-term trajectory of students at this school. This type of information would be particularly needed in a decoupled system where students and parents assemble their educational package based on individual needs as opposed to preassembled whole-school requirements.

In high schools, the data challenge grows. Parents of potential students would want to know Advanced Placement (AP) passing rates, controlling for students' incoming academic performance. They would also want to know how many students go to college, where, and whether they ultimately graduate. While sometimes AP passing rates are reported (though not controlling for either the percentage of students taking the test or students' incoming academic achievement levels), none of the other data above are collected or reported for public schools in a systematic way.

Finally, before choosing educational services, parents might want to know how other parents feel about the school. While it is extremely simple to find both overall ratings and detailed user commentary on books, music, and electronics on Amazon. com, such robust feedback communities do not exist at scale in education.

Challenge 2: Poor Information on Third-Party Providers and Products

When we turn from parents selecting schools as aggregators of services to schools (or parents) selecting individual educational programs and services to meet student needs, the data situation is even worse.[1] Virtually all providers are able to produce some evaluation that purports to show how their services have a positive impact. Unfortunately, many or most of these evaluations do not provide either reliable or useful data.

That this is so should not be surprising. First, much of this evaluation work is executed by the providers themselves—an obvious conflict of interest. In these situations, the analyst, either consciously or unconsciously, may search especially hard for positive news while glossing over or explaining away any negative results. Second, even external evaluations performed for a provider can have serious challenges. Typically, the provider pays for the evaluation themselves, which creates an incentive for the evaluator who wants continued employment not to find negative results. This structure is not so different from the current way bond issuers pay ratings agencies or from the relationship between auditors and those they were auditing in pre-Enron days.

Choosing external evaluators also creates a challenge for providers. Generally, we would not expect providers themselves to be expert in evaluation. However, there are hundreds of small evaluation firms out there of widely varying quality and competence. In selecting the right evaluator, providers, unfortunately, have to judge on technical issues that they do not understand, resulting in many poor choices driven by sales or fit rather than rigor. While one could get around this by only utilizing brand-name evaluation firms such as Mathematica, MDRC, or RAND, small providers will not have anywhere near the resources needed to hire such powerhouses.

Finally, even if bias and quality issues are overcome, it is often hard or impossible for third-party providers to get the information they need to be able to determine impact. Impact evaluations require carefully constructed comparison groups that did not receive the treatment in order to distinguish between changes caused by the program and those that would have occurred anyway. To be confident a program is working, one generally needs individual student- or teacher-level data to avoid errors of composition. Unfortunately, third-party providers are often denied access by education agencies to detailed data on those who did not participate in their program, and sometimes they are denied critical data (such as prior performance) even on those who did participate. As a result, these programs really have no way to determine whether they are effective or not—other than simply asking their participants. This is not the best methodology.

The outcome in the education market is that purchasers or consumers of educational services are faced with a barrage of unsubstantiated claims mixed in with some claims backed by rigorous research. Unless the consumers happen to be experts in evaluation, all of this information (reliable and unreliable) will be of limited utility because they cannot differentiate between the two categories.

But this paints too rosy a picture. Since providers typically perform their own evaluations using their own outcome measures, results from evaluations coming out of two different providers are unlikely to be comparable. For instance, one provider of a math tutoring program may look at student improvement on an assessment tightly connected to what is tutored—say, an assessment focused on understanding and manipulating fractions—while another provider may report results against a broader assessment, such as the yearly state assessment. Even if both tutoring offerings had exactly the same effectiveness on a given topic, we would expect far more growth on the first assessment than the second. As a result, the two claims are noncomparable and essentially useless for making intelligent choices.

Challenge 3: Existing Data Does Not Illuminate Academic Needs and Family Preferences

The theory behind a student needs–driven approach to reform is that those who supply educational goods and services can tailor and target their educational services to schools, teachers, and students and thus better meet their needs than the current command and control systems. Ideally, some form of market discipline will force suppliers to identify and segment that market to provide consumers the specialized services they require.

As Kim Smith and Julie Peterson note in chapter 1 in this volume, for this to work well, potential suppliers need to be able to identify just what the needs of students and schools are and how they differ. In other words, in order to craft products and services that are responsive to the customer, suppliers need to understand and segment the market that they face.

Leaving aside the logistical and legal difficulties of third-party providers capturing or using this data, the data that could be used to segment students largely do not exist. School districts themselves, the entities best positioned to do this, often capture in their IT systems only crude data on students: enrollment, attendance, grades, demographics, and test scores. The list of what is generally not captured is long and somewhat disheartening. Some districts capture only the relatively blunt measures found in state tests but do not capture more sophisticated diagnostic test results that would allow one to know not only that Johnny can't read but why Johnny can't read (e.g., a lack of phonemic awareness, a lack of sufficient vocabulary, trouble with fluency). Parental (and student) satisfaction with schools and their concerns are also infrequently captured. Districts that do survey parents often have appallingly low response rates to the surveys, making any conclusions based on them unreliable.

In a demand-driven system, districts will often find themselves in competition with third-party suppliers. As a result, we might look to states or other potentially neutral oversight agencies to provide competitors the appropriate data. Unfortunately, states usually capture far less data than districts, with the likely result that student, teacher, and parent needs simply cannot be identified from the current data. Substantial new data collection and analysis efforts are needed to segment and identify the needs of students and their families. School systems are unlikely to do this on their own.

A related challenge for suppliers, one familiar to anyone who has implemented interventions in a large district, is that very few district data systems accurately capture the interventions (individualized or not) *already under way* with students and teachers. In other words, what types of professional development teachers are already receiving and what specific strategies have already been used with specific students are rarely known at a level above the individual school. Very few districts track professional development centrally above the level of credits received to increase teacher salaries. Likewise, many student information systems (SIS) do not track student pull-outs, afterschool programs, and so forth. In fact, many SIS systems capture only the homeroom teacher in elementary school. Since elementary school teachers often either team-teach or specialize in math or reading, this means that many districts do not even know who is teaching a given child a particular subject. This critical lack of data has two detrimental effects on the supplier market.

First, third-party providers may be hesitant to enter the market at scale as they have no idea what are actually the *unmet* needs within districts and schools. Indeed, the massive number of microscopic nonprofits in education may at least partially be the result of the fact that these organizations can focus entirely on one or a few schools and invest the time to know what the unmet site needs are. While this ability to understand context and needs at the micro level has some positive aspects, it does inhibit the development of scale competitors for supplying educational services. In addition, it inhibits the spread of successful innovations. Innovations are either copied, often poorly and without quality control from other locations, like the spread of small learning communities, or are rediscovered at each site. It is hard for best practice providers to gain scale.

A second, more important, issue that arises from the lack of data is that it is exceedingly hard, given the data systems in place, for individuals, schools, districts, and states to measure for themselves the efficacy of the services they are purchasing. It is simply impossible to know if you are getting a good value from Wise Action Professional Development, Inc., if you do not know who received the training, when, and why. Even if one provider is outperforming another in terms of raising student achievement, parents, the district, or the state will never know.

In many ways this situation is similar to the health-care landscape before John Wennberg and others began to explore geographic differences in practice and treatment. Prior to the 1970s, it was assumed that the underlying health of local populations drove treatment and, with treatment, the cost of health care. However, once health policy researchers began to look at the prevalence of treatments and their relation to the population's underlying health issues, massive variations in medical treatments of the same conditions began to appear, apparently largely driven by local medical culture. While these variations in care still persist (and are hotly debated), at least they are known. In the field of K–12 education, we do not even have the data to show who receives what treatment.

Challenge 4: Existing Data Are Decentralized, Captured by Specific Providers, or Unavailable

The fourth challenge to demand-driven education reform is that even when good data on student and school needs do exist, the information is often not available to be accessed by service providers outside of the district. Larry Berger and David Stevenson have aptly noted the quite decentralized demand that exists in the education sector—14,000 school districts, each of which needs to be sold independently.[2] Part of a good sales presentation is showing how one's product or service can match the needs of the customer district. However, given the paucity of publicly available data on students and schools, many potential suppliers will need access to nonpublic data to make their case. This puts an immense information burden on the supplier. School districts are rightly very hesitant to share protected, private data with third-party vendors. If we think of suppliers not selling to districts but rather to schools, teachers, and students individually, the data requirements go up dramatically.

There is, however, one class of supplier that has a clear advantage in this system. Companies that design, administer, and score assessments should, over time, build incredibly powerful and potentially longitudinal datasets that allow detailed insights into emerging student needs, trends, and challenges. Mining this wealth of data should allow companies such as the Educational Testing Service (ETS), Pearson, Houghton Mifflin Harcourt, and others to target products and services particularly well and have the data to back it up. Who better than Pearson to sell item banks for benchmark assessments leading to end-of-course tests that they themselves designed and score?

Given the immense competitive advantage that testing companies have, it is unlikely that they would be willing to share this data with potential competitors even if they could ensure appropriate privacy and confidentiality. To use Berger and Stevenson's coinage, "Big-Edu" has a clear and, thanks to state testing regimes, mandated information advantage over attackers trying to enter the market.

Finally, the Family and Educational Rights and Privacy Act (FERPA), as well as numerous state laws, can prevent entrepreneurs from gaining access to the data they need to adequately understand and meet demand. While it is obvious that these privacy protections are needed, they raise the challenge bar for entrepreneurs. Moreover, it is often the case that entities inside the walls of privacy are competing with attackers from outside. Districts—no less than testing companies—may be less than eager to share critical information about their student body with charter schools or third-party providers that threaten to drain students and revenue.[3]

Challenge 5: Data Collection Methods Are Not Compatible with a Decoupled System

A final challenge demand-driven school reform faces is the collection and administration of basic tracking, compliance, and achievement data. In the current system, state education agencies (SEAs) typically depend on districts and charter schools (local education agencies [LEAs]) to collect, aggregate, and report required administrative data to the state. The state in turn provides some data back to the LEAs (e.g., test results) and reports data to the federal government. The LEAs are responsible for tracking student progress, ensuring that students receive appropriate services, and delivering the vast bulk of the child's educational experience. Under such a system, schools (with district support) act as unified deliverers of services to students and, as a result, generate, collect, and hold the majority of the administrative data required by most students. However, who collects the data and how they are assembled would need to change dramatically in a fully decoupled world.

Consider three high school students in a fully decoupled system. Student A is happy with her local high school, appreciates the community it provides, and takes advantage of the school for its offerings across all subjects. Student B is also basically happy with the local school; however, he has a particular fascination with biology and is more advanced in science than many of the students in his grade. As a result, he and his parents decide that an introductory course in biology at the local university would be more appropriate to his needs. Thus, he does not take any science at the high school but goes three days a week to the university to take Biology 101. The family of Student C takes a more radical approach to her education, looking for best-in-class offerings in each subject. As a result, Student C goes to a local and highly respected writing center for her language arts and takes an online biology course offered by a company such as K12 Inc. instead of the courses offered at her school. Since Student C is very self-disciplined, this cafeteria approach allows her to accelerate her learning and assemble a learning plan that suits her needs.

The administrative data implications of these hypothetical students' choices are substantial (and depicted in figure 9.1). Schools and districts—the traditional collectors and aggregators of student enrollment, transcript, progress, and program participation data—may no longer be able to serve this role effectively, especially if they are merely one competitive offering among many. The reason that they performed this

FIGURE 9.1
Data requirements in fully decoupled system

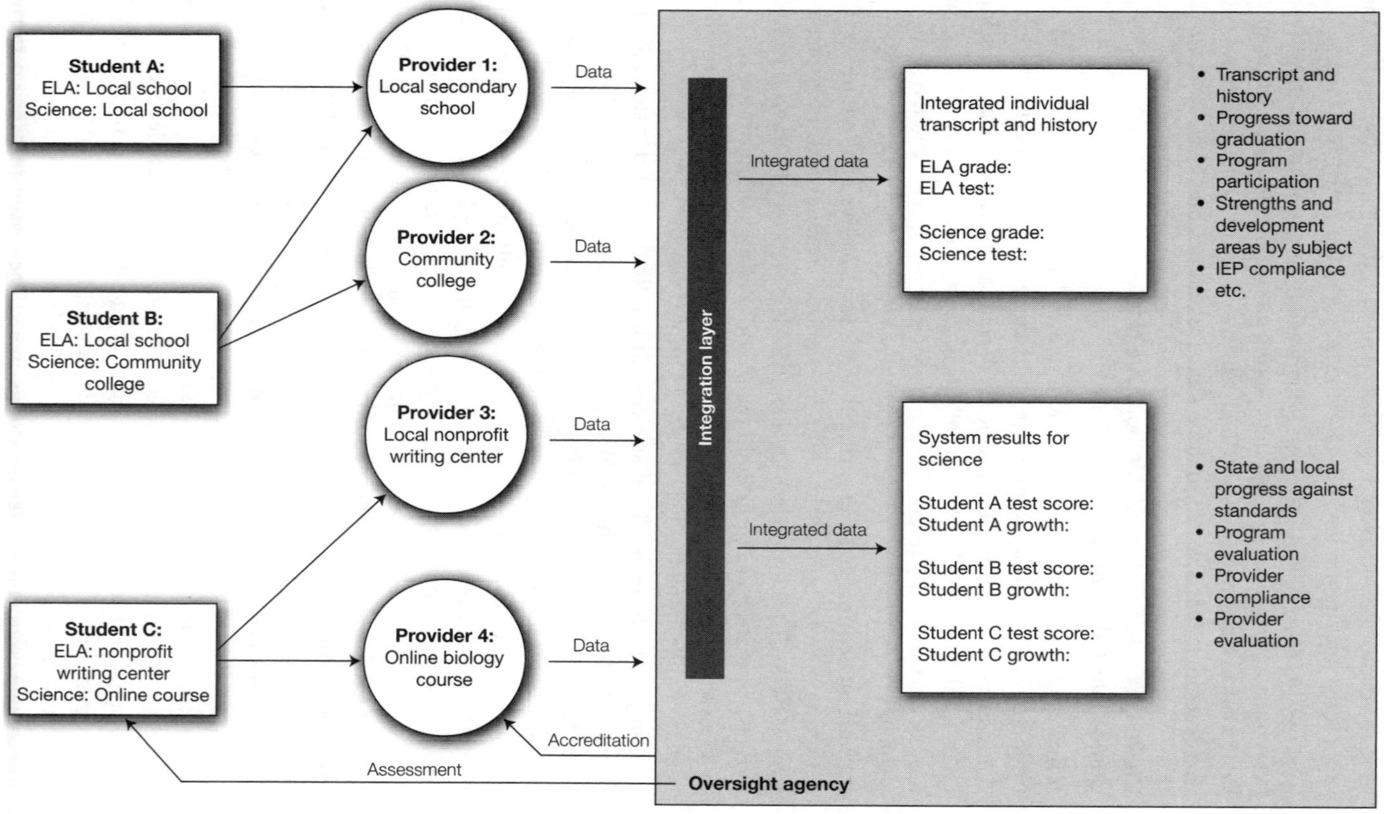

Student A:
ELA: Local school
Science: Local school

Student B:
ELA: Local school
Science: Community college

Student C:
ELA: nonprofit writing center
Science: Online course

Provider 1:
Local secondary school

Provider 2:
Community college

Provider 3:
Local nonprofit writing center

Provider 4:
Online biology course

Data

Accreditation

Assessment

Oversight agency

Integration layer

Integrated data

Integrated data

Integrated individual transcript and history

ELA grade:
ELA test:

Science grade:
Science test:

System results for science

Student A test score:
Student A growth:

Student B test score:
Student B growth:

Student C test score:
Student C growth:

- Transcript and history
- Progress toward graduation
- Program participation
- Strengths and development areas by subject
- IEP compliance
- etc.

- State and local progress against standards
- Program evaluation
- Provider compliance
- Provider evaluation

role in the first place is that they did in fact aggregate and provide the vast majority of educational services. However, in our example, this is no longer the case. Other agencies (most likely the state) may be more adept at integrating the data and providing oversight for student and system outcomes.

To do so, however, schools and districts will need to solve the following data challenges:

Many more providers would need to be connected to student data systems. Information about an individual student's performance now has the potential to come from many sources, not just a single school district.

The system providing oversight of student progress would now need to integrate multiple data sources to produce a single student record. In our example, Student C might have as many as five or six different providers, requiring data from all to be combined in order to determine her progress toward graduation.

If the oversight agency wants to do any quality control or monitoring of providers, it would need to integrate student outcomes by subject and provider.

A neutral oversight agency would likely need to generate and collect data in new ways. Most obviously, the delivery of assessments, which have traditionally been pushed out to schools to handle, might need to be rethought. Provider willingness and security issues would prevent all the new providers of educational services from becoming state testing agencies. (Indeed, this would be impossible for many online providers.) Instead, the oversight agency itself may need to develop its own testing centers to deal with nontraditional providers.

There are substantial data requirements around the monitoring, accreditation, and reimbursement of all the new providers. If there is to be quality control, the state would need procedures to accredit multiple providers and to ensure that parents and their children know who is a legitimate provider and who is not. In addition, reimbursements become more complicated in a demand-driven system. Rather than providing a per-student level of funding to a single provider, one could imagine individual student accounts (the size of which would be driven by a student need formula) that are distributed to multiple providers according to the type and amount of services provided. In chapter 8 in this volume, Burck Smith describes more fully what the end-user experience of such a system might be. To implement this system would likely require fairly dramatic changes in the financial and staffing systems of all the impacted districts in the state.

From a technology perspective, none of this is impossible, or even difficult, to imagine. Consumer-driven manufacturers commonly integrate their supply chain's systems with their own. That said, this would require a fairly radical rethinking of data systems in most states. In fact, to really decouple education from schools and districts, the states themselves would need to provide fully functional SIS systems that could integrate across multiple providers, and providers would need to embrace common data transfer standards aggressively. This would require significant reworking of the IT systems at both the state and local level and significant funding for the changeover.

But just because a system can be imagined does not mean that it can be built or sustained. The first, and perhaps the most significant, challenge here is the organizational one: states, districts, and schools fundamentally rethinking their role in the larger education delivery system. States would have to give up dictating inputs and take on the demands of building the IT structure to allow differentiation of delivery and monitoring of individual student choices. Districts, schools, parents, and students would get unprecedented levels of choice and flexibility but in turn would have to participate in more rigorous, standardized, and thorough data collection than ever before. The creation of an adequate data system is not just the installation of a sophisticated suite of computer programs; a well-implemented system has to tackle the problem of making sure accurate and reliable data is entered on a consistent basis and is sustained over time. This means building a system of incentives, consequences, and checks to ensure that data are collected and validated consistently for all students and all services and all providers.

Finally, note that even if we do not move to a system of individual, decoupled choice, allowing choice at other levels of the system creates similar, if less daunting, difficulties. Presumably, if schools can choose their own support providers, those support providers will need relatively seamless access into district data and management systems. The boundaries of who is inside and who is outside the school district begin to blur.

WHAT CAN BE DONE (AND WHAT IS BEING DONE)?

This argument suggests that there are some very significant data and information challenges that need to be solved for a truly demand-driven system based on student needs to be practical or desirable. Luckily, a number of these challenges are beginning to be solved in isolated pockets within education. Others are solvable but require political will and investment to overcome.

Collect Better Data on Students and Teachers and Use It

First and foremost, to have a system truly driven by student and teacher need, the amount of data typically collected on student performance and challenges will need to grow exponentially. At a minimum, just for students, the system should be collecting longitudinally:

- Student summative assessment results
- Benchmark and formative assessment results (finely grained enough to determine specific learning needs)
- Diagnostic test results
- Courses taken, grade, and teachers' information for the above
- Additional interventions and pullouts, the responses to intervention
- Afterschool program participation
- Student learning preferences
- Parental preferences and information about frequency and type of contact

This information on students is well beyond what most districts (not to mention states) collect and store on anyone who is not a special education student with an individual education plan (IEP). With teachers, the situation is somewhat worse, with very few districts able to track what an individual teacher's strengths and weaknesses are.

However, a few providers and districts are experimenting aggressively with the power of collecting and leveraging data to actively meet their population's needs. The New York City Department of Education has two important data programs that can serve as exemplars. The first, Achievement Reporting and Innovation System (ARIS), is a data warehouse that collects and links detailed student achievement, performance, and progress data from a variety of sources and provides tools to teachers and, importantly, now to parents to track student progress and analyze data. The level of detail available in ARIS is probably the minimum needed to realistically understand and track student needs.

The second program, New York City's experimental School of One, is an excellent example of taking data to the next level to meet student needs. Currently being piloted in math, this program gives students a diagnostic test at the beginning of the term to determine what they know and do not know relative to a learning progression mapped to state standards. Using this information, the computer generates a "playlist" of standards that need to be mastered for each student. Students are then dealt up lessons and accompanying assessments that teach to these standards in sequence. What form these lessons take (online, small group, individual tutor, virtual tutor, or other options) is determined by a survey taken by the student to determine his or her learning style. The speed with which the student progresses through the material is determined by the student's mastery of the material, not by an externally set pacing plan.[4] The result of this, at least in theory, is a completely individualized learning plan built entirely around individual students' needs.[5]

Thus, there *are* systems that do collect the type of data needed to build a system around demand. One could easily imagine a similar human capital system that identified teachers' development needs and provided a list of options for teachers to improve their skills relative to these development needs. However, these systems are expensive and still in their infancy.

In addition, many districts and charter schools have also begun to use numerous formative assessments and assessments that provide real-time feedback (such as those provided by Wireless Generation) to better understand their students' learning needs. While not at the level of School of One, there is a welcome focus on identifying more about actual student learning and needs. However, it is notable that most of these solutions (including those in New York City) are being built by integrated, not decoupled, systems. The real challenge will be collecting this information so that it is not captured only by districts and schools but is also usable by families and alternative providers.

Ensure That Neutral Third Parties Provide Evaluative Data on Approved Provider Offerings

One experiment with demand-side reform that has been taking place over the last decade has been the provision of supplemental educational services (SES) under NCLB. Families are entitled to enroll their children in SES if their children attend a school that has not made adequate yearly progress for more than one year. These tutoring services are intended to improve the learning and academic outcomes of the students who choose to enroll in them. Students are allowed to choose any provider from a state-approved list, and the fees are paid from the sending district's Title 1 funds. Districts are required to make students aware of their options under this NCLB provision.

One might assume that states would embrace this, run a rigorous selection process for third-party providers, and, most importantly, monitor how students who enroll with various providers do relative to those who do not. This has not been the case. Very few states provide any effectiveness information on providers. In Massachusetts, for instance, parents can access information on providers' evidence of effectiveness, but that evidence is simply whatever the provider chooses to highlight. One provider notes that students' "poems showed an overall improvement in creativity/ideas, voice, and the use of poetic devices over a six-month period,"[6] while another provider asserts that "four out of five of our students improved their scores by more than 10% [on what scale or measure?] from pretest to posttest [on which test?], and half of our students improved by more than 25%."[7] This is not terribly useful information. This state of affairs is disappointing, as most states are well-situated to track which students receive what services and then to compare their academic growth to those in other services or to those who did not take advantage of these services.

A welcome exception to this abandonment of the consumer can be found in the Chicago Public Schools (CPS), which leveraged its student data to compare provider impacts using relatively sophisticated multilevel modeling techniques. It then took the next step and actually put the results for each provider in terms of Illinois Standards Achievement Test gains in the documentation of provider options distributed to parents.[8] While the meaning of the results is not made terribly clear in the documentation, at least some relevant data are being provided. The only challenge is that CPS is itself an SES provider—indeed, by far the largest provider to CPS students—and thus may not be the best organization to be supplying this information.

As demand-driven reforms begin to accumulate, states need to step beyond their traditional compliance role and begin to play a role as neutral and trusted providers of high-quality evaluative information to consumers.

Encourage the Creation of Better Forums to Allow Consumers to Connect to Suppliers and to One Another

Online technologies and the collaboration tools developed as part of Web 2.0 have transformed the amount of information available to consumers. One can see what others think of any given album, book, or camcorder instantly on Amazon.com; market estimates of a house on Zillow.com; and reviews of professional and trade services on Angie's List. None of this information is infallible; online reviews tend to be biased upward, Zillow's read of the market is an estimate at best, and interpersonal relationships between consumers and professionals can distort what does and does not get posted on Angie's List. Nevertheless, all of these sources provide helpful information and feedback both to potential purchasers and to producers that was not available before.[9]

Education does have a number of sites that attempt to provide this type of consumer information to parents. SchoolMatters.com, GreatSchools.org, and Education. com, for instance, all provide school information, the ability to compare school stats to one another, and customer reviews of schools. However, these sites, while better than nothing, do not have the consumer usage or review and discussion activity one might expect. Often schools have a few very general reviews, some of which are either completely information-free ("I like this school") or clearly written by children who are mad at their teachers. The level of discourse around Lady Gaga's latest offering on iTunes is far higher than the review discussions around schools.

There are a number of reasons for this anemic discussion around school ratings. First, because the discussion is around whole schools and not finer-grained school offerings, there may be little beyond banalities to say. Second, the choice of school is not one that is made frequently, thus there is nothing to draw in repeat users over time. Third, many parents do not have any comparison points: if their kids all go to one school, how are they to know what it is like in other schools and whether their school rates highly relative to these other schools? Finally, the data on schools that most states provide and that is reproduced on these sites are not really that useful. Thus, there is not a particularly strong draw over time to the sites in the first place.

Demand-driven education has the potential to change this. Where we do find lots of user activity and collaboration is in sites that serve individual schools and on sites that help students make a real choice. While there are many issues with both the reviews and reviewers, RateMyProfessor.com does provide active and ongoing feedback to college-goers about their potential instructor choices. Teacher networking and collaboration sites show early promise as well. For instance, BetterLesson is creating a searchable and structured platform for teachers to share and rate lesson plans and content, substantially easing their ability to find and use the information they need with at least some assurance of its quality.

If, and as, states take on the role of becoming neutral evaluators of schools, programs, and services, they should either establish their own easy-to-navigate consumer sites, with user feedback and discussion groups, or (more likely) work with one or more third-party community providers to get their evaluation data onto sites that can then host much richer user discussions than are currently available.

Work to Develop Third-Party Market Researchers and Allow Them Access to Cleaned Data Sets for Analysis of Student Needs

One important tool used by companies considering entering new product spaces are reports by market researchers. In the IT industry, the Gartner Group, Forrester Research, and IDC, among others, provide market size estimates, trends, and guideposts for companies in the space. While there is some activity in the education sector by companies such as Market Data Retrieval and Simba Information, most of the reports produced are on technology purchases, textbooks, and materials—not on service needs. Given the almost completely nascent status of this market and the lack of good data discussed above, there is little reason to expect more.

However, if we want suppliers to enter this market and not provide one-size-fits-all solutions, they will need to gain some insight into the various segments of the market and their likely size. One solution here could be to set up and fund third-party market researchers who focus on student educational needs and services that could be provided. To be effective, these researchers would need access to detailed, individual, student-level data and thus would need to work in partnership with states and districts. Setting up such data-privileged relationships with governmental agencies will not be easy, but states and districts themselves simply do not have the capacity to produce this type of analysis. Startup funding itself may be difficult to obtain, and foundations may need to provide the initial proof-of-concept support. If a market for providers does develop, then those providers should be able to support the market research organization themselves.

Transform the Role of the States to Be the Providers of Full SIS Systems and to Have More Responsibility for Assessment Administration

Finally, if we are truly interested in decoupling education from single school buildings, states will need to dramatically transform the type of support and services they provide. As discussed above, states will essentially need to become SIS providers, data integrators, and testing coordinators for all students inside their borders, unless they want to dramatically loosen regulations around graduation requirements, testing requirements, and comparability between student programs.[10] For most states, this is a very new level of IT commitment and overall responsibility, one that could easily challenge their capabilities. However, the current regime in which districts each implement their own SIS systems results in a great deal of variation across districts in terms of system capacity and data quality. It is also somewhat expensive, since hundreds or thousands of redundant implementations are taking place. The state becoming a provider of SIS services might be more efficient whether or not education becomes truly individualized or demand-driven.

CONCLUSION

The data challenges to discovering needs and unleashing demand are significant. Better data on students need to be captured and used in more proactive ways (and by more organizations), and states need to take on new and uncomfortable roles to allow data on student needs to flow efficiently and to make true student choice a possibility.

That said, while the needed IT systems are not in wide use now in the education sector, they do not require particularly cutting-edge technology. What they do require is funding and significant political will—a will of major players (e.g., districts) to act against their own short-term self-interest to provide their potential competitors information and access to students. To better understand the likelihood of the data challenges being solved, we need to ask several questions:

1. Do (or could) state education agencies have the operational capacity to take over the management and collection of individual student data on a real-time basis, a job traditionally performed by schools and districts?
2. Do states and state education agencies have the political capacity to implement expensive, new IT solutions that fundamentally undermine districts and schools

as the owners of data (and, by extension, as "owners" of students)? Or, are state education agencies too dependent on district cooperation and the legislators who represent districts for this to be possible?

3. Are consumers ready to be responsible for assembling individual education programs, and, if so, which consumers (parents, teachers, students)? How can such demand-driven education be shaped so that it does not dramatically favor students with sophisticated parents and teachers who can best leverage the new information and choices available?

10

Will Policy Let Demand Drive Change?

Curtis Johnson and Ted Kolderie

SINCE ABOUT 1980, policy has both stimulated and responded to demand mainly by expanding parent and student choice of school. This was useful, but limited.

This approach held constant most of the givens of traditional school. Indeed, for some in the supply-oriented movement, the point of choice was less to change the form of school than to escape the confines of the district and its politics. And in recent years the concept of school has been further constricted by a program of standards and accountability that pressed for the mastery of select academic skills and subject matter content and that defined achievement mainly in quantitative terms using scores on tests.

The effect was to make it increasingly difficult for teachers, schools, and especially the innovatively inclined to develop and test different forms of school and different approaches to learning. In effect, policy constrained the demand for change.

So it is surely now time for policy to break outside traditional school, to be open to forms of school that depart from the conventional bureaucratic organization; that abandon the dominant age-graded, course-and-class approach to learning; and that break with the conventional roles of adults and students as instructors and instructed. New concepts of school, of learning, and of achievement will begin to expand and drive the demand for change.

There is latent demand for doing school differently. This can be seen in the cries from schools whose organization—whose concept of achievement and whose departure from the traditional givens of what students should know and be able to do in this twenty-first century—makes them appear illegitimate in the eyes of conventional education policy and threatens, in fact, their continued existence.

The need is for policy, in the interest of getting the gains so obviously overdue, to open wide the definition of *school* and let the demand for change, reform, and innovation come through.

SHIFTING POLICY ATTENTION TO DEMAND

Clearly, at least within schools, parents and students cannot choose what is not offered. And the school industry will likely not get by, over time, by offering what is not wanted. Inside those converse realities lie the mysteries of demand.

Policy conferences, if they focus on demand at all, are usually about getting school into different arrangements—perhaps pulled out from under bureaucracy's thumb or liberated from constraining union contracts or given yet another way to link performance to pay. Reform pushes have value, but most remain too far ahead of the core question. What matters fundamentally is a focus on the demand for *learning,* in the fullest sense of the term. If that demand can be assessed, understood, and molded into a driver for change, then the reform question follows naturally. The system will face the pressure to change in order to respond to the demands for learning that are present and growing. The scope for innovation and entrepreneurship will be far wider.

Further, we suggest that broadening the focus to take in the full scope of demand for learning exposes the nation's currently narrow definition of what needs to be learned. The persistent prime target is language and math, with a heavy focus on content mastery as opposed to skills development. Despite the nobility of its intentions, the No Child Left Behind Act (NCLB) has been implemented in a manner that has resulted in school districts deciding to concentrate resources on what is being tested. A pattern of shedding other areas of interest and forms of learning is now discernible. Much of high school curricula increasingly looks susceptible to what NCLB critics call "test prep." Meanwhile, whatever demand there is for learning is absolutely not confined to the narrow goals to which NCLB has been practically reduced. The gap-closing needle on achievement may have moved slightly, but another gap between the nature of demand for learning and what is offered may have widened.

As we write, a majority of states are on record embracing a commitment to common core standards. While common standards might reduce confusion, there is no evidence that they will close the gap between what school does and the demand for learning. And the policies emerging under the flag of the Race to the Top competition seem heavily top-down driven. Committing to standards, to effective teaching, to better data systems, and to forcing changes in failing schools are all laudable goals, but they are largely disconnected from practical strategy and not even associated with whether or how students and their parents might respond.

Any serious examination of demand simply must get beyond what is required for accountability purposes. It also must escape the confines of the school itself. In this rapidly evolving information technology age, young people are connecting with knowledge earlier and faster than any previous generation. They are learning every day, and some significant proportion of what they are seeking and learning is happening outside the framework of formal schooling. Is it not obvious that the demand for learning exceeds the demand for schooling?

In this chapter, we make a modest effort to describe the wider world of learning it is now possible to observe. We suggest how customers for learning might be better understood. We point to signs of a nascent shift in what teachers might demand and to how policy makers can use demand to design a system that accommodates the way young people learn and thereby stimulate the supply of schools aligned with their needs. If policy welcomes entrepreneurial, innovative designs for learning, demand can be a constant driver for improvement.

MOST LEARNING IS OUTSIDE SCHOOL

Consider first the raw economics. If *learning* were a discrete industry, it would log in at some $2 trillion (some claim a much higher figure, but no one really knows) a year. Compare that with the formal K–12 and postsecondary systems, collectively a $700-billion-a-year sector.[1] Data about the gap may be elusive, but clearly there is more to what is spent in search of learning than booked and paid for through the formal system or through the institutions that are public or publicly financed.

Then consider the myriad institutional sources on the supply side. Once they are in the workforce, young people encounter how American business sponsors a huge and growing education sector consciously designed to meet its own demands for developing human talent. Business leaders chronically complain that K–12 educators live in a totally disconnected universe, emphasizing the content of their preferences while ignoring what young adults will need to know and be able to do. Does the typical teacher of English really care about cultivating skill in writing a succinct set of instructions or comprehending a technical manual? Few employers are looking for mastery of the nuances of a Chaucerian tale. For work and life, young adults need to be able to apply mathematics to multiple disciplines, to see the connections to problems that cannot even be anticipated; the call for parsing the Pythagorean Theorem or calculating Cartesian coordinates is confined to a relatively small set of adults in the work world.

The military runs a major education track. Unions and other associations run their own training and apprentice enterprises. Of course, most of this is aimed at people beyond their nominal school years, but clearly these sponsored learning arrangements augment if not actually supplant what is done or not done in earlier years.

Academic eyebrows might rise skeptically, but some claim that organized sports is a response to demand for learning, and that as much is learned there relevant to success in life as in the regular school curriculum. More than a decade ago, ethnographer Herb Childress spent a year observing more than a hundred teens in a northern California high school. In a memorable essay published by *The Kappan*, he described the stark contrast he found between the behavior in school and out of school among so many clearly talented students.[2] More boredom than learning happened at school. Outside school, he was astounded at the energy and focus these same teens put into everything from video games (even then requiring mastery of intricate rules and capacity for rapid decision-making) to jobs to sports. Teachers, he found, wrote off poor performance as teenage lassitude, even moral laxity. Childress suggested that rather than ask why teens are so immature as not to invest as much interest and time in algebra as they do in out-of-school activities, the system should pose the opposite question: what is it about school that makes it unworthy of that kind of devotion?

While he might have picked music or theater to press his point, Childress chose something for which he admits he had absolutely no affection: football. "I hate football," he confessed. But unfolding a list of attributes he found in teens' participation in football, he offered the provocative conclusion that football looked like a superior learning regime, compared with school academics. In football the teens are contributors, not passive recipients. In football the drill is constant improvement—practicing until you get it right or drop from exhaustion (not fifty-minute periods shifting when the bell rings). Football offers a full menu of recognition along with the reality that it is a group undertaking; one player can help the team rise up, and one player can let the team down, compared with the traditional academic focus on individual outcomes. Players largely choose the roles they believe fit them; the better players help those who have less skill or need longer to develop. And players, as well as their coaches, have the opportunity and the imperative to show off their work at regular intervals.

What Childress was onto is hardly limited to sports. Just Google *student competitions* and stand by for the deluge of descriptions and opportunities—from Lego construction to robotic applications to chess. Students do not spend extraordinary time each week on these activities because they have nothing to do, or even for social reasons. There is a lure of learning alive in these activities.

Parents consistently seek learning opportunities for their children outside of school. A Minnesota policy enacted in 1997 offers one window through which to see this push. A tax credit program has allowed lower-income parents to claim tax credits up to 75 percent of tax due for expenses outside of school for supplementary courses, tutoring, books, musical instruments, even computers and software—almost anything except tuition in private schools. The average credit is only $274, but the number of claims has been consistently above fifty thousand.

Even if nothing else was affecting demand for learning, a revolution in information technology has been accelerating over the past decade. Schools are now populated by a whole generation of young people who have never known a world without cellular phones and Internet access. The latter may be yet unevenly accessible, but a condition of universal access can hardly be far off. That young people are learning more, earlier, and faster than any generation in history might have seemed a startling declaration back in 2001 when Marc Prensky's essays called today's generation "digital natives."[3] Surprise would be out of order today, as the differences in today's teens—extended even to neurological evolution—are routinely acknowledged.

In 2006, the MacArthur Foundation launched a five-year research effort aimed at better understanding how digital media affects learning and how these remodeled brains of today's teens are operating. This $50 million MacArthur investment naturally attracted a sizeable number of scholars and organizations with similar interests. One such scholar, Katie Salen, associate professor in design and technology at Parsons The New School for Design, reported on MacArthur-sponsored research for members of the Cleveland Conference at a recent Chicago gathering.[4] She said that more interactive design is increasingly moving into the "space for learning"—not rapidly, though, largely due to misunderstanding and resistance from educators who are not among the digital natives. Today's young people, Salen said, migrate a predictable path that starts with just "hanging out" on the Internet, including some emailing, Instant Messaging, surfing, and checking things out. For many, though, this phase rapidly graduates into a stage when "serious tinkering" starts: downloading software, manipulating or mashing up video, creating new Web sites. For some, energized by a compelling interest in some subject, then comes the real "geeking out." This amounts to a deep dive into the universe where the young person's passion lies, whether that's metaphysics or motorcycles. It's an "old thought" that deep learning of this sort requires the direct assistance—or even the presence—of someone we call a teacher. Critics see this as a solitary journey; more often, Salen said, it is highly interactive and involves complex social contacts.

Since almost all of this activity resides in a universe that is outside school, a potentially permanent separation may evolve between the way young people are driven to learn and what school is. This is what academic analysis considers *discontinuity*, according to Lauren Resnick, who, in her 1987 presidential address to the American Educational Research Association, managed to collapse the problem into one summary paragraph:

> Briefly, schooling focuses on the individual's performance, whereas out-of-school mental work is often socially shared. Schooling aims to foster unaided thought, whereas mental work outside school usually involves cognitive tools. School cultivates symbolic thinking, whereas mental activity outside school engages directly with objects and situations. Finally, schooling aims to teach general skills and knowledge, whereas situation-specific competencies dominate outside.[5]

The swell of learning beyond school, outside the curricular boundaries, invites a predictable riposte: how do we know young people are in fact becoming more literate, more aware of how the world works, better acquainted with numbers and measurement, more appreciative of history, or more savvy about basic science? As other chapters have pointed out, the art and science of assessment badly lags behind the nascent reformulation of what achievement means. Bill Tucker of Education Sector puts the problem plainly and suggests where assessment is headed:

> These new technology-enabled assessments offer the potential to understand more than whether a student answered a test question right or wrong. Using multiple forms of media that allow for both visual and graphical representations, we can present complex, multi-step problems for students to solve, and we can collect detailed information about an individual student's approach to problem solving. This information may allow educators to better comprehend how students arrive at their answers and learn what those pathways reveal about students' grasp of underlying concepts, as well as to discover how they can alter their instruction to help move students forward. Most importantly, the new research projects have produced assessments that reflect what cognitive research tells us about how people learn, providing an opportunity to greatly strengthen the quality of instruction in the nation's classrooms. Other fields, such as military training and medical education, are already using technology-enabled assessment to enhance teaching and learning.[6]

Further, technology, through software with metrics and data, is feeding a small revolution in formative assessment and individualization of learning that helps those with learning difficulties catch up and succeed.

STUDENTS HAVE THEIR SAY

Marie Gentile, who represents the Siemens Westinghouse competition in math, science, and technology, told our Education|Evolving colleague Kim Farris-Berg that young people participate in this competition year after year because it taps their motivation to compete. "They aren't playing computer games," she said, "they're writing them. They're not playing with electronic toys, they're buildings them . . . they do six-hour math marathons because they enjoy it."[7]

Choirs and chess, along with organized sports, are familiar activities living at the margin of school and the outside world. But the universe of competitions and projects that are essentially academic in character and content is not only outside the program perimeter of most schools, they exceed what inside-school typically accomplishes in tapping the intrinsic motivation of young people.[8]

Project Tomorrow does focus groups on what students think about school. Julie Evans, its CEO, told Farris-Berg that too many students "see school as something they have to get through to get somewhere else . . . though most love school as a social place." They see a stronger connection with what they learn outside school in getting them ready for twenty-first-century skills than inside. Evans shakes her head at what she hears at education conferences—that students are not ready for, and do not really want to get into, an online platform for their schoolwork. She says back, "Students are interested in learning; they're not interested in the way you are presenting it."[9]

A freshman from Southwest High School in Minneapolis shared some insights from her out-of-school project with Farris-Berg. She had joined a social justice film-making group, TVbyGIRLS, helping to produce a documentary called *The Greatest Girls* in collaboration with the Minnesota History Center. "I learned tons of history," she said, which made what she studied in class seem "so much more relevant."

While interest in actually listening to students (as customers) seems to be rising, exemplified by the Citizens League SpeakOut project, it remains a small part of the policy picture.[10] What industry with an eye to a better future is not engaging in market research? How will innovators and entrepreneurs design better forms of learning, absent what is always gleaned from market research?

THE DILEMMA FOR SCHOOL DISTRICTS

The states, along with increasing federal participation, set standards for achievement, as well as the arrangements for resources and the regulatory framework. School districts are in the business of responding, complying, trying to do what is expected. But the educators in school districts could set themselves apart by agreeing to get expected results while doing more, going further by arranging school to elicit the maximum discretionary effort from both students and teachers.

Let us assume that there is no stopping the expanding world of learning opportunities showing up outside of traditional arrangements for school. How long will it be before the demand arrives at the doorsteps of boards of education and superintendents of schools for them to devise or adopt a system by which young people can demonstrate what they already know? The calls for certifications of competency have a long history, but voices seem to be growing louder and more impatient. And more sophisticated capacity for such assessments is emerging.[11]

Some scholars, notably psychologist Robert Epstein, take the case further, questioning the very cultural foundation of the Western notion of adolescence. Indeed, this country has less than a century's worth of history of required high school. American schooling finds itself in a century of stark new realities, one burdened with a school arrangement still essentially custodial in nature and still mostly tied to an agrarian calendar.

Epstein argues forcefully that these arrangements sequester teens from adults and infantilize them all while expecting an epiphany of adult attributes at adolescence's end. His data assert that roughly the same proportions of adult attributes are present among teens as are found among age-defined adults.[12]

The GED test has been around a long time but is age-constrained; it cannot be taken until students reach the age of normal graduation. In a sense, it is a protectionist policy for high school enrollments, though this does not appear to diminish the propensity to quit school. What if the GED was made more rigorous but was offered at an earlier age, say sixteen or even earlier?

Further piling on this pressure are the nation's employers, who are, as we already observed, not filtering for facility in quadratic equations as much as looking for people who know how to get information and work with modern media, how to work with others, how to think critically and solve problems (the so-called soft skills, which on reflection are anything but soft), along with a competent command of core subjects. But witness the furor over the embodiment of this notion in the work of the 21st Century Skills project, which, in seeking a balance between subject knowledge and skills needed in work and life, is often portrayed as not tough-minded enough, as just a dodge around rigorous standards.

Government, of course, is the ultimate demander. While the federal government seeks to leverage its 8 percent support of schooling into the demand for higher proficiency in reading and math, states remain the staging ground for the multiple demands by parents, employers, elected representatives, and, to some degree, students themselves. State governments—the legislature and the governor—are essentially the board of directors for the schooling enterprise. They establish the goals, set the regulatory framework, write the rules, and provide, directly or indirectly, the resources. This fabric of state control is often characterized as a web of constraints. But state direction is equally capable of becoming a platform for innovation, for aligning how school is arranged with the demands for learning.

MOTIVATION AS EVIDENCE OF DEMAND

Undeniably, this is a learning generation. But concerns persist over whether young people are learning what they will need to get work they can succeed with and enjoy, while also having the kind of education that prepares them to live in a democratic culture.

What ought to be clear is that motivation is key—not the easy, reflexive kind that's nearly always demonstrated by people who are hungry, desperate, or anxious, but the intrinsic kind. Without setting whatever conditions it takes for students to be motivated to learn, all reforms of schooling simply rearrange the furniture, tinker with structure, tease with promises.

Mary Metz puts plainly what is at stake with student motivation: students essentially "hold a veto over all reforms."[13] Educational leader Jack Frymier was even more direct. "Students learn when they're motivated to learn. If they want to learn, they will. If they don't, you probably can't make 'em." He went on to say that "any successful effort to improve learning will therefore be fundamentally about improving students' motivation . . . Different kids are motivated by different things. No effort at motivation will succeed unless it works with these differences."[14] Educators often complain about this general condition, that students are just not motivated enough. Some of the reason for this may have much to do with why they come to school and, even more, what educators think they're coming for.

A professor at Harvard Business School and author of multiple books about innovation, Clayton Christensen always points out that at least 75 percent of all the new products and services introduced every year are failures. People (i.e., the market) reject them. Providers typically conclude that the product or service was not good enough, so they scramble to make improvements. More often than not, the market still fails to materialize. Why is this? Christensen concludes that it is fundamentally a failure to understand what the customer is looking for, and this failure starts with how industries think of the market segments they serve.

> Most marketers behave as if the world is structured by product category or by customer category. Auto companies, for example, typically segment their markets by product category: there are sub-compacts, compacts, mid-sized and full-sized sedans; minivans, SUVs, luxury cars, sport cars, light trucks, and many more. They can tell you how big each segment is, how fast it is growing, and who has what market share. Other companies (and these are not mutually exclusive) frame their market's structure in terms of customer characteristics by using demographic attributes like age, gender, marital status and income level. Business-to-business (B2B) enterprises typically use corporate demographics like small, medium and large enterprises or industry "verticals" to define the structure of their markets. The reason these choices are salient to innovation is that they define the targets, in terms of customers and competitors, for the innovation. Slicing markets along these dimensions makes sense because when you're inside the company looking out on the market, this indeed is how it appears to be structured. What is more, when data are collected about the size of markets, it comes structured by product and customer category, because that is the easiest way to collect and analyze data.[15]

Segmentation schemes such as these are static in that customers' behaviors change far more often than their demographics do. The population segment between eighteen and thirty-four is often used in consumer marketing, for example. That's seventeen years—during which time attitudes, behaviors, and needs change dramatically.

Demographic data cannot explain why a man takes a date to a movie on one night but orders in pizza to watch a DVD from Netflix the next.

The reason why it often seems difficult to explain whether a customer within a given demographic category will buy a new product from within a given product category is that from the customers' perspective, *the market is not structured by product and customer category*. Rather, customers just find themselves needing to get things done. Jobs arise in their lives that demand resolution, and they hire products or services to help them do these jobs. Marketers who seek to develop products and services that their customers will buy predictably need to see the world through the eyes of those customers. This means that they need to understand the basic job that their customers are confronting and the results they need to achieve for which their products might be hired as a solution. In other words, the *job*, and not the customer or the product, should be the fundamental element of a marketer's understanding.[16]

But nothing like that happens in the "industry" of K–12 education. The customer is not the student, or even the family. They are not even the employers, and certainly not the economy. The customer role is played out by the political expressions of the adults who preside over the system. And that system is not driven by student motivation.

So, to play with Christensen's parlance, what is the job students might hire schools to do? "A core reason why so many students languish unmotivated in school or don't come to class at all is that education isn't a job that they are trying to do. Education is something they might choose to *hire* to do the job – but it isn't the job," say Christensen, Horn, and Johnson.[17] They suggest that there are good reasons to hypothesize, given what school is today, that the job teens have in mind is to feel successful and have opportunities for good experiences with friends. School has to compete with everything from clubs (or gangs) to video games to get this job done. Pointedly, most of the arrangements associated with school that appear to do this job best are the athletic teams, music groups, debating societies, clubs for hobbies—all explicitly *not* a part of the curriculum. They are *extracurricular*. It is the content of the curriculum that wears the badge of importance, and good grades are reserved for those who achieve in that framework. All others are invited to consider themselves failures. Why would a self-interested adolescent "hire" school to do that? And taking seriously Epstein's indictment of the very concept of adolescence, why would anyone, seeing the way their worlds are categorized and constrained, expect a different response from teens?

If we assume that many students have the motivation gene but see school as something other than a facilitator of their success, would we not suspect a *design* problem? Wouldn't we see that we need somehow to integrate knowledge and skill development with the realities of adolescent motivation? Even as school fails to connect with close to half its customer base, the nation's mood reflects an opposite reasoning: school is all right, but students (and teachers) are just not performing well enough. We must hit them with the cold bath of rigorous standards, frequently confront them with assessments, and label them as "making it" or not. The assumption must be that motivation will be aroused through fear and threat.

National policy seems further to assume that achievement means the same thing for every young person. But what if LaKeesha loves dance more than dictionaries? What about Robert, who, finding school slow and boring, wants to pick up the pace and looks to Sylvan or K12 Inc. or Capella to catapult him to the next level? Jack has a passion for motorcycles—not just riding them but building them, working on them, using his natural sense of mechanics and discovering how things work. Can he learn what he needs to know from this starting place?

What if school as it is predominantly defined and arranged is badly out of alignment with the job the customer would want to be done? Perhaps there is abundant demand for learning, for acquiring knowledge and skills, but not enough takers for the way school is arranged and offered to students and parents?

LATENT DEMAND FROM TEACHERS

The nearly 40 percent of teachers who quit in their first five years of service make the easiest case for a demand-driven system. Teachers just entering the system, expecting to find a motivating environment and an opportunity for a professional career, find a dominating management-labor model that tells them what to do, how to do it, and when it will be evaluated. Some sizeable proportion of these teachers, plus veteran teachers long frustrated by the arrangements they work in, are a potential force for change. The evidence: nearly every teacher-led school created in the past decade elected a different learning model, reflecting almost directly a market demand for a wider variety of learning strategies.

Meanwhile, as a wave of baby boomer–led retirements looms, there are repeated reports that the nation has a teacher recruitment problem. Demonstrably not true. A cursory look at turnover in teacher ranks and the underlying causes behind it suggest that recruiting is not the problem, but, rather, retention is. If Richard Ingersoll is right, the root cause is the recognition, especially by the newest to arrive at teaching, that for most aspiring young professionals, it is not a very good job. Few want to make a career out of an unsatisfying job.

No one has studied this problem more than Richard Ingersoll, a professor of education and sociology at the University of Pennsylvania. Ingersoll is a data-hound, constantly on the lookout for evidence among the statistics for what others merely argue over. When it comes to why teachers—particularly those who have a wider range of career choices—do not stick with education, his data offer a clear explanation. Controlling for age, seniority, school size, geography, finance, the teacher's "sense of power" (or lack of it) determines whether a teacher will want to stick with the job. Most professionals—consultants, architects, attorneys, accountants—have a reasonable amount of control over their work. If they had a management structure organized to tell them what and how and when to do everything, those professions might look like they also had a retention problem. According to Ingersoll, if teachers can control their work, the results are better performance and lower turnover.[18] Anticipating disbelief, his research had a robust sample and used advanced statistical methods to control for all the factors usually associated with teacher turnover including age, seniority, school size, geography, finance, and poverty characteristics. He concluded that his correlation between the degree to which teachers control their work and the likelihood of turnover was "as clean and overwhelming as any you will ever see."

Back in the mid-1990s, in a small community in south central Minnesota, a group of teachers, using Minnesota's statute governing cooperatives, organized themselves to run schools.[19] They could hardly have known they were starting a movement. Today that coop, called EdVisions, can point to several dozen schools formed with the expectation that teachers will be in charge.[20] While there are fewer than a hundred teacher-run schools in the United States, it is a growing segment of schooling. Most of these schools were founded as charter schools, but there are thirteen inside the Milwaukee public school district that operate with a memorandum of understanding with the teachers union. Nearly all such schools make some kind of arrangement to complete the administrative work that teachers decide they cannot or prefer not to do; but in no case do they revert to the still-dominant management-labor model. And it is striking to see that none of these schools to date has elected the conventional course-and-class learning model. Many are project-based schools, but all are different as they work to line up with what today's students need.

TEACHERS UNIONS IN THE LEAD?

What if this small base of teacher-run schools begins to spread, gains the attention of key union leaders, and becomes an opportunity for professional leadership? Consider the scene as we write: the growing sense of "better teachers and better teaching" as the new magic wand for improvement is playing out as a strengthening of management's role in assigning teachers, in assessing performance, in setting teacher compensation, and in holding teachers accountable. Developments like these challenge a number of things the unions have won for their members over the years. The pressure about scores and the growing tendency to tell teachers how to teach will, if nothing intervenes, turn teaching into a job that teachers will increasingly hate. Their impulse will be to resist. But resistance would make the conflict worse and would strengthen the sense that is widespread already that union resistance to accountability is the principal obstacle to the progress the country so badly needs to make. For teachers and their unions, the more appealing opportunity is to reframe the debate and to leverage the accountability pressure in a way that will help them win professional status for their members. They should say, teachers will take responsibility for student and school success if teachers can control what matters for student and school success.

Unions might assert that the teachers' inability to control what matters for learning is the root of the system's difficulty. And the way things are drifting, they will be even less able to shape what is taught or how it is taught. No more than other sensible people do teachers want to be held accountable for what they cannot control. So conflict looms. Prospects would change in very important ways if the school and its teachers were given real control over the practices in the school. Authority and responsibility go together. If they are not combined at the school, at what level *can* they be effectively combined?

It is in the union's interest to suggest the country cut this new deal with its teachers. They have long said they seek professional status as well as economic security for their members, yet they have never been able to win them that professional role through negotiation or legislation. Increasingly their younger members want this larger role; they want better work and a better career. We know that where teachers do control their work their (and their students') attitudes and behaviors change dramatically. By seeking this professional role for teachers, the unions can make the push for accountability work for them.

This would be in the public interest as well. Rising conflict in the traditional labor/management model would not help improve achievement. Nor can the country realistically expect highly qualified people to move into teaching if teaching does not become a really good job and a really good career—professionally as well as economically. If placing greater authority for learning with the faculty of professional teachers produces the attitudes and behaviors that induce greater effort and improve learning—as it does, where it operates—this clearly seems like what the country should want to do.

A startling proportion of the nation's teachers would apparently like a professional role: a Public Agenda survey in 2005 found two-thirds of the under-five-year teachers and half of the over-twenty-year teachers would be somewhat or very interested in working in a school run and managed by teachers—a school organized, in effect, on the partnership model.

The idea is to enlarge in some way the teachers' role in decisions about how the school runs and how learning is handled. This might mean that teachers form the kind of partnership we see in other professional occupations, fully in charge and with the administrators working *for* them. Equally, it could mean simply larger roles for teachers in schools that continue to be administrator-led. What form it takes, or how the arrangement evolves over time in a particular school, can be left to the people in the school and decided based on what they prefer and believe will best ensure school and student success.

THE POLICY RESPONSE: NEW SCHOOLS THAT
CAN BE DIFFERENT SCHOOLS

If the demand for learning is the policy challenge, new forms of school are the logical response. Up to the 1980s, U.S. schools continued to become more alike even as the American population was becoming more diverse. Then came the charter movement with its promise for greater diversity of learning opportunities. In the 1990s, state after state withdrew what was an exclusive franchise through which only the local school district could offer public education.

Chartering schools as a means of getting new and potentially different schools from which to choose had its origins in a 1991 Minnesota law, with the first such school opening in St. Paul the following year. Charters spread rather quickly to what is now forty states and the District of Columbia; today there are nearly five thousand such schools enrolling over a million students each year. Indeed, the advent of chartering has shown, perhaps more than any other modern policy shift, that latent demand for more choices, for change, exists among parents and students.

But much misunderstanding persists over what chartering is and what it means. Research almost always falls into the trap of regarding charter schools as a *type* of school. This generates worry over whether charter schools do better than district schools or district schools do better than chartered schools, which is like comparing getting a fishing license to catching fish. Chartering is a means of creating a school; it tells you nothing about the type of school it will be or what the learning model will be. Will it be organized along the highly structured, high-expectations model of the Knowledge Is Power Program (KIPP), or will it be a Spanish immersion school or perhaps one based on an International Baccalaureate (IB) model?

With its statutory assurances to operate somewhat outside the usual regulatory framework, chartering is essentially a platform for trying things. It is a kind of research and development sector for education, a potential source of innovation. This is true despite the relatively low percentage of charter schools that are substantially different from the traditional district schools.

Over the past decade, a second platform for new schools has been built. In mostly large urban areas such as Boston, Baltimore, Chicago, and Los Angeles, a new schools sector seems to be finding a home inside the structure of school districts. Boston's Pilot Schools date back to 1994 and were essentially begun by leaders of the Boston Teachers Union as a competitive response to the growing popularity of charter schools. These schools have special autonomy within the district, and teachers, still members of the union, sign annual work agreements to demonstrate their understanding that their schools may operate differently from the practices contemplated either by the central administration or the master labor contract.

In the spring of 2009, Minnesota became the first state to enact the authority for any school district to approve new, autonomous schools (charter-like, not charter-light) within the district. Districts can issue requests for proposals (RFPs). A group of teachers and parents might take the initiative to start a new kind of school. If districts agree to allow a new school to the degree of autonomy spelled out in the law, and the local union chapter agrees to its members' decisions on work practices, then the school has the same relative freedom from state regulations enjoyed by charter schools. Under this new law, all the state and local support, except for a negotiated percentage for central services, such as facilities, insurance, and transportation, go directly to the school's budget. The educators there decide how to use their resources, what learning strategy they will select, who will work there, and the mechanics of the length of the school day and year. In effect, they are getting authority and accepting accountability. No teacher would be there who is not wanted or who does not want to be there. And for students, these are schools of choice.

Think of the new Minnesota statute as opening up a second platform for innovation, challenging every school district to allow educators in these new schools the right to control their work and to be judged strictly on results. If the results are unsatisfactory, close the school.

Structure, along with terminology, vary in this emerging sector. Baltimore's effort falls under an Office of New Initiatives. New York City has "portfolio" schools. Chicago and Los Angeles have been closing failing schools and allowing new ones to open. In Los Angeles, Green Dot has taken over some failing schools and radically restructured them. Green Dot actually secured authority from the state to establish a separate chapter of the teachers union and negotiated a contractual agreement with considerably more flexibility, and it consumes only about thirty pages compared to the L.A. Unified School District's seven-hundred-page contract.

Slowly, states have recognized that chartering as policy is not sufficient to getting enough new and different schools. Legislators hear from educators who have ideas for new schools but who do not want to go the charter route; they hear from superintendents that districts ought to have a shot at the level of flexibility enjoyed by charters. West Virginia, one of the hold-out states on chartering, passed in 2009 a policy for "innovation zones," extending to the fifty-five districts in the state a new opportunity to create schools that operate under different rules. The law is devastatingly top-heavy with layers of approvals required to get this permission, but it is a start. Colorado passed a somewhat stronger law in 2006. The Denver school district has opened an Office of School Reform, through which it approved in late 2008 the district's first school to enjoy special autonomy and be run entirely by the teachers who organized it. Opened in the fall of 2009, this school emphasizes math and science and serves a largely Latino, lower-income part of the city.

SCALING-UP THE DEMAND

Scaling-up in the context of the nation's education goals is a direct response to demand for more variety of learning opportunities.

Innovation—trying things, finding what works better—is not worth much if improvements are stuck at the margin of the school industry, are small islands of success that attract visiting delegations but little replication. Sometimes, of course, replication itself is seen as innovation, which it is usually not. But the question is, always, how might scaling-up happen? And what role does demand play in the likelihood and velocity of scaling-up?

Pressure will predictably scale-up any improvement more rapidly—especially when grants are at stake. Lately, federal money has been a primary lure. Patience is running thin, and all the rhetoric reinforces a new urgency. There is a kind of yearning for big organizational approaches. Much of this push may prove misguided. In nearly every industry, scaling-up happens from a gathering cascade of small changes. In consumer markets, despite a persistent bias against small buyers, scaling-up from these roots seems to happen at great speed. Something happens. Then a growing number of small enterprises try out variations on the idea. Some succeed. Others fail. Only gradually do the successes consolidate into large organizations. In education, the notion persists that the scaling-up to large organizations happens right away. That it can be done politically.

In fact, all the modern evidence suggests that the more radical the change, the less likely it is to be done politically. Politics merely opens closed doors. Years back, the telephone system was structured as a public utility. We were told this was essential to ensure universal service. Under that system, the emergence of telephones available in any color other than black was regarded as a major innovation. Then the door opened in the mid-1990s, and telecommunications blossomed into a self-improving, innovation-driven industry. Microwave towers dotted the skylines; satellites swirled around the Earth's atmosphere. And the telephone became the tiny complex computers we carry in our pockets and purses.

What ought to be clear is that demand is the fuel that drives the scaling-up. And if that is so, there must be space in which the scaling-up may occur. Policy space, political space. That is what chartering laws did. New laws now creating opportunities for autonomous schools are essentially defining new space in which what is started can be scaled. It is reassuring to see the growing demand for learning. And it is helpful to see parents pushing for more choice, business employers urging a more robust effort, and government finally getting religion on this vital dimension of the entire nation's positioning in the world. But demand alone will be just that—alone—without the space for expression. State policy making remains the key to defining that space.

To get the most from demand, states must keep the system open to creating new schools, put a stop to the narrowing of what is needed, broaden the definition of achievement, and be sure that the door is open to innovation.

And teachers are the actors with feet on either the brake or the accelerator. Whether in unionized settings or not, teachers are in a position to *demand* a change in how they are seen and what they can do. Innovation proceeds with great speed in arrangements where work and ownership are combined. One only has to recall the amazing innovations in American agriculture to see this. There was huge demand for better machinery, better animal husbandry, better cropping practices, and better seeds because farmers had a stake in making their operations more productive and thus more profitable. Their demand spawned an explosion in the supply side, as McCormick, Deere, DeKalb, and other companies grew and a new consultancy was born.

It is now in the interest of teachers particularly—and their unions—to demand a different arrangement of relationships and responsibility. Teachers might, as some are already doing, offer responsibility for the quality and the success of outcomes, in return for real authority over the conditions and terms that contribute to success. The deal society has with teachers today is, We don't give you authority; in return, you don't give us accountability. Reversing those terms has the power and capacity to take demand to scale. Money will always matter. But there is already enough money in the system if state policy produces a system that runs on the demands of both professionals and young learners.

Conclusion

Frederick M. Hess and Olivia Meeks

IT HAS FREQUENTLY BEEN noted that schools and schooling today look remarkably like they did a century ago. One would not say that about the practice of medicine or engineering or about commercial sectors like air travel, farming, or auto manufacturing. In each case, dramatic shifts in the labor force, management practices, technology, and communications have transformed familiar institutions and comfortable routines. Much of these shifts are the consequence of unbundling, whereby innovators take apart established structures and routines and reassemble them in newer, smarter ways. Consider how mundane advances like outpatient clinics, the ability to purchase plane tickets on Kayak.com, or the ability to visit the neighborhood Jiffy Lube have reshaped services in ways that are more convenient, beneficial, and efficient.

Despite these larger shifts, the notion of harnessing new technologies or modes of coordination in schooling has too often morphed from a question of finding smarter solutions to emotionally charged denunciations of school choice, for-profit providers, or computer-aided instruction. Here, we endeavor to sidestep these contentious debates and instead delve into some of the possibilities and complications presented by efforts to unbundle schooling.

There are two dimensions along which we can think about K–12 unbundling. The first is *structural unbundling*, in which we loosen our grip on the regularities about what it means to be a teacher, a school, or a school system and explore the ways in which we can rethink how schooling is delivered.

The second dimension is *content unbundling*, or the unbundling of the stuff of learning, in which we revisit assumptions about the scope and sequence of what students are taught and what they are expected to learn, thereby enabling the emergence of new, more varied approaches to curriculum and coursework.

This distinction may not be immediately clear, so consider a couple of examples. A virtual classroom in which a distinguished math instructor in Boston is teaching students in Birmingham online represents a clear change in the structure and delivery of schooling. However, there is no reason to expect that the math lessons will be sequenced or organized any differently than in a traditional classroom setting.

Conversely, efforts to adapt curriculum content and schedules to better suit individual student and teacher needs in real time, as has been done in New York City's School of One, have effectively sliced and diced the familiar block of learning that persists in most classrooms. Allowing for customized learning objectives and sequences, though, does not necessarily require redesigning the structure and delivery of schooling.

These challenges and opportunities are not unique to the United States, though our technology, wealth, international stature, and workforce have left us admirably positioned to lead this transformation. As Chris Whittle makes clear in chapter 3, the economic and social rewards for successfully devising promising solutions are not just educational but will also position the United States to be a leader in what is sure to be an explosive and culturally powerful sector in the century ahead.

The goal for customized, unbundled school reform, as has been laid out in the preceding chapters, is not to develop a new model of what a good school should look like in 2030, but to cultivate a flexible system that emphasizes performance, rewards success, addresses failure, and enables schools and more specialized providers to meet a variety of needs in increasingly effective and targeted ways. Abandoning the quest for a new "one best system" requires avoiding the temptation to enshrine the best of today's new models and instead focusing on identifying various kinds of demands in increasingly powerful ways and then working to erect a system of schooling that addresses those demands effectively.

In this volume, contributors consider reforms that cross both dimensions of unbundling. In this brief conclusion, we will try to highlight a few of the key points that have been raised and flag their import for policy makers and practitioners seeking to cultivate a more customized world of learning in the twenty-first century.

NEW PROVIDERS RARELY UNBUNDLE TODAY

Despite the opportunities posed by unbundling, the slew of nontraditional suppliers that have entered the education market in recent years has generally taken the shape of familiar, bundled provision. Most entrepreneurial ventures have tended to deal in running whole schools or in recruiting teachers to serve in those schools. Terrific charter schools like the Knowledge Is Power Program (KIPP) Academies and Achievement First have attracted national attention for their successes in boosting achievement and getting kids into college, but their comprehensive whole-school solution can be tough to replicate, does not deliver much in the way of new cost efficiencies, and relies on impassioned do-everything educators.

For many would-be entrepreneurs capable of helping meet a particular need for students or educators, the prospect of retracing the paths of the successful whole school providers—and of finding facilities, training staff, policing students, and the dozens of other requisite tasks—is a strong incentive to direct their energies toward a more inviting field of endeavor in a more hospitable sector.

The expectation that schools and school districts can themselves find ways to serve a wealth of kids in a variety of ways has led to overburdened educators and institutions that have trouble doing anything very well. This expectation has proceeded hand in hand with limited attention to identifying the discrete needs or desires of students and families, all the while stifling the ability of specialized problem solvers to relieve some of the burdens placed on the conventional school.

Outside of K–12, nimble entrepreneurs with particular talents or targeted goods are free to meet needs and solve problems. When planning vacations, Americans now find it odd to think of traipsing across town to sit down with a travel agent and pay her to book flights, make hotel reservations, and provide travel materials. Not so long ago this kind of bundled provision was the norm. Today, however, most people would sit down at their computer, visit travel sites like Travelocity or Expedia, and then book their own flights, hotels, and car rentals. Customer service is available in a pinch, and travel agents still exist for those who prefer them, but evolving technologies and approaches have made it newly possible to customize services more readily, in less time, and at a fraction of the cost of the old model.

If a new provider wants to sell books online but not in stores, or to play live music without selling recordings, they are free to proceed as they see fit. In education, outside of those providers who sell directly to affluent families, ventures offering online tutoring, language instruction, arts classes, and much else are dependent on their ability to convince district or school administrators that their service is useful. They must also make the case that it is worth finding ways around accumulated policies, practices, and guidelines which can make that kind of arrangement difficult and politically fraught. This is why many of the most dynamic providers of online education, like SMARTHINKING and Tutor.com, are selling directly to families in higher education, or selling to libraries and the U.S. Department of Education, and only rarely selling to K–12 schools. The result is perverse, trapping educators and students in a ghetto where powerful new tools and services are curiosities rather than routine parts of the school day.

By using new tools and technologies to disassemble and then reassemble service provision, entrepreneurs have devised new efficiencies and found new ways to customize services according to the needs and preferences of the individual. Unlike industries where we have pulled apart and customized provision, however, schooling is still delivered in one indivisible and largely identical mass to most students, regardless of need or learning preference.

This stagnant bureaucracy has been the product of poor information, barriers to entry and exit, monopsony power of districts, political forces, and the public nature and corresponding externalities of the good. What the contributors have presented in the preceding pages is not only an alternative vision but a roadmap for how to use data, policy, market research, and new tools to address these challenges.

While the obstacles confronting new providers seeking to enter K–12 schooling have been examined in recent years, little attention has been paid to understanding the demand for education—a key ingredient to catalyzing innovative, customized services. The chapters seek to break new ground by sketching the pressing questions, challenges, and opportunities on that score.

KEY TAKEAWAYS

To our eyes, six ideas emerge most clearly from the preceding chapters. Together, they offer a framework for thinking about schooling in a very different way. We will here focus particular attention on the impact of data, technology, choice, teacher and administrator demand, the availability of new tools, and the role of finance.

The Critical Role of Data

The first takeaway deals with the vital need to collect and monitor data in ways that reflect individual needs and performance, and not merely that of aggregates. For individualized services to be feasible and useful, end-users—whether students, parents, teachers, or district leaders—must be able to obtain reliable and comparable information on their options. Meanwhile, providers must have reliable information on the needs and characteristics of those they will be serving. In the absence of such information, one-size-fits-all provision will remain the inevitable norm.

As Jon Fullerton deftly outlines in chapter 9, today's data systems are typically unable to meet the information needs described above. Current standardized assessments are helpful but lacking, and while value-added measures are an improvement, they remain imperfect indicators of teacher quality even in the few districts where they are available. School report cards distributed by districts provide parents with some semblance of comparable data on school quality, but the measures are often blunt and frequently do not contain the kind of granular information that a parent might be most eager to know. Web sites like GreatSchools.org that feature reviews on local schools make information more accessible, but they too are limited in the data they report. Assessment rubrics remain standardized and often do not allow for independent consumer reviewing, unlike other service provider review sites like Angie's List or Zillow.com. These data shortcomings persist in a high-stakes accountability environment where federal and state mandates for comparable data for every child in the country become the mold for most of a district's performance assessment efforts.

For students ill-served by the conventional school model—especially those with learning difficulties, behavior problems, or those who fall outside the conventional age range—the shortage of individualized data is particularly acute. Today's standardized tests have proven insufficient in fully capturing these students' needs, and one of the thorniest issues for educators is getting enough data to successfully create a customized learning plan. Without the necessary data to make a strategic plan for meeting the particular needs of at-risk or special-needs students, districts are often forced to try to make up for information limitations with greater manpower and additional classroom support. While this may have been a plausible, if inefficient, strategy in decades past, such resource-intensive approaches are increasingly untenable in the current fiscal environment.

How are we to overcome the challenges posed by insufficiently sensitive data in an unbundled education system? Looking across the preceding chapters, several pertinent policy suggestions emerge. First, longitudinal data on student achievement and school completion must be augmented with information on teacher effects, student and parent learning preferences, student demographics, and information on outside-the-classroom work, such as academic interventions or afterschool programming. As Fullerton points out, the New York City Department of Education has addressed this need for more robust data on two fronts: the ARIS data warehouse, which aggregates and links a number of different data sources to better track student achievement over time, and the city's pioneering School of One model, in which a student's progress across multiple modalities is tracked and modeled in real time allowing for constant updates on personalized lesson plans and early interventions. Such innovations represent tremendous strides forward relative to most data systems and serve as admirable examples for other districts. But as many authors have noted throughout this volume, more needs to be done to better capture parent and student preferences as well as activities outside the classroom.

Second, it is vital that states develop systems of data collection and manipulation that extend beyond simple tracking of test scores. States and districts also need to get in the business of nurturing and employing third-party assessors to provide evaluative data on approved providers. As services become decoupled from the traditional schoolhouse model, the need for quality control, reliable monitoring, and credible benchmarks becomes more critical. Without these supports, consumer choice in K–12 schooling will continue to be stunted by a lack of reliable, comparable information, and new providers will face daunting barriers to competing fairly with traditional offerings.

Third, consumer review sites should be bolstered to create a better forum for service users to engage with suppliers and their fellow customers. As services proliferate and consumers enjoy more options, the need for information on services increases. While authoritative sources like *Consumer Reports* have long fulfilled this need for commercial goods, standard evaluation metrics must be supplemented with consumer feedback in the case of services. This goal is far from out of reach. Angie's List—which serves as an aggregator of consumer reviews for local services like doctors, mechanics, and beauticians across the country—demonstrates the viability of such a service in other sectors, while the ten million opinions registered on RateMyProfessor.com have shown that consumer reviews have a role in education as well.

Despite such gains elsewhere, K–12 schooling still lacks a vibrant and accessible forum for consumers to share important information. Chester Finn and Eric Osberg note this need in chapter 2, suggesting, "Education could do more to emulate sectors that have such robust feedback loops enabled by, for example, Web or phone surveys, hotel and restaurant complaint cards, chefs asking their patrons how they've enjoyed the meal. By doing more of this, schools would enhance their capacity to deliver solid academic results while fostering better-informed and more engaged parents."

Technology and the Rise of Virtual Schooling

Rethinking the 1:25 teacher-to-student classroom that has persisted so stubbornly would be impossible absent the power of new technologies. As has been noted by authors like Clayton Christensen, Michael Horn, and Curtis Johnson in their influential *Disrupting Class* and by John Chubb and Terry Moe in *Liberating Learning*, adopting new technologies can allow for a greater customization of coursework driven by real-time, sophisticated assessments; a freeing of education from the constraints of geography; a deeper engagement of parents and teachers in their student's progress; and a more efficient means for educating more children with lower costs.[1] In the words of Finn and Osberg from chapter 2, technology "helps remove the physical, logistical, and geographic constraints created by school locations, classroom capacity, teacher availability, calendars, and more." As they and others make clear, customization is not just about a fascination with the potential of technology or virtual schooling but also the power of tools like these to spur a larger, more fundamental shift in our approach to educational policy.

One of the most celebrated technologies to emerge in education recently has been virtual schooling, in which students participate in school using online forums, video chats, and other computer-based means. Virtual schooling is an especially appealing option for at-risk or off-track students, as Tamara Battaglino and JoEllen Lynch assert in chapter 4: "Online courses allow scheduling flexibility for both the school and the student, as well as important economic benefits for the district. Even with in-person teacher supervision of virtual credit recovery, a school can consolidate a full classroom of students who may need to be studying half a dozen different subject areas."

Clayton Christensen has boldly forecast that by 2019, 50 percent of high school courses will be delivered online, and we are already seeing evidence of this at the state and district levels. The Florida Virtual School, as Finn and Osberg note, now enrolls 84,000 students, and New York City's School of One, which integrates virtual learning with a number of other learning modalities, has received high praise for its efforts. Supplemental providers, such as Tutor.com and SMARTHINKING, have also had success in serving students outside the bounds of the traditional classroom. While some virtual charters around the country do provide fully online educational experiences, many chapters emphasize that virtual schooling's strength is in its ability to not only provide more choice among schools but to provide more choice within schools at the subject and course levels.

Intraschool choice and the ability to supplement school offerings with those of outside providers hold significant promise in an unbundled world, and the technology needed to track and manage such schooling arrangements from multiple sources has finally caught up. As Kim Smith and Julie Petersen note in chapter 1, two decades ago education professor Frank Smith described a way to track and manage assessments from nontraditional services: students would be given an ATM card that they would swipe at various locales after assessments and with different providers in order to track their mastery of the subject matter. Thus, student performance information would be consolidated while still allowing for students to take advantage of multiple providers. While futuristic at the time, the advent of barcode-scanning cell phones and other digital scan technologies make such ideas entirely viable for today's students. Indeed, the New Hampshire Department of Education, in figuring out how to manage the increased numbers of educational options now available, has developed a system of tracking students' use of and performance in nontraditional services, like internships, community service, and independent study, as well as assessing their progress on competency-based exams for those contexts.

If the aim is to ensure that technology helps promote customization, and that today's new technologies do not become merely one more innovation layered atop the familiar school model, it is necessary to update our notions of policy and accountability to better fit the new era of schooling. First, policies that limit the size and scope of providers based strictly on their modality—such as the enrollment caps placed on virtual charter schools in several states—should be scrubbed. Selectively discriminating against virtual and other nontraditional providers discourages potential investment in new technologies for the field, displaces regulatory resources from needed areas like judging provider effectiveness, and unfairly bars students from the programs they and their parents demand. Second, as noted earlier, data systems must be restructured to cover multiple providers and gather comparable data across a number of modalities. Technological advances now make it possible for schooling to move past the one-size-fits-all model and more nimbly address discrete needs. But doing this at scale requires high-quality assessments that allow families to make good choices and that provide convincing public accountability.

Not Just Choice, but Informed Choice

Efforts to increase parental choice and thereby foster greater demand for high-quality providers outside the traditional schoolhouse will likely fall flat if parents are unable to reasonably research and compare options. If families do not have a firm grip on their children's needs and what schools offer, an understanding of how to make their demands heard, and some sense of efficacy, choice may not do much to help get students into a suitable learning environment.

The availability of choice without information on provider quality or on aggregation of services to support parents is not enough. Chapter 5 provides a cautionary example of the limits of choice. Comparing the market of schools and other providers to a shopping mall, Thomas Stewart and Patrick Wolf assert that most parents, after visiting a few stores and gathering some information, will tire of the search and settle for a convenient choice. Those parents willing to complete the entire "mall crawl" and check with every provider before settling on the best choice only total 15 percent or so of all shoppers. The pressures for quality control that this 15 percent exerts on providers make for a useful lever. But in the case of searching out customized educational providers with tools that meet the specific needs of a student, relying on the 15 percent may be insufficient.

Instead of hoping that families bereft of crucial information will make good choices, policy makers and educators can learn from this shopping mall analogy and figure out how to better collect and communicate information on schooling options. Whether this takes place in the form of consumer reviews, more detailed school scorecards, third-party market research reports, or any number of other information platforms, the forces that could create a high-functioning, individualized schooling system for every student will never come to fruition if reformers rely on choice alone.

Given the need for granular, customizable information in making choices for one's child, third-party reviews and providers themselves need to be more proactive about telegraphing what services are available to a broader, heterogeneous audience of consumers. As Smith and Petersen note in chapter 1, "We will need to strike a delicate balance between an increased number of options and the complexity of those decisions and come up with ways to present information in much more transparent and user-friendly ways." The Success Charter Network (SCN), a charter management organization formed in Harlem by Eva Moskowitz, has confronted the information shortage by staging extensive awareness campaigns in neighborhoods around the city. As Joe Williams describes in chapter 7, through its parent focus groups, public advertising, and hosting of an annual school choice fair for Harlem parents, SCN nurtures demand among parents by soliciting feedback and accessibly sharing information. They and other parent-organizing groups are playing a vital role in improving the mechanics of school choice, Williams notes, "by collectivizing the voices and frustrations of parents, creating a new political force for better schools that has been missing in the policy-making process for a generation."

Customized Education for Teachers and Administrators

Much of the discussion around customization is focused on students, but the intuitions apply equally to educators and administrators. Teachers in need of specialized lesson plans or wishing to import specialized support for a handful of advanced students could use new resources to become more effective. As The New Teacher Project's influential 2009 report *The Widget Effect* thoroughly recounted, the current system's tendency to treat all teachers as indistinguishable cogs neglects their individual demands.[2] Acting as if educators were a monolithic group and refusing to recognize and segment the ranks according to need and ability hinders a more effective allocation of teachers and denies them access to nontraditional preparation methods that may be better suited to their talents.

Teacher preparation would do well to look to Teacher U at Hunter College, which serves teachers working in particular New York City schools; High Tech High Ed School, which trains teachers eager to work there or in similar schools; and Columbia University's Klingenstein Center, which trains those who seek to work in independent schools. By signaling their pedagogical and technique leanings clearly to aspiring teachers, these preparation programs are able to draw in those students who most demand and admire their approach, quickening the preparation process while allowing the program to further build specialized expertise. Likewise, note Smith and Petersen, nontraditional teacher education providers like Teach for America have succeeded at customizing their training and attracting fresh talent.

Much like students, parents, and teachers, districts have specialized needs that are largely neglected by the traditional one-size-fits-all model. District leaders seeking to staff their schools are often frustrated by their inability to find enough candidates who are a good match for their needs. Joe Williams documents the case of demand commandoes like The New Teacher Project who swoop in to meet these needs. Districts have special needs for their schools, and these needs are often left unmet by the traditional talent recruitment methods. The New Teacher Project, writes Williams, "meets that demand by acting far beyond the scope of a typical employment recruitment arrangement. Mere recruiters would scour the countryside in search of hidden pools of excellent teacher candidates to 'fill the pipeline' for school district human resources departments. [The New Teacher Project] digs deep, acting as if the surface-level demand provides them with a mandate to push more lasting changes that will eliminate the root causes that lead to the strong demand in the first place." By identifying and better fulfilling the individualized needs of districts, The New Teacher Project and other district partners can help get the right bodies in the right schools and in front of the right kids, where they will be most effective.

Such customization of teacher placement, as Curtis Johnson and Ted Kolderie point out in chapter 10, may also help to mitigate the high turnover rates that are endemic to the profession. Engaging teachers' specific gifts more fully in the job placement process and giving them more autonomy over how they teach and manage their classroom is not without precedent. For instance, organizations like EdVisions—a Wisconsin-based co-op where teachers collectively take charge of administrative and governance duties—have listened closely to teacher demand and are designing learning environments and positions that are suited to professionalized teachers in the twenty-first century.

Tools for Customization

The efficiencies that customized learning promises are often incumbent on robust specialization. Allowing outside providers to augment traditional classroom offerings means that schools can take advantage of their expertise and leverage those skills to provider services at a much lower cost than developing such expertise on their own. For tool providers such as Wireless Generation and SchoolNet to succeed, as Douglas Lynch and Michael Gottfried detail in chapter 6, it is essential that they be able to identify and gauge demand for their products among their consumers, including the schools that chose to use their products and the parents who choose their school based on the tools that such schools offer.

The potential role of such providers is illustrated, as Lynch and Gottfried show, by the private-sector example of Intel Pentium processors. Intel markets itself to computer producers as a high-quality component that will make their computers more efficient. Computer producers, in turn, leverage the power of the Intel brand when selling to consumers, drawing on the good reputation to distinguish themselves from competing producers. For education tools to be successful in signaling quality and thus stimulating demand among consumers, parents must know about them, know that they have a reputation for being high-quality, and be able to choose those providers who use the tool. By creating a brand identity, toolmakers can better communicate their benefits to choosy families and thus bolster the market with a greater awareness of quality providers.

The current state of parental awareness of nontraditional providers makes this challenge all the more pressing. Lynch and Gottfried's survey work in brand identification revealed some disheartening truths: while 98 percent of all the respondents who self-identified as educators could tell surveyors if they had an Intel processor, only 23 percent of that group had heard of either Wireless Generation or SchoolNet, two of the largest education software companies in the country. The same trends were evident among educators who actually worked in the ten largest districts who partnered with one of these two companies: while 100 percent of these educators knew if they had an Intel processor, only just over half (53 percent) had heard of the software companies whose products they were likely interacting with daily. Because districts often obscure the brands of such organizations by renaming and repackaging their services, providers like Wireless Generation and SchoolNet find it difficult to take full advantage of the possible windfall in the customized market. As Lynch and Gottfried note in chapter 6, "With the lack of information on the entire landscape of demand, there is simply no demand for the suppliers to evaluate. As a consequence, the supply of effective educational tools remains limited."

What does this mean for customization? If third-party companies are to gain any traction in partnering with districts, they must develop a brand identity among both district and school leaders and among the families they serve. When consumers are not aware of a brand and its performance, they will be unable to distinguish it from shoddy providers. This ensures that the market forces for identifying and rewarding quality will go unutilized. For customization to drive healthy competition and reward quality, third-party providers and district partners must be much more aggressive in communicating their presence and the essence of their brand. SchoolNet district partners in Philadelphia, Denver, Atlanta, and Albuquerque have masked the software product and renamed it. In such cases where district partners have masked the software product and renamed it—even when an active consumer base inclined to take advantage of brand signals exists—there is no conceivable way for a provider to reap the benefits of delivering a high-quality service.

Breaking the Whole-School Funding Assumption

Finally, breaking the stranglehold of the whole-school model ultimately requires that states and districts shift away from a vision of choice in which students merely choose between schools. Moving instead toward a model of intraschool choice would result in a system more akin to that of the Health Savings Account in health care. Rather than just paying for students to go to approved School A or B, the state would deposit dollars in a virtual account in the name of each student and then allow parents to use those dollars to procure services from an array of state-approved providers. If families simply wanted to direct all of their funds toward the local school—and most might choose to do so—that would be fine. But families might also choose to use the school but opt out of foreign language instruction, electives, or math in order to utilize alternative programs.

In chapter 2 of this book, Finn and Osberg go into greater detail to explain how such a program might work on a wider scale:

> The flow of resources must be student based and fully portable rather than tied to teacher salary, staff position, or program. When a dissatisfied family switches schools, one school's budget shrinks and the other grows. In that way, every school's future is tied to its success in attracting, satisfying, and retaining students rather than its success in

appealing to the district office for dollars, personnel, or programs. And if the amounts that follow children are adjusted according to their needs—attaching more dollars, for example, to youngsters who cost more to educate for any number of reasons—the system further empowers those parents who today are the least powerful.

Such a system would give families cause to start paying attention to the cost of services, would enable families to happily continue to attend a local school even if they disliked its math program or wanted richer arts instruction, and would permit approved providers to serve families directly without necessarily having to negotiate school district bureaucracies. It would also create new incentives and opportunities for school systems and alternative providers to identify accurate financial information on the cost of services down to student and course levels—creating opportunities for new efficiencies and permitting educators and parents to more effectively make apples-to-apples comparisons of programs and their relative cost-effectiveness.

CONCLUSION

It is our hope that this volume can shed light on the path toward this new environment and stimulate a shift in focus toward delivering the instruction and services that our children need rather than those that fit into the conventional school. The one-size-fits-all school system has passed its expiration date. It is not that there was anything innately wrong with the "one best system" or the conventional schoolhouse. Indeed, they represented the best practice solutions of an earlier, more bureaucratic era. Today, however, heightened aspirations, the press of student needs, and the opportunities presented by new tools and technologies mean that old arrangements are no longer a good fit. The charge is for schooling to make the same shift from the centralized, industrial model to a more nimble, customized model that we have made in so many other areas of life.

Today's schools are a huge hindrance to the ability of educators to address the multiplicity of student needs. Developing a system in which an array of providers can play a more robust role in the sector requires a dramatic reconfiguration of K–12 schooling and fresh thinking as to how states and systems go about their business. Our hope is that this volume can play a role in helping to promote that shift.

Notes

Introduction

1. National Commission on Excellence in Education, U.S. Department of Education, *A Nation at Risk: The Imperative for Educational Reform* (Washington, DC: Government Printing Office, 1983).

2. Frederick M. Hess, *Educational Entrepreneurship* (Cambridge, MA: Harvard Education Press, 2006); Frederick M. Hess, *The Future of Educational Entrepreneurship* (Cambridge, MA: Harvard Education Press, 2008); Frederick M. Hess, *Education Unbound, The Promise and Practice of Greenfield Schooling* (Alexandria, VA: ASCD, 2010).

3. Terry M. Moe and John E. Chubb, *Liberating Learning: Technology, Politics, and the Future of American Education* (San Francisco: Jossey-Bass, 2009); Clayton Christensen, Michael Horn, and Curtis Johnson, *Disrupting Class: How Disruptive Innovation Will Change the Way the World Learns* (New York: McGraw-Hill, 2010).

Chapter 1

1. Thomas Friedman, *The World Is Flat: A Brief History of the Twenty-First Century*. (New York: Farrar, Straus & Giroux, 2005).

2. Chris Anderson, *The Long Tail: Why the Future of Business is Selling Less of More*. (New York: Hyperion, 2006).

3. Barry Newstead, Joe Doctor, and Don Howard, *Communities of Opportunity: Case Study* (San Francisco: Bridgespan Group, 2006).

4. Robert Weissbourd and Christopher Berry, *The Market Potential of Inner-City Neighborhoods: Filling the Information Gap* (Washington, DC: Brookings Institution, 1999); Jamie Alderslade, *Hidden in Plain Sight: How Different Data Yield Vastly Different Understandings of the Same Market* (Washington, DC: Social Compact, 2005); *District of Columbia Neighborhood Market Drill Down* (Washington, DC: Social Compact, 2002); and Elsie Achugbue, "Nontraditional Market Analyses: Dismantling Barriers to Retail Development in Underserved Neighborhoods," *Research Review* 13, no. 3 (2006).

5. Alex Taylor, "Porsche Slices up Its Buyers," *Fortune*, January 16, 1995.

6. Mark Schneider, Paul Teske, and Melissa Marschall, *Choosing Schools: Consumer Choice and the Quality of American Schools* (Princeton, NJ: Princeton University Press, 2000).

7. Kim Smith and Julie Landry Petersen, "What Is Educational Entrepreneurship?" in *Educational Entrepreneurship: Realities, Challenges, Possibilities*, ed. Frederick M. Hess (Cambridge, MA: Harvard Education Press, 2006), http://www.newschools.org/files/EducationalEntrepreneurship.pdf.

8. Albert O. Hirschman, *Exit, Voice, and Loyalty: Responses to Decline in Firms, Organizations, and States* (Cambridge, MA: Harvard University Press, 1970).

9. Marc K. Landy, Martin A. Levin, and Martin Shapiro, *Creating Competitive Markets: The Politics of Regulatory Reform* (Washington, DC: Brookings Institution Press, 2007).

10. Barry Schwartz, *The Paradox of Choice: Why More Is Less* (New York: HarperCollins, 2004), 99–100; Barry M. Staw, "Knee-Deep in the Big Muddy: A Study of Escalating Commitment to a Chosen Course of Action," *Organizational Behavior and Human Performance* 16 (June 1976); Christopher Peterson, Steven F. Maier, and Martin E. P. Seligman, *Learned Helplessness: A Theory for the Age of Personal Control* (New York: Oxford University Press, 1993).

11. David Ferrero, "Why Choice Is Good for Teachers," *Education Next* 4 (Winter 2004), http://educationnext.org/whychoiceisgoodforteachers/.

12. Kaya Henderson, interview with the author, October 2009.

13. Steven Farkas, interview with the author, September 2009.

14. Jean Johnson, Andrew Yarrow, Jonathan Rochkind, and Amber Ott, *Teaching for a Living: How Teachers See the Profession Today* (New York: Public Agenda and Learning Point Associates, 2009), http://www.publicagenda.org/pages/teaching-for-a-living.

15. "Star-Teacher Pre-Screener," http://www.habermanfoundation.org/StarTeacherPreScreener.aspx.

16. Cathleen Benko and Anne Weisberg, *Mass Career Customization: Aligning the Workplace with the Nontraditional Workforce* (Cambridge, MA: Harvard Business School Press, 2007).

17. Elena Silva, *Teachers at Work: Improving Teacher Quality Through School Design* (Washington, DC: Education Sector, 2009), http://www.educationsector.org/research/research_show.htm?doc_id=1058462.

18. Stacey Childress, *Leading for Equity: The Pursuit of Excellence in the Montgomery County Public Schools* (Cambridge, MA: Harvard Education Press, 2009).

19. Tom Toch and Chad Aldeman, *Matchmaking: Enabling Mandatory Public School Choice in New York and Boston* (Washington, DC: Education Sector, 2009), http://www.educationsector.org/usr_doc/ChoiceMatching.pdf.

20. Cami Anderson, interview with the author, November 2009.

21. Richard H. Thaler and Cass R. Sunstein, *Nudge: Improving Decisions About Health, Wealth, and Happiness* (New Haven, CT: Yale University Press, 2008)

22. Clayton Christensen, Michael B. Horn, and Curtis W. Johnson, *Disrupting Class: How Disruptive Innovation Will Change the Way the World Learns* (New York: McGraw-Hill, 2008).

23. Stacey Bielick, *1.5 Million Homeschooled Students in the United States in 2007* (Washington, DC: National Center for Education Statistics, 2008), http://nces.ed.gov/pubs2009/2009030.pdf; Anthony G. Picciano and Jeff Seaman, *K–12 Online Learning: A 2008 Follow-Up of the Survey of U.S. School District Administrators* (Newburyport, MA: Sloan Consortium, 2009), http://www.sloan-c.org/publications/survey/pdf/k-12_online_learning_2008.pdf.

24. Fred Wilson, comments, Hacking Education conference, March 2009, http://publicusv.wiki.zoho.com/Hacking-Education.html.

25. Leland Anderson and Michael B. Horn. *Alpine Online School: A Utah School District's Move into K–8 Online Education* (Newton, MA: Innosight Institute, 2009), http://www.innosightinstitute.org/innosight/wp-content/uploads/2009/08/Alpine-Online.pdf.

26. Frank L. Smith, "New American Secondary Schools Ventures (Grades 7–14)" (unpublished manuscript, St. Johns University, 2009).

27. New Hampshire Department of Education, "Supporting Student Success Through Extended Learning Opportunities," http://www.education.nh.gov/innovations/elo/success.htm.

28. Chris Anderson, "The Long Tail, in a Nutshell," http://www.longtail.com/about.html.

29. Barry Schwartz, *Choice and Happiness: Why More Is Less* (New York: HarperCollins, 2004).

Chapter 2

1. Ted Kolderie, "Young People Are All Right," *Education Next* 9, no. 3 (2009): 72–73.

2. Profiles are available at www.Schoolmatters.com and www.greatschools.net.

3. Terry M. Moe and John E. Chubb, *Liberating Learning: Technology, Politics, and the Future of America Education* (San Francisco: Jossey-Bass, 2009).

4. National Alliance for Public Charter Schools, "Public Charter School Dashboard 2009," June 2009, p. 7, http://www.publiccharters.org/files/publications/DataDashboard.pdf.

5. Education Commission of the States, "Open Enrollment: 50-State Report," 2008, http://mb2.ecs.org/reports/Report.aspx?id=268.

6. "Open Enrollment: 50-State Report."

7. Office of Planning, Evaluation and Policy Development, Policy and Program Studies Service, *State and Local Implementation of the* No Child Left Behind Act, vol.7, *Title I School Choice and Supplemental Educational Services: Final Report* (Washington, DC: U.S. Department of Education, 2009).

8. Moe and Chubb, *Liberating Learning*, 176.

9. Bill Tucker, "Florida's Online Option," *Education Next* 9, no. 3 (2009), 12–18.

10. Moe and Chubb, *Liberating Learning*, 123.

11. Utah Electronic High School, "Frequently Asked Questions," http://www.schools.utah.gov/ehs/faq.htm; Anthony G. Picciano and Jeff Seaman, *K–12 Online Learning: A 2008 Follow-Up of the Survey of U.S. School District Administrators* (Boston: Sloan Consortium, 2009), 11; John Watson, Butch Gemin, and Jennifer Ryan, *Keeping Pace with K–12 Online Learning: A Review of State-Level Policy and Practice, 2008* (Evergreen, CO: Evergreen Consulting, 2008), 12.

12. Watson, Gemin, and Ryan, *Keeping Pace,* 13.

13. Clayton Christensen, Michael B. Horn, and Curtis W. Johnson, *Disrupting Class: How Disruptive Innovation Will Change the Way the World Learns* (New York: McGraw Hill, 2008), 98, 100–101.

14. Moe and Chubb, *Liberating Learning,* 175.

15. Bill Bishop, with Robert G. Cushing, *The Big Sort: Why the Clustering of Like-Minded America Is Tearing Us Apart* (New York: Houghton Mifflin, 2008).

16. E. D. Hirsch Jr., *The Making of Americans: Democracy and Our School* (New Haven, CT: Yale University Press, 2009).

17. *State and Local Implementation of the* No Child Left Behind Act.

18. Hans B. Thorelli, "Philosophies of Consumer Information Programs," in *Advances in Consumer Research,* vol. 4, ed. William D. Perreault Jr. (Atlanta: Association for Consumer Research, 1977), 282–287.

19. Buckley and Schneider, "Shopping for Schools: How do Marginal Consumers Gather Information About Schools," 121–145.

20. Jack Buckley, *Choosing Schools, Building Communities? The Effect of Schools of Choice on Parental Involvement* (New York: National Center for the Study of Privatization in Education, Teachers College, Columbia University, 2007).

21. Michael Alison Chandler, "So Many Dreams, So Many Diplomas," *Washington Post,* June 18, 2009.

22. Montgomery County Public Schools, "Walt Whitman HS, Art Department," http://www.montgomeryschoolsmd.org/schools/whitmanhs/academics/departments/art/art.shtml.

23. Christensen, Horn, and Johnson, *Disrupting Class,* 105.

24. Kristin Kalning "Teachers Invite 'Wii Music' into the Classroom," MSNBC, February 10, 2009, http://www.msnbc.msn.com/id/29127548/.

25. John M. Bridgeland, John J. DiIulio, Ryan T. Streeter, and James R. Mason, *One Dream, Two Realities: Perspectives of Parents on America's High Schools* (Washington, DC: Civic Enterprises, 2008).

26. Paul T. Hill, Marguerite Roza, and James Harvey, *Facing the Future: Financing Productive Schools* (Seattle: Center on Reinventing Public Education, University of Washington, 2008).

27. Not surprisingly, a study by The New Teacher Project found that few teacher reviews amount to much; most teachers get similar ratings; and principals seldom invest much time or effort in this activity. These could be much improved if they incorporated market signals from parents and students regarding teacher performance. See Daniel Weisberg, Susan Sexton, Jennifer Mulhern, and David Keeling, *The Widget Effect: Our National Failure to Acknowledge and Act on Differences in Teacher Effectiveness* (Washington, DC: The New Teacher Project, 2009), 20.

28. Even in brick-and-mortal schools, size need not be an overwhelming barrier. If one pictures a school of 360 students, with twenty pupils per classroom, a K–5 school would have (on average) three teachers per grade, enough for some choice. Of course, any form of team teaching and other constraints on which students can be placed in which classrooms would add to the challenge.

29. Moe and Chubb, *Liberating Learning*, 173–174.

30. Christensen, Horn, and Johnson, *Disrupting Class*, 142.

31. Bridgeland, DiIulio, Streeter, and Mason, *One Dream, Two Realities*.

32. Buckley and Schneider, "Shopping for Schools: How Do Marginal Consumers Gather Information About Schools?" 121–145.

33. National Center for Education Statistics, *Digest of Education Statistics, 2008* (Washington, DC: U.S. Department of Education, 2008).

34. Yoav Gonen, "Head of the Class!" *New York Post*, June 25, 2009.

35. Bryan Hassel, "Cutting Edge Strategies from Other Sectors," in *A Byte at the Apple: Rethinking Education Data for the Post-NCLB Era*, ed. Marci Kanstoroom and Eric C. Osberg (Washington, DC: Fordham Institute, 2008), 218–244.

36. Of course, there are myriad ways to reduce budgetary uncertainty, such as setting enrollment deadlines and devising budgetary rules that cushion the short-run impact of sharp decreases (or increases) in student numbers.

37. Chicago Public Schools, "Local School Councils," http://www.cps.edu/Pages/Localschoolcouncils.aspx. Jillian Melchior, "Harlem Parents Rally for More Charter Schools," *School Reform News*, May 2009, http://www.heartland.org/policybot/results/25162/Harlem_Parents_Rally_for_More_Charter_Schools.html; Douglas McGray, "The Instigator," *New Yorker*, May 10, 2009.

38. Moe and Chubb, *Liberating Learning*, 175.

Chapter 3

1. "Top 200 World Universities," *Times Higher Education*, October 7, 2009, http://www.timeshighereducation.co.uk/Rankings2009-Top200.html.

2. David Graddol, *English Next: Why Global English May Mean the End of "English as a Foreign Language"* (London: British Council, 2006).

3. The Outstanding Schools Initiative Office, Supreme Education Council, *Qatar's Outstanding Schools Program: Supporting Excellence in Education*, http://www.english.education.gov.qa/section/sec/outstandingschools.

4. *The Harrow Foundation Overview*, http:// www.harrowschool.org.uk.

5. "An Overview of Shanghai's International Schools," *Shanghai's International Schools Shanghai Finder*, http://www.shanghaifinder.com/schools.html.

6. Nick Paumgarten, "Our Far-Flung Correspondents: 'Deerfield in the Desert,'" *New Yorker*, September 4, 2006, 102.

7. Meritas Family of Schools, *Leman International School in Chengdu*, http://www.meritas.net.

8. United World Colleges, *Alumni profiles*, http://www.uwc.org/uwc_life/graduate_profiles.

9. Kim Hyun-cheol, "12 Jeju International Schools to Accept 10,000 Students," *Korean Times*, May 29, 2009.

10. Ibid.

11. M. Paul Lewis, ed., *Ethnologue: Languages of the World*, 16th ed. (Dallas: SIL International, 2009), http://www.etnologue.com.

12. Graddol, *English Next*, 62.

13. Ibid., 14.

14. Philip G. Altbach, "The Imperial Tongue: English as the Dominating Academic Language," *International Higher Education* 49 (Fall 2007): 2–4.

15. Atlantic College, "Dynamic Education for Freethinkers," http://www.atlanticcollege.org.

16. Kathleen Kennedy Manzo, "Worldwide Education Achievable, Study Says," *Education Week* 26, no. 20 (2007): 16.

17. Shabana Hussain, "Higher Education Spending: India at the Bottom of BRIC," *Rediff India Abroad*, February 5, 2007, http://www.rediff.com/money/2007/feb/05edu.htm.

Chapter 4

1. Christopher B. Swanson, *Cities in Crisis: A Special Analytic Report on High School Graduation* (Bethesda, MD: Editorial Projects in Education, 2008).

2. All district-specific data cited are based on Parthenon engagements with the New York City Department of Education (2005–2006), Boston Public Schools (2006–2007), and Chicago Public Schools (2006–2007).

3. See Elaine Allensworth and John Q. Easton, *The On-Track Indicator as a Predictor of High School Graduation* (Chicago: Consortium on Chicago School Research, University of Chicago, 2005); Ruth Curran Neild and Robert Balfanz, *Unfulfilled Promise: The Dimensions and Characteristics of Philadelphia's Dropout Crisis 2000–2005* (Philadelphia: Philadelphia Youth Network, Johns Hopkins University, and University of Pennsylvania, 2006).

4. Henry Levin, Clive Belfield, Peter Muennig, and Cecilia Rouse, *The Costs and Benefits of an Excellent Education for All of America's Children* (New York: Teachers College, Columbia University, 2007).

Chapter 5

1. This list includes Washington, DC, Milwaukee, and Baltimore, among other cities.

2. Thomas Stewart, Juanita Lucas-McLean, Laura I. Jensen, Christina Fetzko, Bonnie Ho, and Syliva Segovia, *Family Voices on Parental School Choice in Milwaukee: What Can We Learn from Low-Income Families?* School Choice Demonstration Project, Milwaukee Evaluation Report No. 19 (April 2010), 4, http://www.uark.edu/ua/der/SCDP/Milwaukee_Research.html.

3. Erin Dillon, *Food for Thought: Building a High-Quality School Choice Market* (Washington, DC: Education Sector Reports May 2009), 9.

4. We base this observation in large part on the first round of U.S. Department of Education–sponsored Race to the Top requests for proposals. See, for example, http://www.socialstudies.org/system/files/Race+to+the+Top+RFP+Final+Guidance+111209.pdf

5. See, for example, John E. Chubb and Terry M. Moe, "America's Public Schools: Choice is a Panacea," *Brookings Review* 8, no. 3 (1990), 4–12; Joseph L. Bast and Herbert J. Walberg, *Let's Put Parents Back in Charge!* (Chicago: Heartland Institute, 2003); John Merrifield, "School Choice Evidence and Its Significance," *Journal of School Choice* 2, no. 3 (2008): 223–259.

6. Tobias Jung and Stephen P. Osborne, "Citizens, Co-Producers, Customers, Clients, Captives: Consumerism and Public Services," briefing paper, University of Edinburgh Business School, http://www.scothub.org/publications/consumerismbriefingpaper.pdf; Chester E. Finn Jr. and Eric Osberg, "Putting Students and Parents First: Reframing the Choice Agenda for Education Reform" (paper, American Enterprise Institute, Washington, DC, December 7, 2009).

7. Patrick J. Wolf, *The Comprehensive Longitudinal Evaluation of the Milwaukee Parental Choice Program: Summary of Third Year Reports*, School Choice Demonstration Project, Milwaukee Evaluation Report No. 14 (April 2010), http://www.uark.edu/ua/der/SCDP/Milwaukee_Research.html.

8. Stephen Q. Cornman, Thomas Stewart, and Patrick J. Wolf, *The Evolution of School Choice Consumers: Parent and Student Voices on the Second Year of the D.C. Opportunity Scholarship Program*, School Choice Demonstration Project, Report No. 0701 (May 2007), http://www.uaedreform.org/SCDP/DC_Research.html; Mark Schneider, Paul Teske, and Melissa Marschall, *Choosing Schools: Consumer Choice and the Quality of American Schools* (Princeton, NJ: Princeton University Press, 2000), 164–184; Bryan C. Hassel and Emily Ayscue Hassel,

Picky Parent Guide: Choose Your Child's School with Confidence; The Elementary Years, K–6 (Ross, CA: Armchair Press, 2004).

9. Finn and Osberg, "Putting Students and Parents First."

10. Schneider, Teske, and Marschall, *Choosing Schools.*

11. Cornman, Stewart, and Wolf, *The Evolution of School Choice Consumers,* vii; Brian Kisida and Patrick J. Wolf, "School Governance and Information: Does Choice Lead to Better-Informed Parents?" *American Politics Research* 38, no. 5 (2010): 783–805.

12. Casey J. Lartigue Jr., *The Need for Educational Freedom in the Nation's Capital,* CATO Institute, Policy Analysis No. 461 (December 10, 2002).

13. Jay P. Greene and Marcus A. Winters, "Leaving Boys Behind: Public High School Graduation Rates," Manhattan Institute, Civic Report No. 48 (April 2006), http://www.manhattan-institute.org/pdf/cr_48.pdf.

14. Valerie Strauss and Sari Horwitz, "Students Caught in a Cycle of Classroom Failures," *Washington Post,* February 20, 1997, A01.

15. Lartigue, *The Need for Educational Freedom in the Nation's Capital,* 9.

16. Public Law 108-199, Title III of Division C of the *Consolidated Appropriations Act of 2004,* Section 303.

17. In 2006, Congress amended the law so that, once in the program, families could earn up to 300 percent of the poverty level and still retain their scholarships.

18. Recent legislative changes to the program now also require that participating schools administer the DCPS accountability test to their voucher students, be accredited, and submit to site inspections by officials of the U.S. Department of Education, among other regulations.

19. Patrick Wolf, Babette Gutmann, Michael Puma, Lou Rizzo, Nada Eissa, and Marsha Silverberg *Evaluation of the DC Opportunity Scholarship Program: Impacts After One Year* (Washington, DC: Government Printing Office, 2007), 17

20. Ibid., 15.

21. Patrick Wolf, Babette Gutmann, Nada Eissa, Michael Puma, and Marsha Silverberg, *Evaluation of the DC Opportunity Scholarship Program: First Year Report on Participation,* U.S. Department of Education, Institute for Education Sciences, National Center for Education Evaluation and Regional Assistance, Washington, DC: Government Printing Office, 2005. http://ies.ed.gov/ncee/pubs/dc_choice.asp.

22. Marc Fisher, "Officials at SE Catholic School Offer an Improbable Prayer," *Washington Post,* June 15, 2008, C01; Michael Birnbaum, "Senate Votes Against Reopening DC Voucher Program," ibid., March 17, 2010, B02.

23. Delbert C. Miller and Neil J. Salkind, *Handbook of Research Design and Social Measurement,* 6th ed. (Thousand Oaks, CA: Sage, 2002), 151–154.

24. For additional details regarding our research methodology, see Thomas Stewart, Patrick Wolf, Stephen Q. Cornman, Kenann McKenzie-Thompson, and Jonathan Butcher, *Family Reflections on the District of Columbia Opportunity Scholarship Program: Final Summary Report*, School Choice Demonstration Project Report No. 09-01 (January 2009), http://www. uaedreform.org/SCDP/DC_Research/2009_Final.pdf.

25. Hispanic Parents focus group, Cohort 2, spring 2007.

26. Gerard Robinson and Leslie Fenwick, *More Than Homework, A Snack, and Basketball: Afterschool Programs as an Oasis of Hope for Black Parents in Four Cities* (Washington, DC: Black Alliance for Educational Options, 2008), http://scoter.baeo.org/news_multi_media/ mottSummary.pdf. In addition to the parents' comments, Khari Brown, executive director of Capital Partners for Education, informed us during an interview that mentors and tutors were essential to the success of OSP high school students.

27. Elementary School Parent focus group, Cohort 1, spring 2007.

28. Hispanic Parent focus group, Cohort 2, spring 2008.

29. For example, Joe Soss, "Lessons of Welfare: Policy Design, Political Learning, and Political Action," *American Political Science Review* 93, no. 2 (1999): 363–380; Anne Schneider and Helen Ingram, "Social Construction of Target Populations: Implications for Politics and Policy," ibid. 87, no. 2 (1993): 334–347.

30. Schneider and Ingram, "Social Construction of Target Populations."

31. Theda Skocpol, *Protecting Soldiers and Mothers: The Political Origins of Social Policy in the United States* (Cambridge, MA: Harvard University Press, 1992).

32. See, for example, Schneider and Ingram, "Social Construction of Target Populations"; Suzanne Mettler and Joe Soss, "The Consequences of Public Policy for Democratic Citizenship: Bridging Policy Studies and Mass Politics," *Perspectives on Politics* 2, no. 1 (2004): 55–73; Suzanne Mettler and Jeffrey M. Stonecash, "Government Program Usage and Political Voice," *Social Science Quarterly* 89, no. 2 (2008): 273–293.

33. Amber Wichowsky and Donald P. Moynihan, "Measuring How Administration Shapes Citizenship: A Policy Feedback Perspective on Performance Management," *Public Administration Review* 68, no. 5 (2008): 908–920.

34. Soss, "Lessons of Welfare."

35. AFDC participant, in ibid.

36. Thomas Stewart, Patrick J. Wolf, and Stephen Q. Cornman, *Parent and Student Voices on the First Year of the D.C. Opportunity Scholarship Program,* Report of the School Choice Demonstration Project, Georgetown University, Washington, DC, October 2005, SCDP 05-01. http://www.uaedreform.org/SCDP/DC_Research/PSV1.pdf.

37. See http://www.pickyparent.com/ and http://www.greatschools.org/.

38. See http://www.symphonicstrategies.com/node/47.

Chapter 6

1. Further information available at K12 Inc.'s Web site, http://www.k12.com/.

2. Paul A. Samuelson, "A Note on the Pure Theory of Consumer's Behavior," *Economica* 5 (February 1938), 61–71.

Chapter 7

1. John Merrow, "Can D.C.'s Search Make the Grade?" *Washington Post*, August 8, 2004, B1.

2. Joe Williams, "MPS May Hire Firm to 'Teach to the Test': Arizona Company's Aid Would Cost $390,000," *Milwaukee Journal Sentinel*, April 21, 1998. This type of marketing seemed to disappear after charges of teaching to the test were aimed at the company.

3. Ibid.

4. Tim Daly, e-mail exchange with the author, November 30, 2009.

5. Further information on Parent Revolution is available at www.parentrevolution.org.

6. Lesli A. Maxwell, "L.A. Gives Parents 'Trigger' to Restructure Schools," *Education Week*, October 30, 2009.

7. Eva Moskowitz, interview with the author, October 5, 2009.

8. Mark Claypool, interview with the author, October 16, 2009.

Chapter 8

1. Sloan Consortium, *Staying the Course: Online Education in the United States, 2008,* Sloan Consortium, November 2008, http://sloanconsortium.org/sites/default/files/staying_the_course-2.pdf.

2. Anthony G. Picciano and Jeff Seaman, *K–12 Online Learning*, Babson Survey Research Group, Hunter College, CUNY, The Sloan Consortium, 2009, http://sloanconsortium.org/sites/default/files/k-12_online_learning_2008.pdf.

3. Ibid. When surveyed, K–12 administrators indicated that the top three out of ten reasons for offering online courses were: (1) offering courses not otherwise available at the school; (2) meeting the needs of specific groups of students; and (3) offering Advanced Placement or college-level courses.

4. There is a lively and ongoing debate about whether distance education is worse, equal, or better than face-to-face education. I make no judgment on the educational merits of distance education. For this chapter it is sufficient that distance education has become an accepted way of delivering and receiving credit-bearing coursework.

5. *Program in Course Redesign (PCR): Outcomes Analysis,* National Center for Academic Transformation, http://www.thencat.org/PCR/Outcomes.htm.

6. *Transfer Students* (Washington, DC: Government Accountability Office, 2005).

7. Many colleges are part of coenrollment consortia that allow financial aid to be paid from a home institution to a host institution. However, these consortia are almost always in-state and

negotiated by the colleges themselves; therefore, most do not allow dramatic price competition between host and home institutions.

8. Examples include Transparency by Design, funded by the Lumina Foundation and run by the Western Council on Education and Technology (WCET), and the Voluntary System of Accountability (VSA), sponsored by the American Association of State Colleges and Universities (AASCU) and the Association of Public and Land-Grant Universities (APLU).

9. Multimedia Educational Resource for Learning and Online Teaching (MERLOT), www.merlot.org.

10. Michigan Virtual School pricing information available at http://www.mivhs.org/content.cfm?ID=125.

11. The University of Oklahoma Center for Distant and Independent Learning tuition and fees information available at http://www.ouhigh.ou.edu/charges.cfm.

12. Picciano and Seaman, *K–12 Online Learning*.

13. In K–12 education, the price is the per-student fee paid to the school in which the student enrolls.

14. Clayton Christensen and Michael Horne, *Disrupting Class: How Disruptive Innovation Will Change the Way the World Learns* (New York: McGraw-Hill, 2008).

15. Picciano and Seaman, *K–12 Online Learning*.

Chapter 9

1. Examples include an afterschool tutoring program, a school redesign such as those promoted by New American Schools, or a third-party provider of teacher coaching services.

2. Larry Berger and David Stevenson, "Barriers to Entry: Tales from a Tool Builder," in *The Future of Educational Entrepreneurship: Possibilities for School Reform*, ed. Frederick M. Hess (Cambridge, MA: Harvard Education Press, 2008).

3. This doesn't refer to individual students.

4. Information retrieved from http://schools.nyc.gov/community/innovation/SchoolofOne/default.htm. See also Ta-Nehisi Coates, "The Littlest Schoolhouse," *The Atlantic,* July/August 2010.

5. Note that the School of One, while completely constructed around students' needs, is still not really demand driven. The students' experiences are constructed *for* them, not selected *by* them.

6. "America SCORES New England," http://www.doe.mass.edu/ses/details.asp?ProviderID=131.

7. Smarties Tutoring Services, http://www.doe.mass.edu/ses/details.asp?ProviderID=135.

8. The Office of Extended Learning Opportunities, Chicago Public Schools, *Supplemental Educational Services Parent Handbook, 2009–2010,* http://www.cps.edu/Programs/Before_and_after_school/ExtendedLearningOpportunities/Documents/SESGuide.pdf.

9. See, for instance, Geoffrey A. Fowler and Joseph de Avila, "On the Internet, Everyone's a Critic, but They're Not Very Critical," *Wall Street Journal,* October 5, 2009.

10. Clayton Christensen, Michael Horn, and Curtis Johnson discuss the need for a new type of testing regime that could get around some of these issues in *Disrupting Class: How Disruptive Innovation Will Change the Way the World Learns* (New York: McGraw Hill, 2008), 121–146.

Chapter 10

1. Estimated by Doug Lynch, at a spring 2009 conference, while admitting that this figure is nearly impossible to calculate definitively. Total expenditures in the public K–12 and higher education sectors are about $760 billion; with private institutions added in, the total is a little less than $900 billion.

2. Herb Childress, "Seventeen Reasons Why Football Is Better than School," *Phi Delta Kappa International,* April 1, 1998.

3. Marc Prensky, "Digital Natives, Digital Immigrants," *On the Horizon* 9, no. 5 (2001).

4. Katie Salen (presentation, Cleveland Conference, Chicago, December 5, 2008).

5. Lauren B. Resnick, "The 1987 Presidential Address: Learning In School and Out," *Educational Researcher* 16, no. 9 (1987): 16.

6. Bill Tucker, "Beyond the Bubble: Technology and the Future of Student Assessment," Education Sector, February 2009), http://www.educationsector.org/publications/beyond-bubble-technology-and-future-student-assessment.

7. Kim Farris-Berg, "Student Academic Competitions," February 2006, Education|Evolving, http://www.educationevolving.org.

8. "How Do Students Learn Outside School?" Student SpeakOut Project, June 30, 2008, http://www.map150.org/sso/pdf/SSOIssueBrief_LearningOutsideSchool.pdf.

9. From an interview conducted by Kim Farris-Berg, Education|Evolving, October 2009, http://www.tomorrow.org/speakup/speakup_reports.html.

10. Student SpeakOut Project, Citizens League, St. Paul, Minnesota, www.studentsspeakout.org.

11. Dennis Carter, "'Credit by Exam' Expands Student Options," *ESchool News,* November 13, 2009, http://www.eschoolnews.com/news/top-news/index.cfm?i=61781&page=1.

12. Robert Epstein, *The Case Against Adolescence* (Fresno, CA: Quill Driver Books, 2007).

13. Mary Haywood Metz, *Classrooms and Corridors: The Crisis of Authority in Desegregated Secondary Schools* (Berkeley: University of California Press, 1978).

14. Jack Frymier, conversation, October 28, 1999, reported in Ted Kolderie, "If Kids Don't Want to Learn You Probably Can't Make 'em," *Minnesota Journal,* November 19, 1999, 1–7.

15. Clayton Christensen, "Why So Many Students Seem Unmotivated," in Clayton Christensen, Michael Horn, and Curtis Johnson, *Disrupting Class: How Disruptive Innovation Will Change the Way the World Learns,* 2nd ed. (New York: McGraw-Hill, 2010).

16. Ibid.

17. Ibid.

18. Richard M. Ingersoll, *Who Controls Teachers' Work?* (Cambridge, MA: Harvard University Press, 2003).

19. Edward J. Dirkswager, ed., *Teachers as Owners* (Lanham, MD: Scarecrow Press, 2002).

20. Information on EdVisions Cooperative available at http://edvisionscooperative.org/.

Conclusion

1. Clayton Christensen, Curtis Johnson, and Michael Horn, *Disrupting Class: How Disruptive Innovation Will Change the Way the World Learns* (New York: McGraw Hill, 2008); Terry Moe and John Chubb, *Liberating Learning: Technology, Politics, and the Future of American Education* (San Francisco: Jossey-Bass, 2009).

2. Daniel Weisberg, Susan Sexton, Jennifer Mulhern, and David Keeling, *The Widget Effect: Our National Failure to Acknowledge and Act on Differences in Teacher Effectiveness* (Washington, DC: The New Teacher Project, 2009).

About the Editors

Frederick M. Hess is resident scholar and director of education policy studies at the American Enterprise Institute. In addition to his *Education Week* blog "Rick Hess Straight Up," he is the author of influential books on education, including *The Same Thing Over and Over* (2010), *Education Unbound* (2010), *Common Sense School Reform* (2006), *Revolution at the Margins* (2002), and *Spinning Wheels* (1998), as well as the coeditor of the new volume *Stretching the School Dollar* (2010). His work has appeared in scholarly and popular outlets such as *Teachers College Record, Harvard Educational Review, Social Science Quarterly, Urban Affairs Review, American Politics Quarterly, Chronicle of Higher Education, Phi Delta Kappan, Educational Leadership, U.S. News & World Report, Washington Post*, and *National Review*. He has edited widely cited volumes on education philanthropy, urban school reform, the impact of education research, and No Child Left Behind. Hess serves as executive editor of *Education Next*, as lead faculty member for the Rice Education Entrepreneurship Program, on the review board for the Broad Prize in Urban Education, and on the boards of directors of the National Association of Charter School Authorizers and the American Board for the Certification of Teaching Excellence. A former high school social studies teacher, he has taught at the University of Virginia, the University of Pennsylvania, Georgetown University, Rice University, and Harvard University. He holds an MA and PhD in government from Harvard University as well as a MEd in teaching and curriculum.

Bruno V. Manno is senior adviser for K–12 systemic reform for the Walton Family Foundation and the former senior program associate for education at the Annie E. Casey Foundation. While at the Annie E. Casey Foundation, Manno directed the Baltimore philanthropy's investments in education since 1998. He played several key roles at the U.S. Department of Education beginning in 1986, as director of planning and acting assistant secretary of the Office of Educational Research and Improvement, as assistant secretary of education for policy and planning under Secretary Lamar Alexander, and as special assistant to Secretary Alexander. He left the federal government in 1993 to become senior fellow in the Education Policy Studies Program at the Hudson Institute, where he served as executive director of the National Commission on Philanthropy and Civic Renewal and as associate director of Hudson's Modern Red Schoolhouse Project. Manno served as executive director of the National Commission on the Cost of Higher Education in 1997 and 1998 and is a director of the Fund for the Improvement of Postsecondary Education. He is coauthor (with Chester E. Finn Jr. and Gregg Vanourek) of *Charter Schools in Action: Renewing Public Education* (2000) and a frequent writer and commentator on education issues.

About the Contributors

Tamara Battaglino cofounded and leads the Parthenon Group's Education Center of Excellence. For over fifteen years she has advised clients on issues related to operational excellence, strategy development, and new venture creation. Her clients include a wide range of organizations from startups to Fortune 100 companies, school districts, government agencies, and some of the world's largest foundations. Battaglino has led dozens of engagements with organizations that include the New York City Department of Education, the New York State Department of Education, Boston Public Schools, District of Columbia Public Schools, and leading education-focused foundations and nonprofits.

Chester E. Finn Jr. has devoted his career to improving education in the United States. As senior fellow at Stanford's Hoover Institution and chairman of Hoover's Koret Task Force on K–12 Education, president of the Thomas B. Fordham Institute, and senior editor of *Education Next*, his primary focus is the reform of primary and secondary schooling. Finn is also an Adjunct Fellow at the Hudson Institute, where he worked from 1995 through 1998. From 1999 until 2002 he was a John M. Olin Fellow at the Manhattan Institute. From 1992 to 1994 he served as founding partner and senior scholar with the Edison Project. He was professor of education and public policy at Vanderbilt University from 1981 until 2002, and from 1985 to 1988 he served as assistant secretary for research and improvement and counselor to the secretary at the U.S. Department of Education. Earlier positions include staff assistant to the president of the United States; special assistant to the governor of Massachusetts; counsel to the U.S. ambassador to India; research associate at the Brookings Institution; and legislative director for Senator Daniel Patrick Moynihan. The author of eighteen books, Finn's latest is *Reroute the Preschool Juggernaut* (2009).

Jon Fullerton is the executive director of the Center for Education Policy Research at the Harvard Graduate School of Education and senior practice expert in the McKinsey & Company social-sector office. He has extensive experience working with policy makers and executives in designing and implementing organizational change and improvements. Before coming to Harvard, Fullerton served as the board of education's director of budget and financial policy for the Los Angeles Unified School District. In this capacity he provided independent evaluations of district reforms and helped ensure that the district's budget was aligned with board priorities. From 2002 to 2005 he served as vice president of strategy, evaluation, research, and policy at the Urban Education Partnership in Los Angeles, where he worked with policy makers to ensure that they focused on high-impact educational strategies. Fullerton previously worked for five years at McKinsey & Company as a strategy consultant.

Michael Gottfried is an associate policy researcher at RAND Corporation. His work focuses on education research using quantitative methods to answer questions related to the economics of education. In particular, he evaluates the educational outcomes of high-poverty, minority populations of underserved youth in urban cities. Gottfried's research has extended to large-scale, longitudinal analyses and uses multilevel modeling for quasi-experimental and program evaluations. Most recently his work can be found in journals such as *Educational Evaluation and Policy Analysis* and *American Education Research Journal*. Gottfried holds a BA in economics from Stanford University and an MA and PhD in applied economics from Wharton Business School, University of Pennsylvania.

Curtis Johnson is managing partner for Education|Evolving, a Minnesota-based organization that assists in the evolution of public school systems at the state and national levels. Johnson coauthored, with Harvard Business School professor Clayton Christensen and Michael Horn, the provocative book *Disrupting Class* (2008). He is also the coauthor of three books about public policy issues in urban regions, most recently *Century of the City* (2008). As a longtime writer with the Citistates Group, Johnson, along with columnist Neal Peirce, has written more than a hundred feature-length articles on a wide range of public policy issues that have appeared in more than fifty newspapers over the past twenty years. He has also been a teacher, a community college president, the head of a citizen think tank, a policy adviser and chief of staff to a Minnesota governor, and the chairman of the board of one of America's only two regional governments.

Ted Kolderie is a founding partner of Education|Evolving. He is most recognized nationally for his work on K–12 education policy and innovation, which he has focused on since the early 1980s. Kolderie was instrumental in the design and passage of the nation's first charter school law in Minnesota in 1991 and has since worked on the design and improvement of charter legislation in more than seventeen states. He has written about the charter idea and its progress in a variety of publications and is the author of *Creating the Capacity for Change: How and Why Governors and Legislatures are Opening a New-Schools Sector in Public Education* (2005). He was previously executive director of the *Twin Cities Citizens League*, a reporter and editorial writer for the *Minneapolis Star and Tribune*, and a senior fellow at the University of Minnesota's Hubert H. Humphrey Institute of Public Affairs.

Douglas Lynch is the vice dean at the graduate school of education at the University of Pennsylvania, as well as an academic director in the Wharton School's executive education program. He was formerly assistant dean for corporate learning, new business development, and international initiatives at New York University. He has also worked at the College Board and at Arizona State University. Lynch's educational programs have won several national awards, including the president's award for exporting, the first time a college was recognized for commercial innovation by the U.S. Department of Commerce. He has sat on presidential, congressional, and state advisory boards both in New York and Arizona and currently is on the board of visitors of the Central Intelligence Agency. He is the chair of the public policy council for the American Society of Training and Development and is on the advisory board of Harvard University's Forgotten Half project.

JoEllen Lynch is a private consultant engaged in educational and community-based efforts to create systemic and model pathways for educational and economic opportunity. Prior to this work, she held the position of CEO for Partnership School Support Organizations and the Office of Multiple Pathways to Graduation in the New York City Department of Education. Lynch designed, developed, and led both of those offices for Chancellor Joel Klein. She was a member of the Senior Leadership Team and initially worked with the senior counselor to the chancellor, Michele Cahill, and held the position of executive director of the Office of Youth Development. Lynch has also served as assistant executive director for community-based programs for Good Shepherd Services and was responsible for their K–12 school-based programs and model schools and served as director of South Brooklyn Community High School, a nationally recognized transfer high school.

Olivia Meeks is a research assistant in education policy studies at the American Enterprise Institute and holds bachelors' degrees in economics and political science from the University of Arkansas.

Eric Osberg is the former vice president and treasurer of the Thomas B. Fordham Institute and a research fellow at the Hoover Institution. He is the coeditor of *A Byte at the Apple: Rethinking Education Data for the Post-NCLB Era* (2008) and has previously directed Fordham's research in school funding, culminating in two reports: *Charter School Funding: Inequity's Next Frontier* (2005) and *Fund the Child: Tackling Inequity and Antiquity in School Finance* (2006). Previously, he worked for Capital One Financial Corporation as a senior business analyst.

Julie Petersen is the communications director at NewSchools Venture Fund, where she oversees the firm's communications and publications strategies. Prior to joining NewSchools Venture Fund, Petersen spent three years as a writer at *Red Herring*, a business and technology magazine, where she covered venture capital as well as a range of other beats, including entrepreneurs, social innovation, and education.

Burck Smith is the cofounder and former CEO of SMARTHINKING, the largest online tutoring provider for high schools and colleges. Founded in 1999, SMARTHINKING serves nearly 250,000 students per year. In 2008 Smith launched StraighterLine, a division of SMARTHINKING that offers affordable credit-bearing online general education courses directly to students. Prior to founding SMARTHINKING, he provided consulting services to a variety of technology and education companies, including Microsoft, the Computer Curriculum Corporation, the CEO Forum on Education and Technology, the Milken Exchange on Education and Technology, Teaching Matters Inc., *Converge Magazine*, and several startup companies. He has written about education and technology for *Wired Magazine*, *Wired News*, *Converge Magazine*, *University Business*, and the National School Boards Association.

Kim Smith is cofounder and CEO of Bellwether Education Partners. Prior to this, she cofounded NewSchools Venture Fund in 1998 to transform public education by supporting education entrepreneurs. She served as chief executive officer of NewSchools Venture Fund from 1998 until fall 2005 and currently serves as a senior adviser and board member. In 1989 Smith became a founding team member of Teach for America and was the founding director of BAYAC AmeriCorps, a consortium of nonprofits in the San Francisco Bay Area working to develop young leaders in education. In 2001 she was featured in *Newsweek*'s report on the "Women of the 21st Century" as "the kind of woman who will shape America's new century." She is also a member of the 2002 Class of Henry Crown Fellows of the Aspen Institute.

Thomas Stewart is president and CEO of Qwaku & Associates and a senior research associate with the School Choice Demonstration Project. Stewart has worked closely with youth, parents, community leaders, policy makers, and other concerned parties about urban social issues, namely public education. A native of Washington, DC,

Stewart holds a bachelor's degree with honors from the University of the District of Columbia and a PhD in government from Harvard University. He has extensive experience with coalition building and community development and has held several senior leadership and other roles in organizations that include the Black Alliance for Educational Options, Edison Schools, Harvard University Society of Fellows, Learn-Now, National Black Graduate Student Association, Next Generation Foundation, Parents International, SEED Public Charter School of Washington, DC, Symphonic Strategies, and World Organization of Resilient Kids. Stewart has authored articles, reports, and other documents that examine cutting-edge approaches in the general area of education reform.

Chris Whittle is an entrepreneur with four decades of leadership experience in the fields of education and media. He conceived and founded Edison Schools (now EdisonLearning) in 1992 and currently serves on its board of directors. The company serves hundreds of thousands of children in the United States and the United Kingdom through its schools and a variety of other educational programs. He is also a director of the Center for Education Reform in Washington, DC. Prior to founding Edison, Whittle was founder and chairman of Whittle Communications, which he led to become one of America's Top 100 media firms. Among his properties was Channel One, the first national electronic news system. Whittle is also the author of *Crash Course: Imagining a Better Future for Public Education* (2001).

Joe Williams is a former newspaper journalist and author of the controversial book *Cheating Our Kids: How Politics and Greed Ruin Education* (2005). He serves as executive director of the political action group Democrats for Education Reform. Previously, Williams covered the New York City school system for the *New York Daily News*. As an education reporter with the *Milwaukee Journal Sentinel*, he won numerous local, state, and national awards for his coverage of the Milwaukee Public Schools and that city's groundbreaking school choice programs.

Patrick J. Wolf holds the Endowed Chair in School Choice at the University of Arkansas. He is the principal investigator of the District of Columbia Opportunity Scholarship Program impact evaluation and the School Choice Demonstration Project. He is editor of *Educating Citizens: International Perspective on Civic Values and School Choice* (2004) and a contributing author to *The Education Gap: Vouchers and Urban Schools,* edited by Paul Peterson and William Howell (2002). Wolf has authored or coauthored more than three dozen articles and book chapters on school choice, special education, public management, and campaign finance. He was a member of the National Working Commission on Choice in K–12 Education and previously taught at Columbia University and Georgetown University.

Index